PORTRAIT OF A PEACE CORPS GRINGO

Paul Arfin

Rita,

I hope you enjoy the book —

Paul Arfin

ISBN: 1-4392-4469-3
ISBN-13: 9781439244692

Visit www.booksurge.com to order additional copies.

Rats, scorpions and cold showers make for a Peace Corps volunteer's life—at least for Arfin, who lived on the edges of poverty while dealing with the arrogance of some of his fellow Americans in Colombia. These experiences deeply influenced him and made him a better person who spent the rest of his life in the arena of nonprofits. This book is about a time and a life that is worth remembering.

Arthur Dobrin, Peace Corps Kenya, 1965-67, Professor of Humanities, Hofstra University

This journey of a restless youth from the Long Island suburbs to the discovery and development of his purpose in life should engage any young person currently struggling with the "Who am I? Where do I fit in? What's next?" questions. The people from small villages and towns in Colombia, South America had a hand in affirming the emotional and intellectual commitment Paul Arfin has to social justice and decent opportunities for everyone. Anyone who thinks the path from Peace Corps to becoming a social work leader and advocate is easy will be in for some surprises.

Dorothy "Dee" Gamble, Peace Corps Colombia 1962-1964, Clinical Associate Professor Emerita, UNC Chapel Hill

Paul Arfin offers a personal look into a life shaped, made more meaningful, and at times complicated by the experiences of a first-generation Peace Corps Volunteer. His compelling journey invites us to examine our own values, decisions, consequences, and rewards. Many of us think about writing our memoirs. Paul may have done it for us.

Jim Brown, PhD, Peace Corps Colombia 1962-1964, Editor, Steadman-Hawkins Research Foundation News; Contributing Editor, Duke Medicine Health News

From the '50s "silent generation," Paul Arfin emerged and found his passion for life through the Peace Corps. As an inspirational idea, the Peace Corps not only shaped Paul's life but it changed the world. Defining and practicing his values by giving to others in a different culture, Paul found his "voice" for developing new social initiatives here and has devoted 40+ years in making Long Island a better place for all of us. As a returned Peace Corps volunteer of the '60s, this book resonated with me over and over again. Paul and my assignments were very different but the impact was the same. We are both products of what we gained from our unique experiences.

Rick Van Dyke, LCSW, Peace Corps Malawi 1964-1966, retired President and Chief Executive Officer, Family Service League, and colleague

¡Olé! Paul Arfin's "Portrait of a Peace Corps Gringo" is a fine work. From a childhood with no experience for support of justice and equality, he joins the Peace Corps, discovers a mission and is able to return stateside to implement the goals for peace and justice he found there. It is a great example of how, through community service, one individual can develop into a "life-long" contributor to community health. I recommend Paul's memoirs to anyone, especially those of us who have labored in the not-for-profit world to improve people's lives.

Thomas B. Williams, MSW, retired Executive Director, Cornell Cooperative Extension of Suffolk County and colleague

This book is a fascinating, challenging look into the heart and soul of a Peace Corps man and his remarkable human service career thereafter. "Driven" is the word that lingers long after reading his story. This is a must reading for anyone considering a career to make the "world better." Fire in the belly, so evident in Arfin's life, is required to handle the roller coaster ride of creating social change.

Richard Dina, DSW, retired President and Chief Executive Officer, Family and Children's Association and colleague

The book is terrific! The details of life as a Colombian Peace Corps volunteer are a wonderful trip down memory lane. Each department in Colombia is so distinct, yet the warmth of the Colombians always emerges.

Betsy L. Bucks, Peace Corps Colombia 1964-66, coauthor of *Tortillitas Para Mamá*

A marvelous tale revealing how a life dedicated to others can still include love of family, friends, and fun!

Paul Mundschenk, PhD, Peace Corps Colombia 1963-1965, retired Emeritus Professor of Religious Studies, Western Illinois University

An engrossing narrative. Paul sets forth his story about how his Peace Corps experience shaped his life and gave it direction. A must read for all those who 'swim against the current'.

Jeff Bloomberg, DDS, Paul's lifelong friend and tennis partner

Arfin's book reveals the lesson of the Peace Corps - that life's greatest reward comes from trying to help others.

Ronald A. Schwarz, Ph.D., Peace Corps Colombia. 1961-63, Professor of Anthropology

DEDICATION

This book is dedicated to the memory of Salomón Hernandez. Don Salomón was my mentor during Peace Corps service in Colombia, South America. He was a major influence on me, both in my adjustment to life in Colombia and my growth as a young man. If there were a board of directors guiding my life, Salomón would certainly be a member of that board, if not its chairman. Don Salomón was a self-educated man who lived most of his life in the tiny village of El Valle de San José in the Department of Santander del Sur, Colombia, South America. It was no surprise when, in 1996, I revisited El Valle that I learned that the village's residents had dedicated a plaque to don Salomón's public life and placed it in their new cultural center.

To me, Salomón represented the heart and soul of the industrious Colombian people. He worked hard, gave his wise counsel to countless people, and saw human suffering and injustice around him and took action to alleviate it. He passed on a legacy of public service to his children, residents of his community, and by extension, to generations of Colombians that followed. His spirit will remain part of me forever.

TABLE OF CONTENTS

PREFACE

The Cat Dancer

Above the playing field
the wire is taut
Cat Dancer moves cautiously;
the stakes are high
Inching forward toward his vision
along his precarious perch
Ever onward, inspiring others
bending this ear,
tweaking that one
Bending, balancing; bending, balancing
Extending a hand, lifting others
sometimes young, sometimes old
A safety net stretched out
by those dearest to him
He shall never fail
come what may

Janet Grossman
Sag Harbor, New York

ACKNOWLEDGEMENTS

This writing project has taken years to complete. It started as an essay about my mother, Jeanette Arfin, who was in her mid-eighties at the time and living in Sunrise Assisted Living in Smithtown, New York. She was filled with rich stories about her childhood that I felt should be preserved, so I asked her a lot of questions and taped our conversations over many months. I typed up eighty pages of reflections as "Jeanette's Story" and gave it to her. She was thrilled to see her early life in writing. I realized that Joanelle's story is one of the keys to my life, so the first person I want to acknowledge is my mother, Jeanette Arfin, who did her best to form me into an honest, hard-working, individual with a sense of fairness and justice.

An equally important acknowledgement goes to my wife, Karen, who has been there for me consistently during the past forty-two years. She was by my side as I struggled to find the ideas, feelings, and words that eventually found their places on these pages. Karen, I love you.

Our two wonderful daughters, Liza and Sari, my son-in-law Jeremy, and our two granddaughters, Davi and Mira, are the inspiration that motivated me to write my life story.

I am grateful to a number of friends and colleagues who kindly read the manuscript and provided me with their thoughts and suggestions, especially to Paul Mundschenk, Dee Gamble, Betsy Buck, Jim Brown, Arthur Dobrin, Rick Van Dyke, David Dichter, Jeff Bloomberg, Joan Spence, Dick Miller, Ron Roel, Tom Williams, Dick Dina, Ron Schwarz, and Paul Mariani for their insights. And much thanks go to my wonderful editor, Victoria Wright of BookmarkServices.net, whose critical eye and perceptive insights brought life to my writing.

FOREWORD

Two years. Two mind-stretching, heart-shaping years that changed everything for Paul Arfin, both the years before, as a Jewish kid from Brooklyn growing up in suburban Long Island Mineola in the Eisenhower years, his young mind focused on girls and baseball and, yes, girls again, and then the four decades after his two-year stint as one of JFK's first Peace Corps volunteers in Colombia, his world forever changed now, as he saw afresh through the eyes of the other. His has been a life—as one who knew him back before his odyssey sees it now in retrospect—of selfless dedication to those whose lives, though in one sense poorer than most North Americans, are so much richer in so many other ways. It's a compelling and vital read, this book, and it speaks volumes about a Whitmanesque vision we North Americans might offer to others, to strangers who turn out after all to be our brothers and sisters. Here is the dream of an open hand, an open mind, an open heart to stir us from the nightmare into which we have too often plunged in the past like full-fed lemmings. Read this book. It will speak to you if only you let it. It might even change your life!

Paul Mariani, PhD, University Professor of English, Boston College, poet, biographer, and critic

INTRODUCTION

In his inaugural address on January 20th 1961, President Kennedy spoke, I felt, to me. "Ask not what your country can do for you. Ask what you can do for your country." His challenge to America's youth occurred at a time when virtually all of those around me chose to realize their parents' dreams to become doctors, lawyers, and captains of industry. Joining the Peace Corps wasn't exactly a decision that leads to a typical, middle-class suburban life, but when the formation of the Peace Corps was announced a few weeks later, it triggered something deep inside of me that needed expression. I was the 10,476th American to apply for admission.

Where do I start? What do I want to say? Who is going to read a memoir about a person from a middle-class background, of Jewish heritage, whose childhood was primarily spent in Mineola, New York, part of suburban America during the post-World War II period? This period saw the return of millions of young men and women from World War II; their purchase of single-family homes in America's suburbs; their pursuit of educations for both their children and themselves; and the passing on of their values to their children. My parents were among the young families who moved to the suburbs in 1948. So, why did I leave the safety and security of suburban Long Island and the vast economic opportunities available to me in the mid-1960s to spend two years in Colombia, South America?

The book attempts to answer three pivotal questions: What motivated me to enlist in the Peace Corps? What was my life like as a Peace Corps Volunteer? How has the Peace Corps defined my life? To understand these issues, I describe my family's history, my parents' lives, my childhood experiences, and my development as a man, husband, parent, grandparent, social worker, and citizen of the world.

I've lived a good life with no significant regrets. Indeed, I've been very fortunate. I am keenly aware that our two-breadwinner family income places us among the wealthiest people on earth. I have a loving wife, two wonderful daughters, a terrific son-in-law, and two fabulous granddaughters. I have been able to do work that I've enjoyed; work that improves the human condition. Meanwhile, my life has consisted of lifelong ruminating about relationships, insecurity about my abilities, strivings for professional recognition, lots of impulsive decisions, a heart attack at age 64, worries about memory loss, and most recently, trying to come to terms with life's finality.

My stories trace my personal development, my thoughts, fears, concerns, experiences, and relationships in the pursuit of balance between understanding who I am while living a happy family life and a purposeful public service career. I discuss my thoughts and experiences in the context of the decades in which they occurred. In the last chapter, I reflect upon my life today and the turbulent times in which we live. I share my concerns for future generations and my ideas for social change that evolved from my perspective as a former Peace Corps volunteer.

As you will see, I am a very imperfect human being. If it weren't for the unconditional love, support, and understanding of my wife, Karen, and the joy that she brings to my life, my life would not have turned out to be as rewarding as it has. I proposed marriage to Karen less than two weeks after we met. However impulsive this decision was at the time, it turned out to be the best decision of my life.

If you would like to contact me, I can be emailed at paularfin@gmail.com.

Paul Arfin
June 2009

CHAPTER ONE
My Family and My Childhood

This chapter is a compilation of information about my mother's and father's families. It was principally provided by Miriam Uhlan, a second cousin, and my mother, Jeanette Arfin. The rest is based on personal memories and reports from other family members.

My mother was born in 1916 in Brooklyn, New York, the first of six children, to Anna and Michael Shocket, first generation, American-born Jews. Anna's mother Esther, who we called "Bubbe" was one of six children of Jacob Ladden and Chaya Sara Katowitz Ladden. Some family members report that the name Ladden was originally Lasnick, while others claim that it was Goldstein. Jacob was born in Grinkiškis, Kovno

Gubernia, Lithuania in 1841. Chaya was born in 1842 in an unknown location. Jacob arrived in America in 1885 or 1886. Chaya and the children joined him in 1887 and established their first residence in a tenement on Elizabeth Street on the Lower East Side of New York City. By 1892, they moved to the Williamsburg section of Brooklyn. Jacob had a factory and was a clothing subcontractor, manufacturing overcoats.

My maternal grandfather, Michael, was born in America in 1900. He had little formal schooling but was self-educated. He was a butcher and did very well. For many years, he owned three shops—in Brooklyn, and Corona and Maspeth, Queens. He was an affable person with many friends, respected by others as a natural leader. In his family, he assumed the traditional male role of the times as leader and sole breadwinner of the family. In 1935, Michael worked with his cousins to found a mutual aid society, the Ladden Family Organization, whose purpose was to provide burial space for family members as well as serve as a vehicle to keep the family together. Burial space was purchased at Beth David Cemetery in Elmont on Long Island.

With respect to religion, Michael attended temple on the High Holy Days. He worked on Friday nights and Saturdays. He appealed to the congregation for donations to a local children's home. Michael was impatient with family members who complained about their lives, believing that there was no excuse for not being successful in America. After all, he felt, he was an uneducated person who couldn't read English, and he had become successful on his own. Michael was a lifelong Democrat, like most Jews, but he never got involved in formal politics. According to my mother, Michael's greatest weaknesses were his heavy smoking and eating. He smoked three packs of Camel cigarettes every day throughout his life. He had several heart attacks but ignored his doctor's warnings about his eating and smoking. Anna had to give him nitroglycerine pills on a number of occasions to reduce the symptoms. Michael died in his sleep at the early age of 49.

My maternal grandmother Anna graduated high school. She was a homemaker, never working outside the home except for short periods when Michael was ill and needed help in the butcher shop. She bore six children: Jeanette (my mother), Sidney, Murray, Helen and Teddy (twins), and Ceil. Anna lived until age 96 and, therefore, spent almost half her life widowed.

My mother feels that she got her spirit and feistiness from her father. She recalls an argument between them. She said to her father, "How can you be angry with me? I'm just like you!" Her father told her that her mouth was going to get her in trouble. She responded, "If my mouth gets me in trouble, my mouth will get me out of trouble."

While the stock market crash of 1929 made millions penniless and there was nationwide economic hardship that continued into the late 1930s, the Shocket family lived well. Butcher shops were necessities even during the Depression and World War II, so the family business produced a living. According to my uncle Sidney, the stores could produce $35 each per week. That was enough in those days to live a middle-class lifestyle. The family went on vacations to Florida. They owned good cars during the 1930s and 1940s.

After Michael died, each of his children chipped in $10 a week to help Anna. This was very hard for my mother and father. My father didn't know how difficult it was for my mother to manage the family budget. At that time, $10 bought a lot of food.

My father's background is a lot sketchier than my mother's. He was born in 1916 on the lower East Side of New York City. He was named Abraham, but everyone called him Al or Abe. My paternal grandfather, Yussell, came to America in the late 19th century carrying a sewing machine on his back. The family lived in a tiny tenement apartment on the Lower East Side of New York City and later in Brooklyn for all of their lives.

Yussell was an Orthodox Jew. My grandmother Jenny's family came from Iowa. She wasn't religious until she married. She went to the synagogue where the women were required to sit upstairs. Yussell never walked arm-in-arm with Jenny. She walked behind, as was the custom. It was clear to mother that Yussell and Jenny wanted my father to marry an Orthodox girl.

After my parents were married and living in an apartment in Brooklyn, my mother told my father that they needed to join a temple. My father said he didn't want to join a temple. My mother told my father that Yussell would always blame her if they didn't join a temple. They joined a temple.

My mother never talked much with her in-laws. She didn't know what to say to them. She felt that they were foreigners. I believe that my mother's attitude represented the common feelings of second-generation immigrants who were busy "Americanizing" themselves and distancing themselves from old world traditions.

Because the family was so religious, my father didn't play ball on Saturdays or go out on Friday nights. As far as his parents were concerned, my mother was an American girl who didn't live up to their expectations since she wasn't "Jewish enough." When my father was courting my mother, he had a new two-door Plymouth coupe with a spotlight on it. He would shine the car's spotlight on my mother's bedroom window to get her attention. Anna and Michael didn't like this.

Michael wasn't worried about his daughter marrying my father. He knew how my father felt about his daughter. He once told Dr. Epstein, my mother's cousin and the family physician, "I'm not worried about Al (my father). He'll sell shoelaces if he has to, to support her."

Yussell and Jenny never became Americanized at a time when most everyone else did. Their customs and traditions were strange to me and no one really ever took the time to make sense of them. I was tentative and uncomfortable with them. It didn't help that Yussell didn't often shave and his beard was scratchy when I kissed him on his cheek. They could not speak English so I couldn't speak with them. They couldn't give me praise for my accomplishments which were mainly on the baseball field. Visits to their apartment in Brooklyn were awkward and boring. Their visits to Long Island were equally strained.

I was born in 1940 in Brooklyn Jewish Hospital on a hot, humid Friday night, the first child of my parent's generation on both sides of the family. To be born on a Friday night is a big honor in Judaism. Following the tradition, the family held a party to commemorate the birth of the firstborn son and a gold coin was bought for me. My mother recalls that on that Friday night, my grandfather brought her to the hospital to deliver the baby. My father hated hospitals and would faint at the smells. My mother remembers being in the hospital after I was born and looking out the window at the steamy hot street and seeing my father and her parents sitting on the curb getting a breeze from the passing cars. She remembers her physician, Dr. Sidney, saying, "This is the day you picked?!"

My mother especially loved her grandmother, her Bubbe. The family really didn't know Bubbe's age. She was born somewhere in Eastern Europe. She said she was named after Queen Esther. Her birthday was the same as Queen Esther's and that's why they gave her that name. Bubbe's first husband and she spoke Yiddish, but they were not practicing Jews. Their sons Barney and Willie weren't bar mitzvah. My mother considered Bubbe to be "a real woman" because she admired her independent lifestyle and her outgoing nature. I recall Bubbe as a warm and friendly person. She went to the movies alone and loved to sit on the benches on Eastern Parkway in the Coney Island section of Brooklyn to generate conversations with people, especially younger people. When her second husband, Max Finklestein, died, Bubbe told her friends to knock on her door every morning and if she didn't answer, they should come in because she had died.

When I was brought home from the hospital, Bubbe brought a cat with her to the apartment and insisted on putting the cat in the crib with me. My mother said, "Bubbe, what are you doing?" She responded, "The cat has nine lives and will bring the baby good luck."

During World War II, my father joined the Army Reserve. He was a Major's Aide at an upstate military camp. He was spared from going overseas because my mother went to the local draft board and described her hearing problem and how she couldn't manage on her own with a child. She never told my father about this.

During my early childhood, my mother didn't work outside our home. My father worked for a large liquor distributor in Long Island City as a route man. He worked at night designing the routes for the truck drivers to make their deliveries to liquor stores and bars within a seventy-five mile radius of New York City. I was always impressed with my father's knowledge of how to get around New York City and the metropolitan area. He knew the state liquor license numbers and addresses of hundreds, if not thousands, of liquor stores, bars, and restaurants. He knew which streets went one way and which stores accepted deliveries in the back.

My parents, 1950

Our family meals featured large portions of food. In the 1930s, '40s, and '50s, excessive eating—by families who could afford it—was a sign of prosperity, of social status, and a way of coping with the pervasive feeling that your life could change at any time due to circumstances beyond your control whether through economic depression or world war. If you were in the middle class, at least you could make sure that your children ate well.

My father loved my mother's cooking. She was a wonderful cook, preparing memorable meals both Jewish and Italian style. My father complained that we made too many special requests of mother regarding her cooking. One of his constant complaints was that we didn't eat enough bread with meals. He would say, "You're going to eat us out of house and home! Eat more bread!"

He would also complain that I didn't eat much dairy food. Lox and bagels, white fish, and eggs were the usual Saturday night family meal. At these meals, he would repeatedly say, "Paul, have another piece of white fish," or lox, tomatoes, or eggs, knowing full well that I wouldn't eat them. I complained about this badgering but to no avail. If I showed or expressed disapproval of his remarks, he would go on with his remarks trying to provoke me—a habit he continued for the rest of his life. To this day, I don't eat any forms of seafood, eggs, or tomatoes.

Nevertheless, sharing my mother's delicious food was the social glue that brought us together as a family. My mother's food was a frequent topic of conversation at mealtimes. Despite my father's criticisms, I remember the need I felt to be home on Sunday afternoons, even as a young adult, to eat dinner with the family.

My mother's passion, one that she has enjoyed throughout her life, is reading. She has always been an avid reader, and as a child, she read late into the night. She loves a great novel that compels her to finish it without putting it down. She enjoys family sagas, comparing these stories with her own experiences. She was especially fond of Pearl Buck, who wrote family sagas about China. At age 93, she continues to read two or three books at a time. Reading has been a wonderful source of escape, relaxation, and enrichment for her.

Her parents never expected anything of her with respect to education or a career. This attitude of low expectations for women was common in the first half of the twentieth century. In fact, her father once told her that all she needed to do was know how to cook, clean, and wash diapers. This hurt her a great deal. When she was growing up, my mother was interested in becoming a teacher which you could do, at that time, by taking teacher training courses. However, when my mother finished high school, Michael would hear nothing about further education for his oldest daughter.

My parents' decision to move to Mineola had to do with someone who lived with a friend of my father's in Brooklyn who had a brother who was building homes on Long Island for low-income families. This woman arranged for her brother to take my mother and father to his home in Jamaica Estates. He encouraged them to come to Mineola to see his houses. When my parents saw the model house, my mother could immediately imagine how she would furnish it. She deeply felt that she had to move from Brooklyn—this would be the start of a new life, and it would be good for the marriage and the children. They would have a back yard. The builder quoted a price of $10,000.

My mother had always dreamed of owning a house. She went to her father and asked him for a thousand dollars for a down-payment and he told Anna to go to the bank to get the money. When my mother's brother Sidney and his wife Ann heard about my parents' plans to move to Mineola, they decided to move, too. They immediately put down a deposit on the house next door.

I remember telling one of my school friends in Brooklyn that we were moving to someplace named Mineola. He said that I probably meant Minnesota. I wasn't exactly sure. I didn't know at the time that Mineola was named after a Native American, Mineolagamika, an Algonquin name for "a pleasant or friendly place." Mineola was the county seat of Nassau County.

The move to the suburbs from Brooklyn placed our family among hoards of postwar families looking for their share of the American Dream of home ownership, a car, home appliances, Little League, a grass lawn, summer vacations, and a college education for the children. After the house was purchased and was under construction, we drove to Long Island every weekend on the Belt Parkway. My mother lined the closets with oil cloth in the new house and put all of the dishes in the cupboards. On the day we moved in, I remember feeling that the trip took forever.

I liken Mineola in the late 1940s to "Andyhardysville." It was small-town America. You felt safe. Neighbors helped neighbors with their heavy outdoor work around their houses whether it was building garages or patios or planting large trees. We went fishing for goldfish with friends and threw rocks at darning needles and frogs in nearby Perks Pond at the corner of Herricks Road and Searingtown Road. We bought frankfurters and cans of baked beans and camped overnight in the woods in what is now Herricks, and, when it rained, we slept under one of the overpasses of the Vanderbilt Motor Parkway. We walked and rode our bicycles from one end of town to the other. We collected beer and soda bottles at the many housing development construction sites in the area and brought the bottles to the grocery stores and delicatessens for refunds. I got my haircuts at Scotty's Barber Shop on Hillside Avenue just like my friends did. It seemed like everyone in Mineola banked at the Franklin National Bank at the corner of Jericho Turnpike and Mineola Boulevard and bought their used cars from Madden Auto Sales located across the street from the bank. We attended the annual Christmas Party Dinners at Village Hall and received presents from Santa Claus. We attended the Saturday movies at the Mineola Theater religiously to see cartoons and full-length movies.

Our house was on Argyle Road, which was lined with houses the same size as ours. Some were Cape Cod style, while others were split levels. The fathers mostly worked in blue collar jobs while the women stayed home taking care of the children, doing the shopping, caring for the house, and preparing the meals. Most of the adjoining streets were the same although, on Foch Boulevard, there were some larger houses built before World War II. I always thought that people who lived there were rich.

Our house was made of reddish brick, on a parcel that was 40 feet wide by 100 feet deep. It had a small kitchen, the dining room, and the living room on the first floor and three small bedrooms upstairs with a bathroom. There was also a full basement that my father built into a family room. When I was young, I spent many hours in the basement room, playing with my Lionel electric trains, watching films on my 8mm Keystone movie projector, and building and repairing things at my father's workbench. Later, the basement was my retreat to listen to music on our phonograph and to neck with girls.

I enjoyed playing basketball with my father in the driveway at the rear of the house. My parents had a small, one-car garage built there and hung a backboard and hoop on the garage's face. Dad loved to shoot foul shots underhand and was good at it. We would compete and he usually won. During college, I worked in the liquor warehouse where my father was employed, unloading trailers with cases of liquor. I also worked as a helper on the liquor trucks delivering liquor throughout the New York metropolitan area.

My father was a person of few words. Probably like most fathers in those times, he never told me about the "facts of life." He never helped me with my homework. That was left to my mother. His lessons were taught by example. He taught me the importance of hard work and perseverance. He accepted his responsibilities as sole provider of the family, working long nighttime hours, often twelve- to fifteen-hour shifts, when overtime was available. He showed me that, sometimes, you just had to do your job even though you didn't respect or like either your boss or the work that you did.

My father loved our house and spent most of his free time at home working on projects. He did much of the repair and maintenance work himself although he made deals with neighbors to do the more detailed work. He worked nights for most of his life, so he had the daytime to get to know storeowners and tradespeople in the area. He befriended the Rubins, owner of the paint store on Jericho Turnpike, the Bucelinos, owners of a gas station on Jericho, and later, the owners of the Esso station on Hillside Avenue. Dad's access to alcohol was the grease that moved the wheels for many tradesmen and merchants who loved to drink hard liquor. He bartered liquor for auto repairs, plumbing and electrical work, and auto parts. Freddie, the mason, built the garage and the front porch for cash and liquor. He made similar deals with Charlie, the plumber, and Ernie, the auto mechanic. Dad built the basement playroom by himself. He had a workbench downstairs and spent many hours tinkering with things. He was always painting, repairing something, doing odd jobs on the car or in the garage, or chatting with one of the neighbors or the friends he had in the neighborhood or in the village. He got along well with a lot of people.

On Jewish holidays, we dressed up in suits and ties and walked to Temple Beth Sholom, about a mile away. My parents couldn't afford to pay the full annual temple membership fee and made a deal with the rabbi for a reduced rate. The tradition was not to drive a car on the High Holy Days, Rosh Hashanah and Yom Kippur. We honored this tradition for a few years. Later, we drove to the temple in our car, parking nearby.

My mother stayed home. I always felt awkward at the temple, even when I attended bar mitzvah classes for two years from age 11 to 13. I never acquired a love for, or belief, in religion. It wasn't that I had something against Judaism or any religion. I just never acquired an appreciation for it as part of my life. This attitude has continued throughout my life. I memorized the Hebrew language lessons and the Jewish studies but I was too busy playing ball, having fun, and being self-conscious around girls.

When some junior high school kids threw rocks through the temple classroom window on Willis Avenue while I was in Hebrew class, I was upset but didn't interpret this act as anti-Semitism. I didn't become aware of anti-Semitism until I was fifteen. I was aware that Mineola had few Jewish families, and was mainly populated by Italian, Irish, and Portuguese families. I didn't know about the Holocaust until I was about seventeen, when I read *Exodus*. I was shocked at the horrendous events, cried at the tragic stories told, and celebrated those who were able to survive and founded Israel.

I clearly remember when a childhood friend learned that I was Jewish. We were walking together to school one day, he to Chaminade High School, the regional Catholic School, and I to Mineola High School. When he asked me if I was Jewish, his face showed his disbelief, as if to say, "How could a Jew, whose ancestors murdered Jesus, be a nice person who is my friend?" This upset me; I did not want to have anything to do with him any longer. I began to see that I was considered different by my Christian schoolmates. They must have stereotyped me according to the stories they heard from their parents about Jewish people. Jews were regarded as wealthy and stingy, neither of which we were. I have wondered sometimes whether my Jewish identity would have been different if I lived in Great Neck, Plainview, or Levittown, Long Island hamlets with large Jewish populations. I'll never know.

I quickly learned that being Jewish was part of the way I was viewed by the coaches in Mineola's athletic department. They were excessively critical of me if I made a bad play. When I played on the freshman and junior varsity football teams, they called me "chicken" in front of my teammates if I was tentative in making a tackle. Their prejudice was subtle, never overt. I saw them as authority figures to be respected who saw my personal weaknesses and insecurities. This hurt me. I also began to see that I was not invited to parties that my teammates went to and that I was not part of the athletic group that hung out at Ringen's Ice Cream Parlor and dated the popular girls. I began to wonder what was wrong with me and worried that I wasn't good-looking enough.

I recall a funny experience having to do with being Jewish in Mineola and my mother's attitudes. One day, a neighbor knocked on our front door selling raffle tickets. Wanting to be neighborly, I bought a twenty-five cent raffle ticket. About a month later, the neighbor came to the house with a smile on her face and my prize in a box. It was a crucifix. My mother couldn't wait to get it out of the house. She thought it was a jinx.

Years later, *Newsday* did an exposé about one of Mineola's athletic coaches, a popular and highly regarded basketball and football coach. He had accumulated an impressive winning record as a high school coach and had many admirers. Thanks to *Newsday*, however, I learned about his critics. The story indicated that the Father's Club at the high school took him to task for his prejudicial attitudes toward black and Jewish players. They censured him, an unheard-of phenomenon, that a Father's Club should take such an action. I bumped into him years later and discovered that he was a member of an extreme right-wing, John Birch Society group in Lloyd Harbor. I've often wondered how many other boys experienced his "character-building" machine.

I never had any relationships with black people until junior high school. I recall when the whole neighborhood was alarmed that a black (called Negroes at the time) family might buy a house on nearby Watkins Drive. Blacks lived in Mineola on two blocks near the Garden City border, sometimes called Garden City South. There were no blacks living in northwestern Mineola where we lived in the late 1940s and 1950s. The owners of the house were angry at their neighbors for some reason and threatened to "sell to Negroes." Everyone was fearful that property values would decline. They were upset that a white family would do this to other white families. There were threats made to this family. The house was eventually sold to whites but the experience was very distasteful to me. I told my mother about my feelings, but she seemed to understand the neighborhood's concerns.

I also remember that when I was in Mineola Junior High School, in 1951, I brought a black classmate, Al Cunningham, home after school to play. He had a Lionel train set like I did. I visited his house once or twice. After he left, my parents discouraged me from getting "too friendly" with him, saying that it wasn't a good idea. I didn't understand why and argued with my parents about how wrong and unfair their attitude was, but they said I was too young to understand.

My upbringing did little to promote political consciousness or involvement. My parents were registered Democrats and religiously voted in local and national elections but I don't recall ever hearing a discussion about Adlai Stevenson, Dwight Eisenhower, Richard Nixon, or John F. Kennedy while I lived with my parents. In like manner, there was no discussion about Senator Joseph McCarthy's hearings about communism in America. My parents were busy earning a living and achieving the signs of success that all the other families around us aspired to: a nice green lawn, a late-model car, a washing machine and dryer, a dishwasher, an annual vacation, and sending the children to college.

During my childhood, vacationing every year was something to look forward to. The trips were always taken in the first two weeks of July when the liquor industry shut down. One summer, we traveled to Washington, D.C. to visit the various presidential memorials. Several summers were spent staying in rented cabins at Lake George in upstate New York and Lake Winnipesaukee in New Hampshire. These were memorable times when I enjoyed playing ball with my brother and father; fishing and rowing boats on the lakes; and eating in restaurants, something we rarely did.

My mother was in charge of the family's finances. Dad brought home his weekly salary in pocket-sized manila pay envelopes and my mother managed every penny. It wasn't easy. Dad's base pay wasn't enough to get by on so he took every advantage of opportunities to work overtime, even though it meant working all night and coming home for a few hours of sleep only to return again to the same schedule. My parents paid cash for everything. It was inconceivable, in those years, to borrow money to buy things. My parents were not able to save anything so when it came time for me to go to college they had nothing.

There were years in which my parents owned two businesses. First, it was a Laundromat on Hillside Avenue near where we lived. My father helped in the store but my mother put in many, many hours there, seven days a week. She handled the accounts, paid the bills, folded laundry, gave change, and talked with the customers. The store never made much money, but it was a way for my mother to get out of the house and be with people.

Later, my parents were offered the opportunity to be part-owners of a liquor store, something my father had always wanted to do. My uncle Shel and one of his friends put up the money and had majority ownership. The idea was that my father, who knew the liquor business and had many contacts in the industry, would run the store. According to my mother, Shel and his partner were really investing in her business savvy, not my father's. The store was in the Bronx, at 170th Street and Jerome Avenue, in a neighborhood that was increasingly populated by blacks and Hispanics. The owners, a husband and wife, were older Jews who were retiring after many years.

For several years, my parents traveled every day to the Bronx to open the store by 8 AM and close by midnight. Sometimes the store made money, but it was a terrible struggle to pay the bills and deal with the employees and customers. For years, alcoholics would wait for the store to be opened at eight o'clock every morning every day of the year except New Year's Day. It was a poverty stricken neighborhood and many scary things happened at the store. On three occasions, my brother Rob was there when the store was robbed. He began to wear a bullet-proof vest at my mother's insistence. For many years, Rob ran the liquor store. After a full day of teaching in a Coney Island elementary school (and on Saturdays), he would drive to the Bronx to manage the store, coming home after midnight. Initially, he worked there to help my parents, because the store was losing money, and they couldn't afford to hire a manager.

Throughout my childhood, I was resourceful about earning money. I recall designing a miniature golf course on the perimeter of our small backyard. It had a wishing-well and other holes with underground masonry tunnels through which a golf ball could roll. I charged neighborhood kids to play the course. I collected empty beer and soda bottles when the tradesmen were building the many new houses in our neighborhood. I brought them in my red wagon to local grocery stories and delicatessens to collect pennies, nickels, and dimes. When I was ten years old, my grandmother bought me an 8mm Keystone movie projector, a very expensive gift. I think it cost $25. I saved my earnings from returning the beer and soda bottles and from admissions to the miniature golf course and bought cartoon film shorts at a drug store on Mineola Boulevard. The films featured Abbott and Costello, W.C. Fields, Mickey Mouse, Woody Woodpecker, and other animated figures. I charged the neighborhood children to watch the films. I built a tiny projection booth under the basement staircase and carved a hole in the playroom plasterboard wall so that the playroom was like a real theater. I bought envelopes of Kool-Aid at a supermarket, mixed it in a big pot of water, and sold it to passers-by at a bus stop on Jericho Turnpike facing Chaminade High School. I also ordered duck and chicken patterns from a *Popular Mechanics* magazine ad, bought wood at a lumber yard with my father, and made wooden lawn ornaments that I sold to our neighbors after I'd cut, sanded, and painted them on my father's workbench. In junior high school, I delivered newspapers in the neighborhood afterschool and on weekends, first the *Long Island Press* and, later, *Newsday*. I was always earning money. It gave me a sense of independence and freedom.

I also liked to take photographs. My uncle Harold gave me a German box camera that I valued. I became the family photographer on vacations and special occasions. I carried this interest into adulthood. I get pleasure knowing that some of the photographs I've taken of our children and grandchildren will be part of my legacy.

Playing cards was one of my father's lifelong passions. He played cards with neighbors on Sunday nights at one another's houses. The women would prepare coffee and snacks. His card playing went to another level for a while. My wealthy uncle Shel had made a fortune manufacturing and selling belt backings. He would stake my father to play with the high rollers at the Old Westbury Country Club. My father would tell stories about how Shel would win or lose thousands of dollars without concern.

My parents loved to go to Roosevelt Race Track. My mother would start out with ten dollars. If she lost it, that was it. She was pretty lucky. She would read the program to learn about the horse—who owned it, what its post position was, when it last ran, whether it won on a muddy track, and who the jockey was. My mother knew the jockeys by name and only bet to win. She used to say, "If the horse can't win for me, let him drop dead!" She always loved the number eight horse. She used to scream at her horse. Once she won the daily double, and she was so excited that she went down to the rail at the winner's circle and begged the driver to let her pat the horse. He let her and everyone cheered. Her love of horses went back to when she was a teenager and rode horses in Brooklyn's Prospect Park.

When I was nine years old, I got a terrible cold that wouldn't go away. We didn't have a local doctor so my mother called her cousin, Dr. Sidney, who lived in Brooklyn. He drove out to Long Island with his wife, Flora. He didn't know what was wrong with me, so he recommended that they bring me to Queens General Hospital in Jamaica because he didn't have privileges at a Long Island hospital. At the hospital, they performed a spinal tap and diagnosed polio. It was late at night and I was scared and confused. My mother and father were in another room and could hear me screaming. I didn't know it then, but my mother was crying and throwing up. The daily newspapers featured stories about a polio epidemic. My mother had seen photographs of children in wheelchairs and with crutches and metal braces on their legs, and she was scared. Finally, Dr. Sidney came out and gave my parents the good news: it was a very mild case of polio and there would be no side effects. My parents were so relieved.

I remained at the hospital for ten days. My parents came to visit every day and brought me ice cream and toys. My mother reports that the ice cream mogul Howard Johnson's son was in the hospital at the same time. He laughed when my parents brought ice cream to me. He said that they didn't need to bring it; his father would bring all the ice cream we wanted.

HE'S THANKFUL: Nine-year-old Paul Arfin, above, of 109 Argyle road, Mineola, looks like any other average boy—and he is! But he has a special reason to be thankful on tomorrow's Thanksgiving Day. Three short months ago he was stricken by bulbar polio and was not expected to live. Today he is completely recovered and is looking forward to spring and baseball. His mother says doctors claim Paul's recovery is "miraculous."

Me in Long Island Press after bout with polio, 1950

When I returned home from the hospital after my bout with polio, my parents were so excited that they bought a 12-inch black-and-white Dumont television set, our first TV set and one of the first in the neighborhood. Soon, my mother contacted the *Long Island Press* newspaper who sent a reporter to interview me and take a picture. That photo of me, wearing a cowboy hat and straddling my new chrome bicycle, appeared on the front page of the newspaper. The story said that I had overcome bulbar (spinal) polio. Many children hadn't been so lucky because their polio was detected too late or was too severe a case and were placed in "iron lungs," to ease their breathing. While in the hospital, I saw many children in "iron lungs."

My mother never told my grandmother about my polio. The silence about my illness was an example of my family's policy of keeping bad news a secret. Silence was also a response to death, along with "protecting the children" from sadness and grief. As a child and young adult, I was never brought to the family cemetery plot.

As I got older, I became very aware how protected and sheltered I had been as a child, especially by my mother. I rebelled against her attitude and saw it as a way to keep me a child and dependent on her. I decided then not to shelter my future children. I made the commitment to myself to enable my children to find their own ways, to handle their own fights, to learn to use words to settle disputes, and not to be too dependent upon their parents.

During my childhood, my parents maintained strong ties with most of my mother's brothers and sisters and their spouses. They had many special times with Harold and Ceil, Sidney and Sandy, Murray and Gloria, Irving and Helen, and Thelma and Shel. My mother was the glue that kept communications going within the extended family. As the oldest child, she naturally assumed this role. She maintained frequent contact with her sisters and brothers and invited family members to our house. I was always impressed with her leadership in family relations. She enjoyed volunteer community service and spent several years involved with Hadassah. She served as editor of Temple Beth Sholom's Hadassah newsletter, and wrote clever rhythmical poems and stories about member activities. I recall helping my mother to fold and package the newsletters on the dining-room table for their monthly mailings.

My parents also attended many meetings and social events of the Ladden Family Organization, the mutual aid society that my grandparents and distant cousins established. I have fond reminiscences of the annual Ladden Family Organization picnics at Hempstead Lake State Park when we played softball with all of

the men in the family. I remember being upset
if it rained and the picnic was cancelled. On
one occasion, I remember the entire extended
family coming to our house when the picnic was
rained out. My childhood was filled with visits
from my cousins and visits to their homes. We
had wonderful times together, especially with
my cousins Lana and Michael, Caroleah, Marsha
and Bruce, Andrea and Michael, Marilyn and
Mickey, and Jeffrey and Michaelyn. As adults, we
don't have much to do with one another but we
share fond reminiscences of the time we spent
together when we were young.

We had little to do with my father's side of the
family. His sisters Esther and Fay married and lived
modest lives in the city. They were very religious
and followed the old traditions. I always felt that
our visits were due to a sense of obligation. My
father's brother Irving, or "Red" (nicknamed due
to his reddish hair), married and had children but
we had little to do with them. Red died at an
early age.

Many years later, I got involved with the
Ladden Family Organization and became its
president. The group had been inactive for
many years. We basically saw one another at
weddings, bar and bat mitzvahs, and funerals. I
organized a reunion which was well-attended,
with some relatives traveling distances to be
there. Not too long after the family reunion,

things broke down. Several of the cousins and I complained to another group of cousins that the two cemeteries where the family owned burial plots wouldn't permit non-Jews to be buried there because Jewish law requires Jews to be buried in ground that's been sanctified by a rabbi. This was an issue to us because some of our cousins had intermarried with non-Jews. First, we suggested a "don't ask/don't tell" policy where it would be assumed that the deceased was Jewish. This offended many cousins who had sworn to their deceased parents that the cemetery would follow Jewish law into perpetuity. So we proposed purchasing another burial plot in an additional cemetery where Jews and non-Jews could be buried together. This became my mission as president of the association.

The purchase of this property generated considerable controversy in the family. Some felt that we were proposing to use funds donated by our ancestors to buy expensive land that few might use. From some of the remarks made during family meetings, I suspected that some of my cousins were prejudiced against non-Jews and didn't want to do anything to condone intermarriage. Who knows, someone might marry a person of color! When I said as much, they got offended. Ultimately, the property was purchased but not without tension and divisiveness.

At eight I developed my first crush, on Audrey Dosé, who lived around the block in one of the big houses on Foch Boulevard. Actually, they were modest homes built a few years before ours, so it was just that the neighborhood looked more settled. I never had the confidence to talk to her throughout twelve years of school. I perceived her as beautiful and unapproachable. I went out of my way to pass her house whenever I could, although I don't know what I would have done if I had actually seen her. Audrey became a high school cheerleader, a classic beauty whose presence always stopped me in my tracks.

Insecurity with girls plagued me throughout my school years. Gail Bender, a girl in junior high school, had been making eyes at me in the hallways, so I took her to a dance. When I walked her home from the dance, it was already dark outside. We went into her backyard where we talked. All I could do was talk and talk even though I wanted to kiss her. I knew she wanted to be kissed, but I couldn't muster the courage to do it. She eventually asked me what color eyes she had. Without a clue, I got real close to her, looked into her eyes, and told her she had brown eyes. She was stunned at my response. I felt like a jerk and went home frustrated at my ineptitude with girls.

Steve Einhorn was a childhood friend. We spent many hours playing baseball together.

Steve went on to be a very good catcher throughout high school. We also played board games, especially Monopoly, and card games. He was very clever and always beat me, which didn't make me feel very smart. His father, Henry, was an insurance salesman, attended all our baseball games, and often praised my play. It was no surprise to learn years later that Steve became a very successful salesman.

One of my friends was Andy Schwartz. Andy was a bad influence. He had "dirty" pictures under his mattress which fascinated me. Andy stole 45 RPM records from the music store on Jericho Turnpike, placing them in his maroon parka. Andy pressured me to join him in this thievery both at the music store and at Korvette's department store, and—I confess—I did it. Andy dated Sally Lubin, who was known to "put out." One time, Andy insisted I go to the movies with him and Sally so I could see how he "felt her up." As I watched, I was astounded by his guts. When he asked me if I wanted a feel, I refused.

Another close friend was Todd Bergman. Todd lived a few blocks away. I met him when I delivered newspapers to his house. Todd went to Chaminade, the Catholic high school, across the street from Mineola High School. We did a lot of silly things together. We imitated skits by TV comedian Louis Nye, whose popular character was named Gordon Hathaway, a ladies man. I played Gordon, interviewing Todd, the straight man who set me up to talk like Louis Nye with his suave, cool demeanor. You had to be there to appreciate it. Todd attended West Point, went to Viet Nam, and later became a successful businessman for one of the big oil companies.

I loved baseball. I watched the Brooklyn Dodgers games on television or listened to the games on the radio. When I was a young boy, I played with friends on the block. We played on a field on Emory Road that we called the "siren" because the water company had a fenced-in metal tower with a siren that shrieked, on the hour, all day long, plus when there was a fire.

From ages 11 to 18, I spent my summers playing on organized baseball teams, I played on the Mineola Elves (a pre-Little League team), the Mineola Little League, Babe Ruth League, and the Connie Mack League. Among my teammates were Ray and George Cross, Al Pedicini, Al Trimborn, Gary Peers, Gerry Asher, Dick Nonelle, Steve Einhorn, Jimmy Dunne, Bob Latham, Jay Kessell, and Dick Hayde. I always played first-string on teams and sometimes stood out as a player.

The Mineola Elves, 1951 (me, second row, third from left)

Growing up, my greatest baseball heroes were Joe DiMaggio and Jackie Robinson. When I was in the hospital with polio, my mother wrote to the Yankees and asked if "Joltin' Joe" could write me a letter, which he did. I treasured it for many years. I particularly identified with Jackie Robinson after reading *The Jackie Robinson Story* and empathized with the struggles he experienced as a black man and his strength of character facing racism. It troubled me to hear how people treated one another based on their race. I admired Jackie's aggressive base-stealing and did my share of base-stealing. Through high school and college, my batting stance was modeled on Jackie's.

In my last year of Little League, I pitched for the winning team at the Fourth of July game and hit a home run with the bases loaded. My father was there and sitting next to Mineola's Mayor. As I rounded the bases, I could hear him yell, "That's my boy!" However, when I struck out at my next at bat, he criticized me in front of my teammates. I was very embarrassed and cried. It ruined the day for me. I never seemed to get it right with him.

I was a member of every All Star Team. I thought I would eventually replace Roy Campanella behind the plate as the catcher for the Brooklyn Dodgers. I went on to be a star player in Babe Ruth and Connie Mack Leagues. One time, I hit the ball over the right field fence at the high school, which must have been a 350-foot shot. I didn't have a very good batting average but excelled as an outfielder and second baseman. My father came to some of the games before going to work. I was very aware of his presence and tried to do well when he was there.

A year before my thirteenth birthday, I began to study for my bar mitzvah. I attended Hebrew School and was tutored by Rabbi Morris Speier for my *haftorah* (a reading from the torah). My parents arranged for a big party to be held on the Saturday evening after morning service.

My mother and me at my bar mitzvah

In high school, I was selected to play on the first-string squad on the varsity baseball team when I was a sophomore, having demonstrated powerful hitting during practices. I was thrilled to be on the same team as high school seniors who I had always admired especially Pete Crispo, Don Golden, Howie Iffinger, and Bill Irwin. On more than one occasion, I hit the ball onto the high school roof in center field. Then, in the first few competitive games, I struck out regularly and ended up on the bench for most of the season. I was a fast runner so the coach used me in a critical squeeze play against Glen Cove in which

I scored the winning run. Our team went on to win the Nassau County Championship in 1956, beating Sewanaka. I also played football for one year and basketball for two years. In my senior year, I stopped my high school baseball career and joined the track team because I concluded I didn't have what it takes to be a professional baseball player. Since I was the fastest runner on the baseball team, I thought I would do well in track. I ran the 440-yard dash and threw the shot put. I found that my track running speed was good but not exceptional. I did come in second and third in some events.

In my junior year in high school, I needed to earn money to buy a car. I found a job at the King Kullen supermarket on Jericho Turnpike where I started off earning eighty cents an hour. I worked after school twenty hours a week and was very enthusiastic about my work. I was first assigned to stock the dairy department and grew to know all of the prices by heart. Soon, I was ordering the products so that we didn't run out of anything. Later, I was taught to be a cashier.

With my earnings, I bought a used car, a 1954 black-and-white, two-door, standard-shift Ford. My parents lent me $400 of the $750 I needed. I paid them back $20 a week for the next twenty weeks.

Me at 17, washing my 1954 Ford

When I was seventeen, I passed the high school driver's education course and test and got a driver's license. That license was very important to me. It represented freedom and independence from my parents. Before I got my own car, I got up early every Saturday morning for the chance to drive my father's 1954 Pontiac. The first time I took the car for an early Saturday morning ride, I skidded off a wet road in Old Westbury and scraped the side of the car against a fence. My father was furious, but my mother calmed him down.

I had other misadventures associated with driving. My father said I had a "heavy foot." My Ford had a standard shift on the column. I loved to rev it up at lights and race away. Once, on Herricks Road, I met up with a fellow student, Dick Mohrman, who had borrowed his brother's gray 1952 Oldsmobile coupe. We approached Jericho Turnpike and signaled to one another to turn east on Jericho to drag race. At each traffic light, we revved and raced. Neither of us noticed the police car behind us. As we approached Mineola Boulevard, he pulled us both over and gave us speeding tickets.

In my senior year, a friend, Carl Anderson, invited me and some other guys to a bachelor party. Carl soon married a girl named Evelyn who was a sophomore and lived in the neighborhood. They had a baby. Evelyn's parents were supportive of their daughter and accepted Carl as a son but the newlyweds were the subject of scorn in the community, which upset me so I became Carl's friend. Carl and Evelyn lived in an upstairs bedroom in her parents' house.

The bachelor party was held in New York City's Germantown. We drank a lot of Lowenbrau dark beer and ate steamed hot dogs with sauerkraut until three in the morning. I drove, probably legally intoxicated over the Triborough Bridge and onto the Grand Central Parkway only to be stopped by a policeman. He gave me a speeding ticket but, fortunately, not a sobriety test. These two speeding tickets put my license at risk, but that didn't stop my heavy foot. A year later, while in college, I got another ticket in the Bronx, where I accidentally went the wrong way up a one-way street. I appeared before a judge who took my license away for one year. I didn't know what to do since I needed my car to get to college and work. My father decided to call in a favor from someone he knew in the motor vehicle bureau. I was given a stern warning and a three-month suspension of my license.

I was a "nester," always looking for the girl I would marry. Myra, a Jewish girl, was my girlfriend for several of my adolescent years. We went to the movies and dances together, and when we stayed in and watched TV, we sometimes played a game where, when an agreed-upon word was said on the TV, we would kiss. The word "the" was my favorite word selection. We hugged and kissed a lot but nothing else. Somehow, I thought "everything else" should wait until after you were married. I was fascinated by Myra's emerging breasts. I went out of my way to get peeks of her bra when her blouse was positioned in certain ways or when she bent over. I felt guilty for looking but couldn't stop myself. I was heartbroken when Myra and her family moved to Massachusetts at the end of my senior year in high school. I drove to see her often for a while. Within a year, the relationship ended, the victim of romance from afar.

When I was a teenager, I was very shy and immature with girls, like most of my friends. I was moody and often stayed in my room for hours at a time with the door closed, staring out the window a lot. I was very critical of my parents. When I was sixteen and a sophomore in high school, our neighbor Lenny Lawrence offered to bring me to El Paso, Texas for the summer. I jumped at the idea. My father and Larry spoke with Ben Wallace, the principal, who allowed me to take my exams two weeks before school closed so that I could go with Lenny. Mother wasn't happy, because she was afraid that Lenny would be too permissive.

The trip was an awakening for me. I made new friends, traveled throughout the beautiful Southwest and came home wanting the family to move. Larry took me along on his travels as a dry goods salesman. We visited trading posts on Indian reservations throughout west Texas, New Mexico, Arizona, and Colorado. We visited Chaco Canyon National Historical Park, Bandelier National Monument, White Sands National Monument, the Taos Pueblo, and Window Rock, the headquarters of the Navajo. It was beautiful country. I wore a white cowboy hat all summer and began to learn Spanish, mainly from the Lawrences' house-cleaner. The Lawrences introduced me to their friends with teenage children. This developed into invitations to parties and playing poker as well as visits to Juarez, Mexico, across the border. Some of the boys went to whorehouses. I reluctantly went inside of one with them and was approached by some girls. Not knowing what to do and worrying about making a fool of myself, I refused to have sex. Fortunately, my friends were joking around, probably because they were also uneasy. We left within ten minutes.

My brother Robert was born in 1944. During the time my mother was expecting, she went to stay with Michael and Anna so that her father, Michael, would be able to take her to the hospital at any hour since the birth could take place while my father was working. When my mother was ready to go the hospital, Michael got his car and my father rushed over and jumped on the car's running board. A policeman saw them speeding down Fifteenth Avenue and escorted them to the hospital with his siren screaming. My mother was immediately admitted to the hospital and a funny thing happened. Dr. Sidney's wife Flora came to the hospital with him. She told Sidney to "make sure it's a girl. She already has a boy!" When Dr. Sidney saw that mother was having another boy he said how lucky she was because he had three girls!

My sister Michaelyn was born in 1948 just after the family had moved to Mineola. My father drove my mother all the way from Long Island to

Brooklyn Jewish Hospital. Dr. Sidney delivered the baby and screamed, "It's a girl!" My mother's first reaction was disappointment. Her father had recently died, and she wanted to be the first of his children to name a child after him. Eventually, each of her brothers and sisters named a child Michael, or a similar name, in memory of their father.

My brother and I got along and had lots of toys and games that we shared. Rob hated to wear my hand-me-down clothing so my mother bought him his own. However, he had no problem with playing with my old toys, which was good because the family couldn't afford to buy new clothing and toys for both of us.

Rob and I shared the same 10' x 10' bedroom with our beds nearly touching one another. I remember playing all kinds of games with Rob. We would play a lot of hide and seek, in the house and outside. We would hide in closets under clothing, in the attic crawlspace, in the loft of the garage, on top of the oil burner, in the closet under the staircase, and in the basement slop-sink. At night, we would play twenty questions before we went to bed. On the weekends, we shaped our pillows and covers as boats or stockades and had imaginary naval battles and conflicts between cowboys and Indians. We had our fights but never seriously hurt one another.

One rainy day when we were very young, we were bored. We didn't know what to do. We were complaining a lot to our parents. Our father scolded, "Go bang your heads against the wall!" —his usual advice at times like those. He warned us that if we kept complaining he would send us to Boys Town Nebraska, which we understood to be a place for "bad" boys. We had seen letters from Boys Town on the dining room table from time to time. But we ignored his warning. Our father, still angry, went to the telephone and asked for long distance, person-to-person to speak with Father Flanagan. He had us believing that Father Flanagan actually got on the phone and spoke to him. We cried and begged, "Daddy, Daddy, we'll be good! Don't send us away!" His bluff worked. We settled down. Little did we know, at the time, that the letters from Boys Town were appeals for donations. It was cruel but effective.

Summers were times to fly kites, play baseball, box ball, stoop ball, and stick ball, flip baseball cards, make scooters out of milk crates and roller skate wheels, play marbles, skate on the sidewalk, and set up forts in the nearby lots and pretend we were soldiers, or cowboys and Indians. We both had holsters and guns and cowboy hats. We made a tree fort in the empty lot adjacent to our house and made campfires.

One time, the campfire we started in the vacant lot next to our property got out of hand. Panicking, Rob and I ran into the house and hid in the basement. Meanwhile, the firemen arrived and put out the fire we had started. It leveled the trees and weeds in the lot. We heard sirens and the commotion we caused through the basement window. My mother found us in the basement and deduced that we were responsible for the fire. We felt terrible.

At times, we buried raw potatoes under a campfire's coal embers. We called them "mickies." It was years later when I connected the word mickies with the Irish. Just as I didn't make the connection between blacks and the N-word as in the phrase: "eenie, meenie, minie, moe, catch a n_____, by the toe, if he hollers let him go..." When I found out, I felt terrible and searched my memory for instances when I had used this racist language. As hard as it is to believe now, the word was common back then, and no one told us not to use it. Who knew?

When Rob was in junior high school, school officials wanted to promote him because he was very smart in all of his courses. The teacher asked my mother to come to the school to discuss the idea, but my mother decided that it was best to leave Rob in his grade level with his friends. Years later, he told my mother that he was glad that she had not agreed to promote him.

Rob was especially interested in playing baseball. We played baseball with a plastic wiffle bat and ball in the backyard and in the front of the house for hours at a time. Rob would represent the players in the New York Yankees lineup and I would represent the Brooklyn Dodgers players. We set up rules for what was a single, double, triple, and homerun. We would argue about who was the best player—Mickey Mantle, Duke Snider, or Willie Mays—and which was the best team. We imitated their batting stances and pitching motions. We knew their batting averages all the time. We watched baseball games on television and kept score cards of every play. As a Brooklyn Dodger fan, I suffered through all of the incredible World Series losses and that awful three-game playoff in 1951 with the New York Giants. In 1955, I had my vengeance when Brooklyn finally beat the Yankees in the World Series.

The day Rob was bar mitzvah, he was worried that when he was standing in front of our family and friends, he wouldn't remember the Hebrew words that he had memorized. He refused to go with the family to the temple. Rose and Bill Cohen, our next door neighbors, convinced him to go with them to the temple in their car. He did fine. The party wasn't as fancy as mine because the family didn't have that kind of money at the time and wouldn't consider getting a loan for such a purpose.

Being the younger son, Rob had to follow many of my paths. In high school, when the Spanish teacher, Paul Ash, called Rob "Pablo," he got angry and wouldn't answer. The teacher called my mother on the telephone to ask for a meeting. She went to the school and told him that she supported Rob's feelings. She told the teacher that if he continued to call Rob "Pablo," she would report him to the principal.

Rob's high school graduation day fell on the same day as my college graduation and Michaelyn's junior high school graduation. Our parents didn't know what to do. The solution: My uncle Sidney went to Michaelyn's graduation, my grandmother went to Rob's, and my parents went to my graduation. We all went to Patricia Murphy's Restaurant in Manhasset to celebrate together.

Rob was a very smart ballplayer and an especially good pitcher. He only wanted to be a pitcher and dreamed of making it to the big leagues. The problem was that he had chronic back problems. In 1963, when Rob was eighteen, my mother wrote a letter to Casey Stengel, the manager of the New York Mets. She wrote, "Dear Mr. Stengel, do yourself a favor. I have a son, that from his birth, wanted to be a ballplayer and my husband thinks he has a good arm. If you could spare the time, please check him out." Rob didn't know that she had written the letter. She didn't tell anybody. When Rob received a letter in the mail from the Mets inviting him to a tryout, he was flying. At the tryout at Shea Stadium, Ed Kranepool, who became a star player on the team, was getting a lot of attention. After the tryouts, Rob was told that he wasn't physically big enough to be a major league pitcher.

During high school, Rob worked at a children's carousel on Jericho Turnpike. After high school, he attended Nassau Community College. He went on to complete his college education at Ricker College in Maine where he graduated and met his wife, Liz. After college graduation, Rob became a successful teacher in Coney Island and, later, an effective school administrator. He is treated with respect by his students and is regarded as a capable school representative to community leaders and parents. He has also worked as a teacher in various yeshivas and as a director of large summer camps. Liz and Rob have three children, Jodi, Jason, and Matthew. Jodi married Lee, a computer technician with his own business. Jason is a CPA for a major wine distributor and married Penny. Matthew is a successful salesman and married Gigi.

While I was in the Peace Corps, Rob and I wrote to one another. I encouraged him to visit. To my happy surprise, Rob did visit, spending three weeks traveling with me to remote villages.

At the time, I didn't appreciate the financial sacrifice that Rob made to travel to a foreign country to spend time together. It was very important to me that my brother share my very special experience. Over the years, we have thought back on this important time in our lives.

My sister Michaelyn was heavily influenced by my Peace Corps service. She was inspired by my commitment to public service and wrote many papers in high school and college about the work I was doing in Colombia. She wrote letters to me while I was overseas. She continues to feel that my Peace Corps work influenced her to help people and to advance her education. She was also affected by my decision to talk with our mother about her hearing problem. I later learned that Michaelyn was in her bedroom with her ear to the air duct so that she could hear my appeal that our mother get medical help to deal with her hearing loss. We were all aware of her hearing deficit and compensated for it for many years. I felt that our mother might respond to my logic. I reasoned with her that she could improve the quality of her life if she could hear better. I convinced our mother to have the operation to correct the problem. Michaelyn points to my intervention as an important event in her teen years that influenced her desire to help people. It was gratifying to know that my action had such an impact.

Michaelyn earned an AA degree in Recreation Supervision at the State University at Farmingdale and later earned her Bachelor's degree in Elementary Education from City College. She worked in community recreation for a period of time and then held a position caring for children with developmental disabilities. She continues to volunteer with many local charities.

When Michaelyn was dating Victor, her future husband, my father would say, "If that boy was Jewish, I would get up on the roof and tell the world how proud I am to make him my son-in-law." My father knew that Victor came from a good family and was intelligent and was a wonderful son who helped his father in his gas station.

It didn't take long for Victor to be more than accepted by my father. Victor is a civil engineer and a very successful partner in a prominent civil engineering firm. My father grew to treat Victor with great affection—I often felt that he treated Victor with more affection and respect that he did me. He never understood what I did for a living or showed interest in it. After the Peace Corps, when I worked in youth agencies, he would frequently try to provoke my ire by asking, "When are you going to get a real job?" Sometimes, I showed him my paychecks to prove that I actually got paid for my work. Intellectually, I understood his inability to appreciate the work that I did, but emotionally his attitude and remarks hurt.

Michaelyn has a wonderful singing voice and volunteers to sing at local nursing homes and assisted living facilities including facilities where my mother has lived. My mother glows with pride to see her daughter on these occasions. Michaelyn and Victor have two daughters, Jessica and Lindsay. Jessica married Alex and has a career in human resources. After college graduation, Lindsay pursued a career as a hairdresser and works at an exclusive salon.

I recall fondly the many good times spent with my brother and sister. We share a common bond and love one another. It's sad to me that we have not been able to sustain a stronger relationship over the years. We came together when our father died and, recently, when our mother became dependent on the care of others. The three of us have lived busy lives with many family and work obligations. At the same time, I know that I have done more than my share to separate us through my judgmental attitudes. For this, I have much regret.

Graduation day for Michaelyn, Rob, and me, 1962

During junior and senior high school and college, I developed a strong friendship with Jeff Bloomberg that continues today. Jeff was one of the few other Jews at Mineola High School. While I was in the youth group at Temple Beth Sholom, Jeff and I dated girls from other temples. In high school and college, Jeff delivered furniture for his father who owned a furniture store in Queens. He and I would double date and go "cruising" looking for girls together in our cars. Jeff had a white Buick convertible with red upholstery. Jeff went to C.W. Post College and I went to Adelphi

College. We were on our college baseball teams and played against one another on at least one occasion, which was strange.

In college, Jeff and I worked together in the Hotel Brickman in the Catskill Mountains (sometimes referred to as the "Borscht Belt" or the "Jewish Alps") one summer. At Adelphi College, I introduced Jeff to his future wife, Joan Lubin. Joan and I were classmates in a drawing course and became friends. I was in the Peace Corps when Jeff and Joan got married and was disappointed not to be at their wedding. After they were married, Jeff studied dentistry at New York University after which he and Joan spent two years stationed in Alaska in the Army. Jeff became fascinated with huskies and raced them, sometimes winning. When they bought an upstate New York home, Jeff bought several huskies, racing them throughout the Northeast and Canada. He named his dog kennel "Kuspid Kennels." Karen and I and Jeff and Joan have continued this close friendship every since, a wonderful gift. When our children were younger, we camped together in the Berkshires. Jeff and I love to play tennis, as does Joan. We cherish the times we spend together. It has been a retreat for us for many years. The door is always open if I need a place to stay when traveling to Albany on organizational business. Jeff became a dentist and administrator of a large dental clinic. Joan became a social worker and director of a county mental health clinic. Jeff later left dentistry to become a professional tennis instructor at various colleges where he built teams. For more than fifty years, Jeff has been like a brother to me, helping me with financial planning advice as well as with unconditional love.

Another close high school friend was the poet and biographer, Paul Mariani. Paul, his younger brother Walter—who had a whacky sense of humor—and I often drove upstate on weekends to get away from the pressures of living in suburban Long Island. Paul was a serious student, with a keen sense of humor. We often spent long hours into the night, as young men will, talking about our nearly non-existent exploits with girls, trying to map out the directions in which our confused futures were going to take us. In any event, girls, both as unattainable ideals and as centerfolds, were an important part of the mix.

The oldest of seven children, Paul transferred to Mineola High School from a year in Beacon, New York with the Marianist Brothers, the Catholic teaching order at Chaminade, where he had "hamletized" over whether to spend his life as a priest teaching high school and college students. His father, also named Paul, had run Scotty's Esso up on Jericho Turnpike for years. According to Paul, his father then decided to make his fortune running a Sinclair gas station on the other side of town. That dream lasted only long enough for the County Highway Department to close down the access road to the gas station, leaving his father to eventually file for bankruptcy.

Having decided that his own future lay in the prospect of getting married and having a family, Paul spent a fifth year of high school at Mineola High, taking courses in math and science, in an ill-directed attempt to prepare himself to become a civil engineer, before he finally opted for his real love: literature and the classics. Paul went on to Manhattan College, then Colgate for his Masters, and then the Graduate Center of the City University of New York for his Ph.D. Today, Paul is a Distinguished University Professor of English at the University of Massachusetts and holds a chair in poetry at Boston College.

I also developed a number of friendships with people who were raised in politically-conscious, liberal families, including Diane Siegal and Dave Simon. I came to share their distaste of conformity and suburban lifestyles. They introduced me to Greenwich Village where we attended poetry readings in coffee houses. I became aware of folk singers including Pete Seeger, Joan Baez, Woodie Guthrie, and the Weavers. I loved their songs of protest against the status quo, war, and social injustice. I was fascinated with Jack Kerouac's *On the Road* and identified with the restless main character.

My college years were very difficult for me. I lived at home and commuted by car to Adelphi College where I did poorly in most of my academic subjects. I barely graduated in four years. My father said I got "an 'A' in fraternity." Fortunately, I had enough B's to offset the many D's and F's that I had accumulated. College was a time when I began to feel more certain that I wasn't as intelligent as many of my friends. I had felt this in high school, too, but in college, it became apparent. I began to feel very insecure about my future. I couldn't imagine what I would do after college. I spoke to no one about these feelings of insecurity but began to identify with outsiders and anti Establishment causes. I was envious of many of my peers who had direction and careers in mind. They were pursuing the paths their parents had prescribed for them to become lawyers, doctors, accountants, and businessmen.

I studied towards a degree in what was called "general business." I had considered getting a degree in physical education to go into teaching but when I saw the science courses that I would have to take, I decided against this course of study. I took a smattering of courses in accounting, marketing, business writing, sales, and economics. I also took many courses in the Spanish language and culture. The only "A" I got in four years of college was in Spanish. The

Spanish classes were socially difficult for me because I was the only male in the room with some very bright female students. I had to repeat the accounting course and the English course in my freshman year. My study habits were terrible. I couldn't seem to absorb the material. I did my share of using the fraternity files to prepare papers that had been written by others.

For two years, I played on Adelphi's baseball team. I was a first-string player but didn't excel. I hit a number of home runs but my average was mediocre. I played the outfield and second base, and I was a relief pitcher. I remember one game against St. John's University where I was the relief pitcher. It was as if I was pitching batting practice. Every batter hit the ball over the outfield fences. I didn't last an inning. Talk about being humbled.

In my senior year, I joined the golf team. I had played golf on and off since age 14 when my uncle Shel gave me his old set of golf clubs. I played at Salisbury Park most of the time. My scores were usually in the nineties. At Adelphi, they remained the same which meant I rarely helped the team win any golf competitions. I do recall winning a match against Farmingdale State University. My opponent and I tied at the end of eighteen holes so we needed to go back out and play until one of us won. On the second hole, I hit a good drive. My second shot landed on the green about twenty-five feet from the pin. My opponent also placed his second shot on the green. I was able to make the putt for a birdie while my opponent missed his. I was thrilled to win and rush to the clubhouse to tell my teammates.

While in college, I continued to work in supermarkets, mostly at the Grand Union located up the block from our home. The manager was very flexible with my hours. I could work whenever I wanted, either as a cashier or as a stock boy. The income I earned at Grand Union provided the tuition and spending money I needed during college so that I didn't have to ask my parents for support. I took pride in this. Most of the people I knew in college didn't have to work in order to pay for their college educations.

I also worked for Peel Richards, the liquor distributor where my father worked. My jobs were both as a warehouseman, unloading trucks and as a helper on a truck, delivering liquor to stores, restaurants, and bars through the New York metropolitan area. I mostly worked between Thanksgiving and New Years Eve, the peak season in the liquor industry as well as at the beginning of each month when purchasers could take advantage of discounts if they paid by the fifth of the month. The work was hard but the overtime pay was great. At first, it was awkward, arriving at the Long Island City "shaping site" as a college kid whose father worked for company management. In fact, my father had spoken to the shop steward and arranged for me to get work. Sometimes, I felt bad when I got work while older men, perhaps married with children, weren't selected. I was also exposed to how truckers pad their pay checks by loafing. It was customary to leave the shape site, go to the warehouse to load the liquor, and then drive to side streets of Long Island City where we had half-hour breakfasts. At the end of the day, we would finish our deliveries and then find a quiet street where the driver parked. We would sleep for an hour or two before returning to the warehouse to clock in. I knew this was wrong but the pay was too good to say something about it. And, if I did "rat" on the men, my father would have been in a lot of trouble and I would lose this opportunity to pay for college, so I figured it wasn't my place to change the system.

In the summer after my sophomore year of college, Jeff Bloomberg and I decided to try to get jobs in a hotel in the Catskill Mountains. We understood that you could earn a lot of money from tips. One Saturday in late June, Jeff and I woke up early and drove Jeff's white Buick convertible up the New York Thruway and onto Route 17 to Monticello/South Fallsburg. Jeff figured that, with so many hotels in the area, one of them was likely to need a waiter or busboy at the last minute before the season began. By late afternoon, we had visited two dozen hotels with no success.

At the Hotel Brickman, we met with the maitre'd who was short two busboys. But there was a problem. He wanted to know our ages (we were both 19) and if we had experience working as waiters or busboys. It seems that the Brickman insisted on their dining-room staff being twenty-one years of age. I think they had this policy out of fear that their guests could accuse hotel staff of seducing their underage female guests.

We had prepared for the question about experience. We told him we had waited tables at Linak's Log Cabin in Centerport, New York. If he asked for references, we would tell him that the restaurant had burned down (which it actually did). But since we weren't 21, we decided to bluff and take our chances. The bluff worked. We said that we had left our wallets in our car's glove compartment. We turned to leave the dining room to go to the car when he called us back, saying it wasn't necessary to get our licenses. I saved two thousand dollars in ten weeks that summer, a lot of money at that time. Jeff didn't do as well and left before the summer was over. It was very hard work—seven days a week, seven o'clock in the morning to nine o'clock in the evening. I learned to cope by taking short naps during morning and afternoon breaks.

I also earned extra income driving one of the hotel's dance instructors to New York City from time to time. I got paid $25 to drive him the two hours to New York's Port Authority Terminal. We all suspected that he was gay and going to the city for a rendezvous. I didn't care about his lifestyle. I just knew that $25 was a lot of extra money.

My first college friend was Norm Reich. We were buddies during our freshman year and pledged the same fraternity. Norm was from a very wealthy family from Rochester, New York. I was invited to spend Thanksgiving at Norm's home and saw, for the first time in my life, what type of life big money could buy. Norm's father impressed me a great deal and was very generous. He was a self-made man. He didn't fit the negative stereotype of wealth that had begun to develop in my mind during college. Norm seemed unaffected by his family's wealth. I admired that a great deal. When Norm began to date his future wife, Judy, I was hurt and jealous. It felt like she robbed me of a friend.

The second fraternity brother whom I befriended was Lionel Simon. Lionel was a strange guy. He was several years older than the rest of us because he was studying on a part-time basis. He joined almost every club on campus because it enabled him to go to their meetings and get free food. He was very intelligent, the editor of the college literary magazine. He wrote poetry and had a dry sense of humor. He loved to pull pranks.

Once, he convinced me to join him in hijacking the college newspaper, *The Delphian,* on April Fool's Day. As a newspaper staff member, Lionel knew the exact details of where and when the paper was published. He knew the exact time of day when the paper was delivered by the printer to the campus. He knew the exact locations where the paper was placed throughout the campus by Bruce Montross, the editor. Lionel and I sat in my car in the dorm parking lot at daybreak waiting for the newspaper delivery and watched Bruce place the newspapers in his car for delivery. As I sat there with Lionel I increasingly thought that this was crazy and that I didn't want to be part of it. Ultimately, I refused, despite Lionel's protestations.

A third good friend at Adelphi was Kevin, one of the few black fraternity brothers. He lived in Hempstead. We studied together and drank a lot of beer at fraternity parties. None of the other frat brothers had close relationships with him. I remember being angry at their behavior. One of them actually used the n-word in referring to him and claimed he couldn't help it since he grew up in a home where blacks were hated. When I heard these remarks, I walked away to show my disapproval since I couldn't ignore the hateful racist references. None of the others did anything. I developed a reputation as an "overly sensitive" liberal and was ostracized from the fraternity group. I withdrew from most fraternity activities by my junior year.

Having sex was always on my mind and the minds of my friends. It was the subject of most conversations. You never knew which guys were actually being honest and which weren't about their sexual exploits. I felt like a loser. I'm sure that promiscuous coeds sensed my insecurity and didn't want to have anything to do with me. Those I did date didn't want to go all the way. I tried lots of rational arguments to convince them that it was okay to do it. While I dated fairly often, I was always looking for my future wife. I would go with one girl regularly until we broke off. Since I worked part-time, I always had my own car so my friends and I would go looking for girls at the bowling alley, beach, ice cream shops and later at the bars. I was never particularly successful in this capacity although I had several extended relationships.

One of those relationships was with Barbara Greene who was two years younger than me. I took Barbara to fraternity parties, to the movies, and night clubs in New York City. We did a lot of "parking" with hugging and kissing, nothing else. Years later, someone who had transferred from Boston University to Adelphi reported that Barbara, who had also transferred from BU, had been sleeping with "everyone wearing pants." Whether this was true or not, at the time, it hurt.

In my junior year at Adelphi College, President John F. Kennedy announced the establishment of the Peace Corps. I applied for entry into a program in a Latin American country when I graduated college. I was the 10,476th American to apply for admission to the Peace Corps. Because of my career uncertainties and my growing concern around social issues, the Peace Corps captured my interest. I had read a number of books about the history and politics of Latin American countries *The Winds of Revolution* by Tad Szulz and *The Great Fear in Latin America* by John Gerassi. I began to understand the significant role that the US played in the region and that the US used its substantial economic and political power to quell communist influences and to support dictators. I empathized with Fidel Castro's grassroots revolution against Fulgencio Bautista.

In the spring of my senior year, I joined the Army Reserve. I didn't have strong patriotic feelings or feel it was my duty to enlist. There were no wars going on at the time that tested my patriotism. I attended a few monthly drill meetings at an armory in Garden City before college graduation. I joined the Army Reserve because I was worried about being drafted into the Army. I couldn't imagine spending two years in the military, much less killing another human being. Joining the Army Reserve entailed a commitment of six months of active duty and five and a half years of two-week summer camps and monthly meetings with a local reserve unit. Six months versus two years. It was a no-brainer. I didn't have to chose among alternatives like young men had to do several years later when the Vietnam War was being fought. Over the years, I have wondered what type of soldier I would have been if the reserve unit was called to active duty. I'll never know.

When I graduated college in June 1962, I went into Army basic training at Fort Dix, in southern New Jersey. Six months of active duty was a terrible experience. I was a poor soldier, disobeying orders, and selling my guard duty and kitchen patrol duty to others so I could go home almost every weekend.

Me in the US Army Reserve, Fort Dix, NJ in 1962

I made friends with other recent college graduates who, like me, were counting the days until we got out of the Army. One of them had been a Reserve Officers' Training Corps (ROTC) student in high school and was, therefore, familiar with military drills and procedures. Once he learned how the weekly schedule of daily assignments was distributed, he figured out how we could avoid senseless duty on Tuesdays when reservists gathered after breakfast to be assigned to various monotonous projects. Our group assembled in front of the headquarters' building and marched to the commands of our ROTC buddy. He led us to an empty barracks building in an isolated section of the base where we would sleep on the floor until it was time to return for dinner. The basic idea was that if you looked like you knew what you were doing, you could get away with a lot. That turned out to be a good life lesson.

After basic training I was assigned to Fort Devens in central Massachusetts. Fort Devens was a military base primarily for men who had volunteered for military service. Reservists like me were in the extreme minority and were not treated as real soldiers. They were mostly assigned to completely menial tasks like kitchen duty (washing dishes), nighttime guard duty, cleaning latrines and offices, and weeding gardens. Officially, I was designated a Tracked Vehicle Specialist but received no track training. In the three months at Fort Devens, I was inside a tank once—just out of curiosity.

My days were mainly spent waking up at 0530 for roll call, eating meals, and standing in an unheated tool shed handing out tools to tank and auto mechanics. In the tool shed, I spent much of my time preparing a wall calendar that showed how many days I had left in the Army and how much time I had already put in. Calculators weren't in common use yet so I did the divisions with pencil and paper.

Most nights were spent off the base. I would get out of my uniform, put on my civilian clothing, and leave the base whether I had a pass or not. If I didn't have a pass, I would drive with another soldier who had a pass to a remote part of the base where I would climb over a chain-link fence. The other soldier, who lived in a nearby town, would drive off the base in my car and meet me along Route 2. I would drive him home and proceed to Cambridge, Massachusetts, about two hours from Fort Devens. At other times, I would hide under blankets in the trunk of the car. I figured that the worst they would do if I got caught was give me more kitchen patrol or guard duty, so I was willing to take the risk.

I had a friend at Harvard Law School, Joe Hirschfeld. Joe and I had worked together one summer at the Hotel Brickman in the Catskills during my college years. He gave me a key to his dorm room and let me stay there whenever I wanted. I joined him that fall with his fellow Harvard students when they attended mixers at Radcliffe, Wellesley, Boston University, Simmons, and Tufts.

I was a nervous wreck in the fall of 1962 when tensions grew to a crisis standstill between the Soviet Union and the US. The US discovered that the Soviet Union had a nuclear missile base in Cuba. The threat of war was in the air. I feared that my time in the Army might be extended. I re-contacted the Peace Corps to notify them that I was available for service after December 1962. I knew that if I joined the Peace Corps I would receive a deferment from military service so Peace Corps service was a way of postponing military service. With the world tensely watching

the daily news, President Kennedy ordered
a blockade of Cuba and demanded the
removal of all military bases. Tens of thousands
of US troops were on full alert and on the
verge of being sent to implement the invasion
recommendations by top US military leaders. The
scuttlebutt at Fort Devens was that the base's
enlistees and reservists would be sent to Germany
should America go to war in Cuba while troops
in Germany would be sent to fight in the invasion
of Cuba. Eventually, an agreement was made
between the US and Soviet Union whereby the
Soviet missiles were removed from Cuba and
American nuclear missiles were removed from
Turkey. The world watched on television to see
aerial photos of the Soviet removal of the missiles.
I felt a tremendous sense of personal relief.
In December, I received a telegram from the
Peace Corps inviting me to join Peace Corps V,
a rural community development group, going to
Colombia, South America in February 1963. Not
having any other plans for my life, I informed the
Peace Corps that I was available for service. My
life was about to change dramatically forever.

When I look back on my childhood and
adolescent years in Mineola and in college, it
was if the world outside didn't seem to exist.
The Korean War, the McCarthy hearings, and
the build-up of the military-industrial complex
under President Eisenhower took place. Efforts to

desegregate schools and register black citizens to vote in the South amidst fierce resistance of white southerners went on but didn't directly affect me and my family. We were another American postwar family trying to get our slice of the pie. My social consciousness of racism, poverty, and income inequalities was limited to my personal experiences with family and friends. Social protest movements came to my awareness late in high school through friendships with my progressive friends.

During my college years, I increasingly identified with anti-Establishment causes. I was troubled by America's love affair with consumerism as depicted in John Kenneth Galbraith's "The Affluent Society," Harper Lee's depiction of racism in "To Kill a Mockingbird," Michael Harrington's description of poverty in America in "The Other America," and William J. Lederer and Eugene Burdick's depiction of how American foreign policy was formulated and implemented in "The Ugly American." I recalled my childhood experiences as a Jew with racial prejudice and my objection to my parents' attitude towards "negroes." I also became aware of the Cuban revolution and viewed it as a positive step toward overthrowing a dictator. Something inside me was being ignited by knowledge of these social and political conditions, something that propelled me to take personal action and set aside the desires of my family that I pursue a traditional business career.

This passion for community service and social justice would continue to grow during the upcoming years. The first major action for me as an individual was to sign up for Peace Corps service. This decision proved to be a life altering one.

CHAPTER TWO
Peace Corps Service: 1963 – 1965

My mother was worried when I went into the Peace Corps. She was afraid that I wouldn't return or that I would marry a native. She actually boarded the airplane to say another goodbye after we had done so in the terminal.

My father couldn't understand what the Peace Corps was and why I would want to "throw away two years of my life." He represented the majority opinion among family and friends who believed that, with a college education, the world was mine for the taking. The Peace Corps didn't advance a career and that was all that mattered to them. My father gave me a handful of promotional pen knives from liquor companies to use if I needed "to barter with the natives." I accepted them not for bartering but for gifting.

When I insisted on entering the Peace Corps despite their entreaties, they took out "the big gun"—they commissioned my uncle Sidney, a successful businessman, to take me out the night before I was to leave for Colombia to try to change my mind. We went to the Roslyn Café and drank twelve-year-old Ambassador Scotch for several hours while Sidney tried to convince me to reconsider. He had no clue about my motivations or the Peace Corps' purpose. He talked about the great expectations that the family had for me, the family's first college graduate. He found that my mind was made up and no one was going to change it. He and my parents had no idea why someone would enter the Peace Corps. For them, life was all about earning a good living and taking care of your family. If I had planned to be a teacher, they would have understood, since teachers have good health and retirement benefits and security. But they knew nothing about careers in public service, social work, or community action.

In some ways I was the typical Peace Corps volunteer. I had graduated college and was from a middle class family, like many others and, like many of them I, too, was unsure about a career. Certainly, being Jewish placed me among a small minority. I was one of only two Jews in a group of sixty-five trainees. There were trainees from the west who had "never met a Jew" and seemed so fascinated I felt certain that they would share this information in their next letter home.

In October 1960, while I was in college, I was struck by presidential candidate John F. Kennedy's widely-publicized speech at the University of Michigan, in which he challenged students,

> How many of you who are going to be doctors, are willing to spend your days in Ghana? Technicians or engineers: How many of you are willing to work in the Foreign Service and spend your lives traveling around the world? On your willingness to do that, not merely to serve one year or two years in the service, but on your willingness to contribute part of your life to this country, I think, will depend the answer whether a free society can compete. I think it can! And I think Americans are willing to contribute. But the effort must be far greater than we have ever made in the past.

I was later captivated by President Kennedy's Alliance for Progress Program and its ambitious goals for peaceful change in Latin America. In 1961, at Punta del Este, Uruguay, President Kennedy proposed a ten-year plan for Latin America. He said:

We propose to complete the revolution of the Americas, to build a hemisphere where all men can hope for a suitable standard of living and all can live out their lives in dignity and in freedom. To achieve this goal political freedom must accompany material progress...Let us once again transform the American Continent into a vast crucible of revolutionary ideas and efforts, a tribute to the power of the creative energies of free men and women, an example to all the world that liberty and progress walk hand in hand. Let us once again awaken our American revolution until it guides the struggles of people everywhere-not with an imperialism of force or fear but the rule of courage and freedom and hope for the future of man.

My motivation was bolstered by a self-inventory that went something like this: Continuing my education didn't make sense. My study habits were poor, as were my grades. I knew that selling insurance was not for me, nor was working as a trainee in my uncle's textile business or becoming a management intern for a supermarket chain. My contemporaries were focused on becoming attorneys, accountants, entrepreneurs, and physicians. I didn't know what

I wanted to do as my life's work but I knew that I couldn't conform to the traditional, acquisitive, lifestyles that surrounded my upbringing.

However, I was able to speak reasonably good Spanish, my most marketable skill, and it made sense to me to build on what I knew. I deducted that living in Latin America could be challenging and fun, and it might be helpful in defining a career path. I saw the Peace Corps as a way station between the pressures and responsibilities of college and beginning the responsibilities of full-time employment and eventual marriage. It struck a chord as a unique way to set myself apart.

I wanted to be on my own. I lived at home while attending college and had only traveled off Long Island during the trip to the Southwest when I was sixteen years old. During my short military service, I came home often. I somehow knew that if I delayed leaving home, I risked falling into an unfulfilling, directionless lifestyle and being further smothered by well-meaning but controlling parents. I had lived a protected life in which my mother was a powerful figure; pleasing her was very important to me. I gathered the emotional courage to follow my instincts, whether it was sensible to my parents or not. This wasn't easy, but in retrospect, it was a major emotional turning point in my life.

Peace Corps training began in February 1963 at the University of New Mexico in Albuquerque and later in Taos, New Mexico which is located about two and a half hours north of Albuquerque. At the university, we were housed in a dormitory, ate in the cafeteria, attended lectures in the classrooms along with the university's regular students, and used the sports facilities. Training was a wonderful, stimulating experience that engendered a sense of freedom. I enjoyed our enthusiasm for the work and the camaraderie with the other volunteers who came from thirty different states. I liked the idea that I would be on my own answerable to only myself.

Our training group, called Colombia V, of all men, was a mixture of recent college graduates, those who had taken some college coursework, or were recent high school graduates from rural communities, as well as a handful of "older" men who were in their mid and late twenties. Some of our teachers were faculty at the university and others were academics from colleges and universities around the nation. I was seriously interested in the various courses and discussions about community development, Colombian history and politics, and the roles we were expected to play as rural community development workers in partnership with Colombian counterparts.

Trainees were expected to extend themselves by trying new and challenging experiences. During the training period, I learned how to float in water for hours at a time, shoe horses, lay bricks, drive a bulldozer, rappel a stone wall, and to understand and apply theories on how to organize a community for self-help. We learned to play soccer, Colombia's most popular sport. We did daily physical education exercises including push-ups, pull-ups, squats, sprints, and running a mile. When I started training, I ran a mile in six minutes and twenty seconds. Over the three-month training period, I reduced my time to five minutes and fifteen seconds.

Community development was the core idea of the Peace Corps advocated by its first director, Sargent Shriver. The Peace Corps hired Richard Poston, a United Nations Community Development consultant, to train our group. Fundamentally, the concept was to "help the people help themselves." We were given the opportunity to apply some of Poston's ideas in villages in north central New Mexico, an area consisting of small, isolated towns with high unemployment rates and poor health care services. The strategy was for teams of Peace Corps volunteers to be bussed to the villages, where they divided into teams of two, to knock on doors in the community. The objective was to engage people in conversation and elicit their participation in efforts to improve conditions in the area. The next step in the strategy was to assemble people from all aspects of the community and help them to organize a parade. Parades included civic groups, the police department, the fire department, the Boy and Girl Scouts, and the churches and schools. Parades culminated in high school gyms with speeches by community leaders who appealed to everyone to work together to make the community better.

The experience was embarrassing and a lesson in how *not* to organize a community. Community development doesn't involve speeches and platitudes. Community development is about listening to people, learning what their "felt needs" are, not imposing your values on them but respecting theirs, and identifying purposeful roles that you could play to help people advance their agenda to make life better. Most volunteers that I knew didn't grasp community development theory or how to apply it, seeing it as amorphous, idealistic thinking. They groped around for two years trying to find useful roles in their communities, often unsuccessfully. One volunteer read all two hundred paperback books in the foot locker that Peace Corps provided for each of us.

The State Department expressed fears that hundreds of young American Peace Corps volunteers could damage America's reputation by drinking too much, having sex with native women, angering local politicians, and perhaps, sympathizing with leftist forces in the country. They remembered that in 1958, just three years before the Peace Corps started, Vice President Richard Nixon was the subject of mass anti-American demonstrations in Latin America. And, of course, there was Fidel Castro, the Cuban leader responsible for the revolution against dictator Fulgencio Bautista just off the Florida coast.

I had grown a goatee while in training and was quite disappointed when Peace Corps officials insisted that I, and others, shave our goatees and beards before going to Colombia. The logic was that facial hair would be associated with Fidel Castro. American public policy towards Castro was negative. He was a communist, with close ties to Russia, who had established a beachhead in the Western Hemisphere from which to expand communist influence throughout Latin America.

Initially, Congress refused to approve funding for the Peace Corps. In fact, President Kennedy sent the first volunteers overseas using funds from his Executive budget not from funds approved by Congress. Shriver, who was President Kennedy's brother-in-law, fought the State Department's attempts to control the Peace Corps. In early 1961, Shriver wrote to Kennedy, "It is important that the Peace Corps be advanced not as an arm of the Cold War but as a contribution to the world community." Shriver felt that the Peace Corps' potential lay in the freedom given to the volunteers, with their high motivation but limited technical skills, to become part of their communities and work with their counterparts as community development workers. The idea was to build lasting community capacity. It was hoped that Peace Corps volunteers would demonstrate America's commitment to peaceful democratic change, while financial aid and technical assistance were provided through the State Department. This part of the Alliance for Progress program basically failed, leaving Peace Corps volunteers on their own to find what they could offer under the circumstances.

My roommate at the University of New Mexico was Paul Mundschenk of Port Washington, New York. We had met at New York's LaGuardia Airport en route to our training in Albuquerque, New Mexico. We hit it off from the start. We shared many childhood experiences growing up on suburban Long Island in the 1950s. He helped me cope with my uncertainties and loneliness. Paul had high expectations, like me, about effecting social reforms in Colombia. His philosophical perspective on life attracted me and provided a balance to my more action-oriented mind. We both searched for meaning in what we were doing. I searched for solutions to social problems more than Paul even though I often felt that my solutions were simplistic and just ways of occupying my time in non-obtrusive ways. In other words, if you couldn't do something positive, don't do something negative.

Trainees were divided into five different language groups according to their ability. Group V consisted of US citizens whose families were from Cuba, Puerto Rico, and Mexico. I was placed in Group IV. My ability to speak and read Spanish grew, as did my self-confidence. Our Spanish language instructor, Hernán Tafoya, liked to breeze through the grammar lessons with us so we could spend more time conversing and reading the newspapers. He told us that the best way to learn Spanish was not to speak English at all—not in the dorm, the cafeteria, in town, shopping, or on the soccer field. Well, I had an idea about how to play a joke on Sr. Tafoya.

One day, in the hallway as we neared our classroom, Paul Mundschenk and I approached him from the rear until we were within earshot. I exclaimed "Seriously, Paul we must speak as much Spanish as we possibly *podemos* (can)!" The instructor turned around to laugh with us. On another occasion, I placed a water gun in the instructor's desk drawer. We were all aware that he had a habit of opening this particular desk drawer to take out an imaginary gun and shoot us when one of us made a grammatical mistake. So, of course, I deliberately made a mistake, causing Sr. Tafoya to do a double-take when he saw the water gun.

A different game that Paul and I played had to do with the use of the two Spanish verbs *ser* (to be), and *estar*. *Ser* refers to an inherent condition or quality of someone or something. *Estar*, on the other hand, refers to a temporary condition or quality. Paul claimed that I was overweight as in *ser*, not *estar*. I would disagree, saying that the proper verb to describe my weight was *estar* since it was a temporary condition. We frequently joked about *ser* and *estar* usage.

Paul and I also came up with a tongue-twister that gave us lots of laughs during training as well. There was a story in our Spanish language book that featured a family who had a pet monkey. It came to pass that one day, the monkey climbed up the wall, much to the delight of the family's child. The child cried, "*Mamá, mamá, ven acá para enseñarte una cosa. Mire como camina con los manos en la pared!*" (which means: Mother, mother come here! Look how he climbs with his hands on the wall!). Well, Paul and I made it a contest to see who could say "*Mama ven acá,*" the fastest. We timed one another and repeated this silly phrase throughout training and during our Peace Corps days.

Paul and I were part of a foursome. Bob Salafia graduated from Brown University with a major in music. He loved Bach and found a piano wherever we went so that he could play. He dated one of the Spanish instructors. John Maier was a psychology major with a cynic's eye. We often ate together and went drinking as a group. One time, all the volunteers went to the ranch near Taos, New Mexico where we were taught horsemanship. Horseback riding was to become our main means of local transportation in rural communities so it was important to be able to ride adequately. One afternoon, after our rides around the corral and guiding horses through gates, we were ready to be bussed back to our dormitory in Taos when I noted our riding instructor, Bill Perkins, watching a long trailer turning off the main road towards the barn. Bill, wearing a handsome but dusty cowboy hat, reminded me of James Dean, the popular actor of the previous decade. When I asked him why the trailer was coming onto the property he said that it was filled with hay which had to be unloaded and placed in the barn that day. I have always loved the smell of hay, as well as the other smells common to farms, so I offered to help him unload the trailer. Bob, John, and Paul joined us. It was tough, sweaty work that I loved. The camaraderie was something special. In the dusk, after the trailer was empty, Bill drove us back to our dormitory in his Chevy truck. We took hot showers, went to the Taos cafeteria for a late supper, and hit the sack, exhausted.

Part of the training consisted of classroom study about Colombian history, economics, and politics. One of the instructors started a lecture by writing *Alianza para el progreso* on the blackboard. We well knew that the words referred to the name of JFK's program of economic development in Latin America, The Alliance for Progress, and that the Peace Corps was a part of the Alliance. To our surprise, we were told to look again at what was written. No one could understand what the instructor was getting at so he underlined the word *para*, which in Spanish has two meanings: for, and deter or stop. Aha! The Alliance deters progress! He went on to suggest that the Alliance may not work due to the depths of poverty and the class structure in existence for centuries in Latin America. I began to see what the instructor was getting at. Good intentions aren't enough, and in fact, could have negative consequences.

Some trainees were deselected during training mostly due to difficulties learning Spanish. In other cases, they resigned due to personal reasons like homesickness. There was also a case or two where it was felt that someone didn't have the psychological disposition for service as measured by two standardized psychological tests given to all trainees. During the last month of training, we anxiously awaited the posting of lists indicating who had been deselected. In all, 42 of the original 65 trainees completed training and went to Colombia. Of this number, 35 completed two years of service. I felt that some of the Peace Corps' deselections were arbitrary and ill-conceived. I believed that the inability to learn Spanish in a classroom didn't necessarily mean that you couldn't learn the language living in the community. Over the term of my service, my point of view was validated as I saw volunteers who attended school districts with no language requirements blossom in speaking Spanish. Others struggled with the language but somehow got their ideas and feelings across and earned the empathy of villagers who spoke slowly to them.

By the time the two-month training program ended, I felt prepared to give the Peace Corps my best effort. I couldn't understand some of my colleagues who were already skeptical about their work and the likelihood that their work would improve the living conditions of poor Colombians. I remained optimistic that our work would be productive and that the experience would help me mature and find career choices. I felt that Peace Corps would be a lot more than a goodwill exchange among nations and a public relations program for the US. I hoped the Peace Corps would help to organize low-income workers to reform their government so that income was more fairly distributed and the nation's substantial resources were better utilized.

My adventurousness was tempered by concerns about whether I would find useful things to do, if I would like Colombian food, and how I would deal with scorpions, snakes, and spiders. I felt that I might not be able to cope with sleeping in a hammock in a straw jungle hut for two years. So, when the Peace Corps asked the trainees if we had any preferences as to what part of Colombia we'd prefer to live in, I requested a meat-producing region with a temperate climate.

Between the end of our training in New Mexico and our departure for Colombia, we had the chance to go home for a week. My visit was uneventful. My parents were resigned that I was committed to stay in the Peace Corps despite their concerns.

Our group gathered at a hotel near the Miami airport for the flight to Colombia. On the flight to Bogotá, the capital of Colombia, I interviewed many of my fellow volunteers using a reel-to-reel tape recorder. I asked them what they hoped to accomplish during the next two years. Over the years, as I have reflected on my question, I could see how naïve I was.

We arrived at Bogotá's El Dorado airport in May, 1963. Bogotá is situated on a large plateau in the high plains of the east Andes Mountains, over eight thousand five hundred feet above sea level. After disembarking from the Pan American airplane, we were greeting by a welcoming party of Colombian and Peace Corps officials. Our group assembled beside the plane to sing the Colombian national anthem, which we had learned during training.

Arriving in Bogotá, Colombia, 1963

We were driven in a bus to the Hotel San Francisco in downtown Bogotá where we stayed for three days of "in-country briefings" with Peace Corps officials. The temperature was cool. Men wore dark suits, often with gray, brown, or black wool *ruanas*, Colombian ponchos. Automobiles were dated usually from the nineteen forties and fifties. I was struck by the large number of children in the streets, many of whom begged for money and offered to shine your shoes. *Regálame cinco* (donate five cents to me) was their appeal. In downtown Bogotá, I could see and hear men hawking lottery tickets on every street corner. Every city and department in the country has a lottery.

We were introduced to Chris Sheldon, the director of the Peace Corps in Colombia. One night, Chris invited us to a get-together in his apartment. He showed us a home movie about the three-mast sailing schooner that he and his wife had owned. The schooner served as a high school for boys, while also providing the boys with powerful life experiences serving as crew mates. Years later, the story of the misbegotten ship was told in the film *White Squall*. Chris lost his wife and some of the boys in a tragic sailing accident. Soon after his crushing personal tragedy, Chris accepted the assignment of Director of Peace Corps in Colombia. Chris encouraged independent thinking and was well-respected by the volunteers.

I was assigned to live and work in El Valle de San José, a small village in the central Andes about eight hours north of Bogotá by road. I boarded a two-engine DC-3 propeller plane in Bogotá and headed to Bucaramanga, the capital of the Department of Santander del Sur —

one of Colombia's thirty-two *departamentos*
(states). A city of half a million inhabitants
situated thirty-one hundred feet above sea
level, Bucaramanga is known as *Ciudad de Los
Parques* (City of the Parks). It is a city of contrasts.
On one hand, it is surrounded by neighborhoods
consisting of cardboard and wooden shacks with
no running water or sewers. On the other hand,
Bucaramanga is a bustling commercial center
with modern buildings, great restaurants, affluent
neighborhoods, and a world-class country club.
The flight to Bucaramanga took about two hours
over mountainous and rocky terrain. As we
began our descent, I could see that the city rests
on a plateau. On its southern end, the plateau
falls steeply onto unstable, rocky land where
you could see that many make-shift houses had
fallen hundreds of feet into rocky ravines.

At the airport, I was met by Brad Whipple,
a member of Colombia I, the first group of
volunteers to arrive in Colombia in 1961. I was
very impressed with Brad's fluent Spanish and his
knowledge of Colombian ways of speaking as
well as his understanding of Colombian politics
and culture. He had married a Colombian
woman from Bogotá whom I met once. She was
spending time with her parents in Bogotá before
she and Brad left for the US. I learned that he
had been in the Marines for three years and was,
thus, a few years older than me. We drove by

taxi to the city's bus terminal located in a heavily trafficked area. We boarded a taxi to El Valle by way of San Gil, a nearby small city about half an hour from El Valle.

Switchback roads, Chicamocha Canyon

The drive to San Gil was memorable. We passed first through fertile fields of cane and corn into narrow canyons where evidence of rock slides could be seen. We passed through a towering mountain range of arid, rocky, hilly terrain. We crossed a two hundred foot long steel truss bridge over the Chicamocha River and then ascended a series of eight switchback curves climbing to a height of five thousand feet above sea level. Most of the roadway had no barriers to prevent cars and buses from falling down the cliffs. I was sitting in the center, rear seat of a full, six passenger taxi. I hid the fear I was feeling as the driver negotiated the many sharp curves and blind spots. Some sections of the road could only accommodate one-way traffic. When this occurred on a curve, drivers used their horns to alert on-coming traffic that they were about to enter the curve. We climbed many steep mountains on narrow, switchback roads lined with funeral stones and religious crosses that indicated the fall of vehicles with their passengers.

Two and a half hours later, we arrived in San Gil and caught a taxi to El Valle de San José. At 4100 feet above sea level, San Gil is well known for its national park, El Gallineral. The park is situated along El Río Fonce and features a network of walkways through beautiful botanical gardens, riverside views, and age-old trees from which long tendrils of Spanish moss hang.

*Spanish moss in El Gallineral National Park,
San Gil*

I am reminded of a wonderful piece of folklore that was popular among San Gil's residents. It says something about the friendly competition among the region's villages. The story goes this way: The Río Fonce passes through San Gil and runs north towards high country. One of the villages to the north of San Gil is Charalá. There is a bridge over the Río Fonce in San Gil which, during the rainy season, becomes a chocolate brown color. It is said that San Gil residents, when looking down from the bridge at the river and viewing the muddy water, declare, "Ay, *se bañaron los Charalenos!*" (Ah, the people of Charalá must have taken baths!).

El Valle sits about three hundred feet above a white-water river that flows through the central range of the Colombian Andes in an area of rolling hills and valleys where peasant farmers raise cattle, cultivate sugar cane, tobacco, coffee, and yucca, working the soil as their ancestors had for centuries. El Valle has a semi-tropical climate where winters featured a good deal of rain and muddy roads and summers featured dry weather and dusty roads.

The region is famous for its *hormigas,* which are over-sized ants that live in two-foot high mounds throughout the area. *Hormigas* are very tasty and serve as a bonus, or cash crop for farmers. During the two months each year when the *hormigas* are at peak size, the farmers stop whatever they are doing and harvest *hormigas.* They break up the mounds with a shovel, and, with their bare hands, grab the insects; break their heads apart from their abdomens; and place the abdomens in burlap sacks. Farmers frequently get bitten during the above procedure, but with their hardened skins they are able to withstand the pain. After the *hormigas* are gathered, they are boiled in oil in large vats and later brought to markets to be sold. They are considered a delicacy and are expensive. There is even a company that sells pressurized cans of *hormigas* throughout Colombia.

Early in my Peace Corps service, I was introduced to *hormigas* at a dinner party in Bogotá. I was led to believe that they were some sort of salty nuts and I found them surprisingly tasty. My friends got a kick at my shock when they told me I was eating ants. I also had *bocadillo,* a candy that I loved. It is made of sweet guava paste which is a puree of guava fruit. Often sold wrapped in dried palm leaves in small wooden boxes, *bocadillo* is dense, almost like a fruit leather, but still soft and easily cut with a knife. It is sometimes served with a soft cheese. Most every food store sells *bocadillo*, but the village of Vélez—in Santander del Sur near the border with Boyacá—is said to have the best in Colombia. It was considered a must to buy some *bocadillo* when you passed through Vélez. More than once, I ate a full box of *bocadillo*. No wonder I needed serious dental work soon after my Peace Corps service. Guava is also the main ingredient in another Colombia treat called "*una oblea*," which is made with sweet milk and served on a wafer.

There is a one hundred foot steel narrow bridge, sort of a miniature George Washington Bridge, which crosses the Río Fonce where the highway turnoff to El Valle is located. From there, it is a short ride up a winding hill into the village of El Valle de San José. I later learned that El Valle had about two thousand villagers and another eight thousand residents in the surrounding rural area. Residents mostly had primary school educations and rarely traveled outside of the area.

I soon caught a very pungent aroma in the air. Brad explained that it was the odor of a tannery, where cattle hides were transported by truck every Tuesday and Sunday after the cattle had been slaughtered for the market days in El Valle's central plaza. At the tannery, the hides were cured for production into various products like chairs, shoes, and boots. Almost fifty years later, I can close my eyes and smell the tannery near the bridge to El Valle.

Main street, El Valle de San José

My first observations of the village of El Valle were of young boys and girls, walking and playing on the cobblestone streets or raised concrete sidewalks bordering the white-painted buildings. Grass and weeds grew in between the cobblestones wherever they could. Green horse and mule droppings in the streets provided a pungent odor common to barn yards. As they noticed that Brad was in the taxi, the children approached us and greeted Brad with warm, friendly smiles. The children wore white shirts and grey or tan pants that were often too small for them. They were mostly barefoot or wore *alpargatas,* white canvas slippers. I was saddened to see that some of the children wore torn clothing.

Children were often seen coming and going into the central square to obtain running water drawn from a narrow spigot in a square concrete structure. They carried the water to their homes in five-gallon tin water cans sometimes on their heads or on poles carried by two children and balanced between them on their shoulders. The one-story homes were connected to one another giving the appearance of continuous warehouses with entry doors interspersed here and there along narrow sidewalks. The houses had red-tile roofs and were constructed of mud and straw and were whitewashed. Houses did not have windows but rather contained colorful green, blue, or pink wooden shutters that brought both light and air into the houses when opened.

I later learned that the color painted on the shutters and on the lower portions of the village's exterior walls indicated the village's political leanings. If a village was liberal, the houses were painted pink or yellow. If a village was conservative, the houses were painted green or blue. This tradition came from the mid-twentieth century. In 1948, the tension between conservatives and liberals erupted after an extremely popular liberal presidential candidate, Jórge Eliécer Gaitán, was killed in Bogotá. The city and the country as a whole went into chaos. Gaitán's death is known as *El Bogotazo* (the Bogotá crisis). During the next ten years, Colombia was struck with *La Violencia,* a political war between liberals and conservatives in which somewhere in between 180,000 and 300,000 people were killed, more than were killed in the Korean War. I heard many stories of senseless killings of innocent people. Buses were stopped and everyone was killed. A village's telegraph and telephone lines would be cut and everyone in the village was murdered, often brutally. The violence ended when a moderate, compromise government was established in which there were four years of liberal-led government followed by four years of conservative-led government. This arrangement continued for sixteen years.

Upon entering El Valle's main plaza, I was struck by the immensity of the small village's church building. El Valle's church was constructed mostly of red brick and unpainted cinderblocks. Its bell tower stood at least ten stories over the surrounding one-story buildings. The smells of nature were sweet, raw, and unfamiliar.

As I traveled through Colombia over the following months and years, I saw many villages with enormous cathedral-like churches, more suitable to churches in a city. Whenever I saw these edifices, I thought that the money and manpower to build these churches would have been better spent to build schools, roads, and bridges and for books for the children.

El Valle de San José's church and central plaza, 1996

Brad brought me to the house that we would share for a month until he returned to the States after his two years of service. The building was owned by the *Federación Nacional de Cafeteros* or *Cafeteros*) the National Federation of Coffee Growers. It was located on a corner of the village's central square across the street from the church. My new home had two rooms off a long interior covered patio. On the hard dirt patio outside my room, there was a 6 x 3 foot concrete wash basin where I washed my hands and face and brushed my teeth every morning. It was built as a wash basin for coffee beans and had an eight foot long narrow pipe that carried cold water to a spigot at the end.

The patio also contained a four-burner kerosene stove with an oven on which I prepared many of my meals. At the end of the patio, there was a wooden stall with a flush toilet and another containing a cold water shower, an amenity that many Peace Corps volunteers did not have. Facing the patio was a backyard filled with high weeds and lemon, banana, and orange trees. From the patio, above the adjoining adobe walls that separated homes, I could see the rolling green mountains looming over the village. It was a very beautiful scene especially when the sun was rising over the hills. In the mornings, I could hear horse and mule hoofs on the cobbled street and the crow of roosters.

Brad's room had a window with green shutters, white walls, a high ceiling, a double bed, a large gray metal desk and bookcase, and a wooden chair with a leather sewn seat and backing. My room, which was adjacent to Brad's, contained a single metal cot and a wooden chair. On the wall above the bed was a large mirror. On another wall, was a large world map. Lighting in each room was provided by one sixty-watt bulb hanging from the ceiling by its electrical wire in the middle of the room. The floors were made of concrete and the ceilings were at least ten feet in height.

Brad introduced me to Antonio Hernandez, an 11-year-old boy. I immediately noticed his smile and the absence of upper front teeth. I later learned that if a village *chino* (child) had a toothache, he or she would go to the small, poorly-equipped village hospital where the ailing tooth would be pulled out by one of the attending nuns. Antonio's hair was well-groomed, his shirt and pants were clean, and there was alertness in his eyes and seriousness of purpose about him. Brad provided a cot for Antonio in a small adjacent room. Antonio, who never knew his father, had been informally adopted by Brad. His mother lived in the village and had ten other children. Antonio, the oldest, was left to fend for himself. He was studious and enterprising and had befriended Brad. He became Brad's helper, doing errands, cleaning the house, bridling Brad's horse and bringing him from a nearby pasture in the morning, and generally following Brad wherever he went in order to be handy. Antonio continued to help me after Brad returned to the US.

Brad ate his meals at El Valle's "hotel," which was actually more like a small boarding house for single men. Each man had his own very small room off an inner brick patio and ate his meals at a communal dining table on the patio. After my first dinner and breakfast, I knew that this type of meal plan wasn't going to work for me. There were a lot of flies and moths hovering around the dining table and loud, unfamiliar music playing on the radio. My first dinner featured a thin, chicken-based soup called *caldo*, along with a piece of dried, tough, grilled red meat, a piece of *arepa* (a cornmeal pancake) and boiled *yucca* (a tasteless potato-like starch). I later learned that meat was commonly treated by evaporating most of its water content, salting it, and allowing it to dry on clotheslines. The beverage was a cane-based drink, a very sweet hot drink made of sugar cane, called *agua de panela,* and *tinto* (coffee), served in a small cup. If you wanted a full cup of coffee, you asked for a *café americano*. Coffee in Colombia is very strong. I acquired a liking for this type of coffee. After dinner, Brad brought me to meet the Colombian man with whom I would work for the next two years. I was very eager to meet him and hoped that we would get along.

Brad introduced me to Salomón Hernandez. Salomón's house was diagonally across from Brad's in the village's central plaza. He was a short man of lean build with thick, dark, black hair. He greeted me as soon as I entered the reception area of the house with a warm and welcoming smile. The reception area also served as Salomon's office. He then directed me into the inner patio of the house and introduced me to his wife Carmela and each of his five children, ages two to seventeen. His wife was also short but overweight. She greeted me with a warm smile and giggled as she made an awkward bow as we shook hands. I felt like she regarded me as visiting royalty. After the introductions, Brad, Salomón, and I returned to the front office where Antonio was waiting.

After supper most evenings, I visited with Salomón in his office. We talked about village news, Brad's work, and how I might be able to replace Brad when he left. I felt welcomed by Salomón but very uncertain about how I was going to be helpful. After all, what did I know that Salomón didn't? It certainly wasn't because I learned to swim underwater for two lengths of a university swimming pool or to shoe horses. No, the Peace Corps strategy to build up my self-confidence was doing me no good. I felt useless — welcomed, but lost. And Brad's self-confidence and apparent many

successful projects were making me feel
unsure.

My first night in El Valle was stressful. I was
fearful of scorpions and other "creepie-crawlies."
I had been warned about them—and in fact, I
would see many during the upcoming months—
and childhood fears were ignited. I surveyed
the room for spider webs and got onto the chair
and used a sweep broom to break up the many
cobwebs in the tall ceiling's corners. I was very
conscious of every sound. I got undressed down
to my shorts and t-shirt and carefully placed
my pants and shirt on the wooden chair that
I placed near the bed. I made sure that my
clothing didn't touch the floor. I killed every moth
that entered the room before I went to sleep. I
also placed my boots and a flashlight near the
bed so that I didn't have to walk barefooted
if I had to go to the bathroom in the night. I
considered sleeping with my boots on the bed
but decided this was going too far. I would make
sure to shake them before putting them on in the
morning since I was warned that scorpions like to
hang out in dark places. The silence in the room
was powerful, making it difficult to get a good
night sleep. The room's mud walls were three
feet thick so you barely could hear other outside
noises until you opened the window. The silence
was only broken by the powerful sound of the
nearby church bells that resonated throughout

the village and surrounding hills beginning at six o'clock in the morning. They sounded as if they were ringing in the next room.

In the following months, another threat to my sense of control would have to be dealt with. My room served as my bedroom, office, and kitchen. The room contained such unrefrigerated comestibles as rice, spaghetti, sugar, coffee, cereals, flour, bread, and cookies. When Brad lived in the warehouse, he'd kept no food in the house since he ate at the hotel.

The food items caught the attention of the hoards of rats and mice living in the ceiling of the coffee grower warehouse's adobe walls. Rodents could crawl through a space of no more than half-an-inch. At night, I could hear them scratching around and honing in on the food in my room. I put some of the food in the small refrigerator. I placed some of it high on the bookshelf. I didn't understand that they could smell the food through cellophane and cardboard packaging. I tried to ignore the rodents but they were heavily on my mind as I went to sleep. I bought "snap" rat traps and placed them along the room's interior walls, with limited effectiveness. My concern, though, was to prevent the rodents' entry to the room, not killing them once they were inside — the one place in my new world that I wanted to control.

I went to bed with a flashlight on the chair next to the bed. When I heard the rats' gnawing through the dirt walls and their imminent entry was apparent from the noises (as if they were about to enter or were actually in the room already), I pointed the flashlight beam towards the target spot. I bought extra batteries so I didn't run out. I needed to see the rats actually enter the room, although I didn't know what to do if I actually saw them in the room. I placed a straw sweep broom next to the bed so that I could sweep them out the door. I figured the best I could do was shine light on them and, thus, discourage their entry. That worked, even though it meant that I was unable to enjoy uninterrupted sleep.

I shared my problem with Antonio and Salomón. They suggested the use of rat bait that somehow made it difficult for the rodents to carry the poison back to their ceiling nests and die there. They would, thus, die in the outdoors, not in the building, which caused terrible odors. Fortunately, the rat bait was effective and enabled me to again get some sleep.

In my first week in El Valle, I asked Salomón if I could tape him on the reel-to-reel portable tape recorder I had bought in the states. I asked him to make some reflective comments that we might want to hear two years later at the end of my Peace Corps assignment. Without hesitation, he said, "My dear friend Pablo, welcome to the

Valle de San José. I hope that your presence here will be of much benefit to the community and of much experience to you. Thank you very much." Simple and eloquent.

In my first month, I learned that Brad was a well-known figure not only in El Valle, but in San Gil and in Bucaramanga, the department's capital. Brad had worked with local officials to obtain official authorization from the Santander del Sur's Department of Rural Roads to build a farm-to-market road that would enable remote-living farmers to bring their fresh produce more quickly to El Valle's market as well as the one in San Gil. He was also successful in making arrangements to borrow heavy equipment from the Department of Public Works. Rights of passage were needed from a number of landowners for the road to pass through their properties. All but one of the landowners agreed, which stopped the construction. Frustrated, one evening Brad drove one of the borrowed bulldozers through the objecting landowner's fence and across his land. The landowner threatened to have Brad arrested, but road construction proceeded, and ultimately, the right of way was secured by eminent domain. This incident resulted in negative political consequences for the Peace Corps and its reputation in the region. The department's governor issued instructions to his department heads not to cooperate with Peace Corps volunteers for a period of time until further notice. Volunteers in other areas of the department were very upset with Brad, who made no apologies for his actions. If the ends justified the means, then Brad achieved a good deal of success.

In another instance, Brad noted the presence of an abandoned steel bridge near the main highway linking San Gil and Bogotá. It appeared to be a bridge to nowhere. The bridge was located in the El Departamento de Boyacá. Brad went to Tunja, the capital of the department and to Bogotá, the national capital, to plead for authorization to move the bridge. This was obviously a complicated transaction. Transferring a bridge from Boyacá to Santander del Sur was an ambitious project testing intransigent political and bureaucratic governmental entities.

Well, Brad did it. It took six months of trips to Tunja, Bogotá, and Bucaramanga to appeal, cajole, and beg to make it happen, but he succeeded. He also arranged for the special trucking necessary to transport the twenty-foot bridge structure over the one hundred miles to its ultimate destination as well as permission to use the national highway for this purpose. Brad's role in securing the bridge was an example of a useful role that Peace Corps volunteers could play to help local people get help from their government. *Campesinos* (poor farmers) were too busy struggling to survive, with no funds to take buses to strange and distant cities. But Peace Corps volunteers could represent them in these dealings. Months after Brad returned to the states, local officials decided to name the bridge the Bradford H. Whipple Bridge. The bridge enables remote farmers in El Valle's most remote *veredas* (rural subdivisions) to easily bring their products to markets in El Valle and San Gil.

Salomón worked for the Cafeteros that had made arrangements with the Peace Corps for volunteer assignments throughout the country. The Cafeteros is a major non-governmental agency, which represented what was at the time Colombia's only exportable product, coffee. Salomón helped local farmers to learn the best techniques with which to grow their crops. He aided them to obtain financial aid and loans from the Cafeteros to build new houses, repair existing houses, and build aqueducts, small bridges, and roads.

I soon learned that Salomón was a very well-respected person in El Valle and surrounding communities. Salomón was often called upon by El Valle's mayor, Ramón Súarez, to make speeches at public occasions.

On most mornings, I awoke to the shrill sound of a rooster's early morning greeting, the church bells, and another sweet-smelling sunny day. I caught the scent of Doña Elena's corn muffins. Doña Elena lived two blocks up from my apartment and was famous for the delicious corn muffins that she baked fresh every morning, which I frequently purchased in a small store down the block. I heard the barking of the village's numerous dogs and, from time to time, the noise of jeeps bouncing along the cobblestone streets. In the morning, I took a cold shower, got dressed in my blue dungarees, brown shirt, and leather boots, and prepared my breakfast. I never got used to the cold showers.

I felt that El Valle was a place as close to paradise as I could imagine but I often wondered what I was doing there, a middle-class twenty-two year old college graduate from suburban New York with no career goals. "Help the people help themselves" was the Peace Corps' stock answer, representing the Peace Corps' vision. But I wasn't an engineer, a teacher, an architect, or a specialist of any kind. I had a bachelor's degree in general business. I had a restless feeling to learn more about the world and myself before settling down but felt lost about how I would spend the next two years.

I shopped in the village market every Tuesday morning, buying cuts of meat and fruits and vegetables from the many vendors who set up make-shift, portable wood and canvas stalls in which to sell their products. Market days featured the sights and noises of chickens, pigs, and goats that were tied to the stalls by their owners. Children seemed to be everywhere, often kicking a makeshift soccer ball around the square. During the first two months in El Valle, I bought a pressure cooker, a tiny refrigerator, a frying pan, pots and pans, dishes, and utensils. Antonio cleaned the kerosene stove so we could cook with it. We made hamburgers, pancakes, french toast, roast chicken, and steaks. I grated yucca and fried it in cooking oil to make yucca pancakes that tasted like potato pancakes similar to the ones my mother made at home. I used the pressure cooker to prepare rice along with chunks of meat, potatoes, and vegetables. I inserted beef bullion cubes in the mix for flavor. The pressure cooker enabled me to make meals in short order.

Over the first few weeks in El Valle, I frequently walked the village's streets to introduce myself. I greeted lots of village residents. I was the subject of considerable curiosity, mostly of children. Virtually everyone asked, *Se amaña aquí* (are you happy here)?" People wanted to know why I came to their village and what I hoped to accomplish. They seemed grateful that I lived in their village. They asked questions about my family and the house that I lived in back in New York. They wanted to know why Americans hated black people—even in remote places the US had a reputation for its internal social issues. They wanted to know how much money I made and why I wasn't married. They were spontaneous and genuine without suspicion or hostility. They went out of their way to make me feel welcomed. Sometimes, I was treated like I was a visiting dignitary; when a government official visited the mayor, he introduced him to me. There was status to a village because they had a Peace Corps volunteer. I drank a lot of beer and rum, ate fried yucca, chicken, meat, and too much of the guava candy called *bocadillo*. I asked everyone how I could be helpful. Everyone promised their unconditional assistance, which made me feel good. Little did I know that these pledges usually meant nothing. It was common courtesy in Colombia to offer your assistance whether you meant it or not. It was another thing to actually get involved. This cultural attitude was difficult for me to accept and understand. Where I came from, you didn't pledge help unless you intended to act on it.

As I spoke to villagers, I often heard that it would be a good idea to develop a project which provided people with something to do on the weekends. The weekend schedule mainly involved the men of the village and the peasant farmers from the surrounding area spending hours at the many small bars, where they would get inebriated on beer and *aguardiente* (anisette) while the women remained at home with the children, sitting on benches in the plaza, or in the church. There was nothing to break the drudgery of six days a week, twelve-hour days of hard work primarily as farm laborers and sugar cane plant workers.

I appreciated that Salomón understood my youthful enthusiasm and desire to be useful while respecting the values and traditions of his countrymen. We sat in his home almost nightly to discuss daily events, plans for the next day, current events, and everything else friends talk about. Salomón was curious about my life in the US. He was abreast of world affairs and balanced in his political views. He knew that the very rich controlled the Colombian economy but was against violent revolution. He saw change as happening gradually and pointed out farm-to-market roads, electrical hook-ups, running water, and telephone service that didn't exist ten years ago. He was grateful for the US' financial aid but was troubled that some funds never reached their intended beneficiaries. Sometimes, Salomón and I traveled on roads in his Toyota jeep where vehicles could no longer pass due to deep muddy ditches or steep inclines. We sometimes mounted mules or horses for the journey deeper into the isolated back country.

On one trip, about a month after my arrival, we traveled by jeep to a remote area called Colacote where we were met by several barefoot *campesinos*. They guided us to an underground water source high in the lush green hills. The plan was to construct an aqueduct for the hundreds of farmers that lived in the area thus enabling them to have running water in their homes and water power for the irrigation of their crops. They had horses and mules waiting for us along the road. We mounted the animals and proceeded to gradually ascend the steep inclines, carefully balancing ourselves on the saddles. Since it had rained the night before, the trail was often muddy. Sometimes, the mud was so thick that it reached our boots in the stirrups. At these times, we dismounted, making it easier for the horses and mules to traverse in the mud.

Typical campesino children on a path overlooking El Valle, 1963

We arrived at a small mud-built schoolhouse. Salomón invited me to go inside with him to greet the teacher and children. Once inside, I was introduced as a North American. As the teacher was making his speech to welcome me, I noticed a color poster on the wall. It had a picture of President Kennedy, the emblem of the "Alliance for Progress," and an American flag on it. Its wording spoke of cooperation between Colombia and the United States. When I saw the poster, and the forty barefoot, smiling children in this isolated, small, dark one-room schoolhouse, I knew that I was about to break down and cry.

I went outside behind the school building and sobbed, my body shaking. Salomón found me behind the building and clasped my hand. His silent support and understanding comforted me. I could see on his face that he understood my sadness at the conditions that the children faced in order to obtain an education. Sobbing, I told him why I was so upset. It was as if this experience was the moment in which I actually came to terms with how different my life had been compared to these children and the depths of poverty in which people lived. Perhaps, it was my first emotional introduction to my life in Colombia.

We left the schoolhouse and walked through fields of tall grass that paralleled a rushing stream. I followed Ambrosio Diaz, the local *campesino* leader. Salomón told me that he and his wife had fifteen children. Ambrosio had albino features, a rare condition in Colombia. At one point, Ambrosio stopped in his footsteps and motioned for me to not move forward. He ran ahead while removing his macheté from its leather sheath. He was chasing a snake that he killed with a rock. After cutting the snake's head off, Ambrosio brought the snake—a venomous coral snake, in fact—to me and offered it as a gift. I thanked him and smiled and said I didn't want the snake. Ambrosio smiled and threw the dead snake into the stream and we continued to the future site of the aqueduct.

Sometimes we visited small farm houses and schools under construction in areas that had no roads outside of El Valle. In those cases, we would go by horseback. Brad had purchased a horse, a tall, tan, well-built steed that I inherited. I would soon learn that he had a terrible temper. If he didn't want to be mounted, he would run away or run circles around you and kick and scream. On one occasion, after taking an hour to corral, saddle, and mount the horse, I rode him into the village. With no provocation, he swerved from the village street onto the sidewalk where he scraped my right leg against the side of a building, trying, I guess, to unseat me.

Typical rural home

On another occasion, several volunteers from Bucaramanga visited El Valle to get away from the city and their work routines. They wanted to visit a rural area and go horseback riding. I made arrangements with Salomón to borrow some horses. I escorted them to La Piñuela, a rural school building on the top of the mountain overlooking El Valle. After visiting the school and speaking with the teacher and children, we mounted our horses and began our decline on the cobblestone road to the village. It soon began to rain heavily, which it often did during summer afternoons. I pulled in the reins and told Nan Kretchkoff, one of the volunteers, to go ahead without me while I put on my grey rubber rain slicker, which I had tied onto the back of the saddle. I remained mounted as I unfolded it. I hurled it away from me so that I could find the hole for my head, which startled the horse. He leaped to a gallop. I grabbed for the reins but it was too late. The only thing left was to cling to the saddle horn.

Me on my horse looking down to El Valle

I tried to ride the horse like a bucking bronco, but my rodeo experience was extremely limited. In less than twenty feet, I was thrown onto the wet, cobblestone and rock surface. I got up and walked towards the horse, and I noticed blood on the ground and on my boots. My arm had a hefty three-inch gash in it. Apparently, I had fallen with the weight of my body directly onto my right forearm. For the first time in my life, I screamed for help. Fortunately, Nan wasn't far ahead and heard my voice. She galloped up the hill to where I stood. With her help, I mounted her horse and returned to El Valle. Nan took the reins of my horse and walked him the short distance into the village. I was rushed in a car to the hospital in San Gil. At the hospital, the wound was stitched and bandaged by the attending nurse-nuns. I spent the next two weeks recuperating from the injury in the home of Dee Neb and Sharon Lake, volunteers living in Bucaramanga.

Salomón provided me with not only friendship but also practical direction. Over a forty-year career in community service organizations I have often asked myself what Salomón would have done if he was faced with situations I confronted. He had a way of simplifying the complex and saying the right thing at the right time.

My other close friend in El Valle was Isbelia Martinez. She was an informed and educated woman with definite opinions and passions for her country, ahead of her time. She drove her own car and matter-of-factly walked the streets of El Valle beside single and married men thus branding her as a "modern woman" in the eyes of villagers. Her husband, Tomás, had been killed in 1948 at the age of 26 during *La Violencia*, (The Violence) when liberals and conservatives battled one another for political power. Tomás was a leader of the Liberal Party in the region, one of over 200,000 Colombians killed during a ten-year period.

Isbelia and her older brother, Carlos Hernán, took over management of El Mesón, the family's 250 *hectare* (618 acre) farm located about twenty minutes outside of El Valle on a narrow, bumpy, unpaved road in the Vereda del Hoyo. El Mesón produced coffee, sugar cane, corn, yucca, and bananas. Isbelia assumed the reins managing El Mesón, no easy job for a widow raising two children, Nohora and Tomás, both teenagers at the time. They attended school in Bogotá and visited their mother during vacation periods and summers. Isbelia made the time to help me organize community development projects in El Valle. She understood how difficult it was for me to quickly adjust from North American to rural Colombian culture and to find fulfillment of my desire to help improve conditions in her country. She could tell when I felt directionless and at a loss as to what to do next. She helped me adjust to the pace of life there, to deal with my impatience, and to better understand the minds of the people I was trying to help.

Isbelia also introduced me to typical Colombian food. At her home, we feasted on *sancocho* (a soup of chicken, plantains, yucca, cilantro, corn, and potatoes), *empanadas* (stuffed pastries), *chorizos* (sausages), and *buñuelos* (cheese fritters).

My primary work project in El Valle was organizing a community movie theater. I hoped that the theater would generate enthusiasm and community spirit and lead to other community betterment projects. I saw the initiative as a good community development project because it could help build leadership and community pride. With Salomón's help, an ideal building was found, one originally constructed as a movie theater for the leisure time diversion of Rodolfo Rueda, a wealthy owner of a nearby farm called La Palestina. It had been abandoned years earlier and was in disrepair. He agreed to lend the building to the community to use as a theater. For equipment, I made arrangements with the international CARE organization to borrow a 16mm projector. Films were rented from a distributor that I located in Bucaramanga and made arrangements for the films to be shipped by bus to El Valle on a weekly basis. White sheets and cotton window curtains were sewed together by a woman in the village for the screen. We used the mayor's public address system, which had speakers positioned throughout the village, to announce meetings.

At meetings with villagers in their homes, I invited their participation. Several wonderful people got involved in the theater including

Antonio Corso, an auto mechanic. Antonio loved to tell me dirty jokes and stories in Spanish. I was amazed at how many more dirty words and phrases there seemed to be in Spanish for sexual body parts and activities. We'd laugh and laugh together. He also loved to tease me about my fear of scorpions and other critters. The theater's burlap ceiling tiles were home to lots of scorpions, which frequently crawled down the walls. Sometimes, Antonio cut off their tails to watch them dance around and delighted in my reaction, laughing all the time.

We named the project *El Teatro Comunal* — The Community Theater. The theater also served as a center for social activities. We sponsored a number of dances at the theater, providing diversion to villagers. Colombians love to dance. It was here that I made my first clumsy efforts to dance *la Cumbia,* a beautiful Colombian dance. I never learned the right steps so I simply moved to the music, trying to imitate the dancers around me. Colombians appeared to appreciate my efforts to dance to their music.

Salomón, Isbelia, and I scheduled the first meeting to organize the theater for a Monday night at seven in the evening in the theater building. I spent the prior week frequently in the village plaza and visiting homes to encourage attendance at the meeting. I told people that the theater could provide something else to do on Friday and Saturday nights besides drinking and staying home. We could also show educational films and raise funds through gate receipts. The funds could be used for community projects like buying needed books for the schoolchildren and placing benches in the village square. Monday night arrived and no one was there at seven o'clock except me. By seven-thirty, Antonio Corso and Lígia Martinez had arrived. They were enthusiastic about the theater. We waited together. I became impatient and decided to go to find out where the others were, those who had promised to come.

The movie theater was my first experience with Colombians' sense of time. Village life moved at a snail's pace. When a meeting was set for eight o'clock in the evening no one except me arrived before eight-thirty and arrivals at nine were regarded as normal.

One individual, Celso Diaz, had seemed genuinely interested in helping to organize the theater so I went to his house first and knocked on the door. When he opened the door he was his normal friendly self but didn't have a clue about the purpose of my visit. I reminded him of the theater meeting. He smiled and said he'd be there shortly. I left Celso's house and returned to the theater to find Antonio Corso and Lígia and Pedro Martinez, the only arrivals. Celso arrived at eight-thirty. Such was the sense of time in Colombia. I can honestly say I never got used to it. And it wasn't just a village-level thing nor an aspect of life restricted to poor people. It was simply a cultural quality at all levels of society.

Eugenia Martinez and Celso Diaz

On the theater's opening night, I was nervous, wondering if anyone would show up. I scurried around between the theater and the mayor's office, concerned that the mayor would be drunk—which was often the case—and unable to make an announcement about the theater opening at eight o'clock. I knew that I shouldn't expect people to arrive by eight o'clock but when no one had arrived at all, I was a nervous wreck. In the next half hour, people gradually arrived, carrying their wooden chairs along the village's dimly lit streets. I shared smiles of relief with Antonio, Lígia, and Pedro.

At eight thirty, Antonio started the first reel. The film was a black-and-white Mexican cowboy film with lots of excitement and mariachi music which villagers loved. I heard laughter at various times as well as singing with some of the songs. That felt good. After the show, we tallied the admission and candy concession funds. Two hundred people attended the first night, earning the theater two hundred *pesos* (about $20US). We reviewed the night's events and discussed how to improve things for Sunday night's show. We were tired but content.

Over the next few weeks, the theater's leaders and I spent many hours in the theater. Receipts from the first few weeks were used to buy wood with which to construct six-seat wooden benches. Antonio designed a cardboard pattern that was used to hand saw the various parts of the benches before they were nailed together. Thirty benches were constructed. After several months, the theater had the money to construct two toilets. Before then, if nature called, men went into the adjacent street and urinated along a wall neighboring the theater. It smelled terribly.

Lígia Martinez handled the theater's ticket sales and got lots of children from the school involved at the concession stand where soda and candy were sold. Her older brother, Pedro Martinez, a carpenter, was a kind and generous man with a sparkle in his eye. He quickly learned to operate the projector and became one of the leaders of the theater group.

Showing the movies had its stressful moments. Sometimes, the village's electrical power shut off or lowered dramatically leaving hundreds of people in the dark theater not knowing when—or if—the lights would go on. On one occasion, the projector's bulb burned out and we didn't have a replacement, so the show had to be canceled. By the following week, I had traveled to Bucaramanga to find a replacement. The only bulb I could find for the following week was a 750 watt bulb, not a 1000 watt bulb, which didn't exactly fit in the slot. That weekend we showed a dim, hard-to-see movie. Antonio and I took turns holding the bulb case in place during the showing. Ouch! By the following week, we received two 1000-watt bulbs from a supplier in Bogotá.

For several years, the theater provided community entertainment, an alternative to drinking oneself into a stupor, a reason for families to go out together, and a place for children to have fun. It was also a source of income for the theater's board of directors who used the modest profits to purchase their own projector, the two toilets in the theater, books for the village school, and for other public purposes. Decisions about how to spend the money were made by the theater's board of directors. The theater's success also challenged the common attitude that the money raised would be misused or stolen. Thus, the theater served to build trust among villagers.

In 1996, when I visited El Valle with Karen and Sari, I learned that the theater had closed many years before. Several of its leaders had been killed in a tragic bus accident when the bus fell off the San Gil–El Valle road into the white water rapids of the Río Fonce. Others had moved to San Gil and Bucaramanga. The building was converted for municipal meetings and health education classes.

The theater project was a turning point in my Peace Corps experience, and in fact, my life. It gave me the self-confidence that I could work well with people despite cultural barriers. It was the first of other community development projects for me over the next two years in the Peace Corps and the beginning of my career in public service.

Villagers became accustomed to hearing the announcements on the public address system. Speakers had been wired to one another and positioned on poles placed throughout the village. Usually, the village mayor, Jaime Súarez, made the announcement. But he could not be counted on since he was a heavy drinker. On one occasion, I was in the theater helping to set things up when I heard Mayor Súarez ranting on and on about *El Teatro Comunal* and how wonderful I was. It was awkward and monotonous to hear his ranting so I ran up to the mayor's office. I thanked him and tried to take the microphone away from him with no success. I finally pulled the plug from the amplifier—much to the mayor's chagrin—and urged the mayor to come to see the show.

During the theater's life, many Mexican and American movies were shown as well as short educational films about health issues. Villagers especially liked Mexican westerns featuring three very popular mariachi singers Miguel Acéves Mejía, Antonio Aguilar, and Pedro Infante. These singers chanted love laments and villagers sang along with them. We also had guest speakers come to talk in between reels about forming a savings and loan cooperative association. We held dances that attracted village residents along with some of the friends I had made in San Gil including some very attractive young women who loved to socialize with Peace Corps men. Indeed, Peace Corps volunteers in and around San Gil became celebrities in the city's social circles. We were invited to private parties and *bailables* (dances). Colombian men were attracted to the female volunteers, assuming that they all "put out" and Peace Corps men caught the attention of Colombian women. Fortunately, Colombia has a lot of beautiful women. I heard many stories of Peace Corps volunteers who married Colombian women, including Brad who married a young woman from Bogotá.

There was another cultural feature that was hard for me, as an American, to deal with. Generally, when Americans are asked to do something, they usually let you know directly whether they are interested or not. In Colombia, it was common for people to graciously express their best of intentions to do something, whether it was to return a call or carry out an activity. They assured you of their commitment but then did not follow through. I came to learn that they wanted so much to accommodate you that they chose graciousness over directness. In like manner, graciousness was also common in how people greeted one another. It was not enough to greet someone by saying hello or how are you. It was very common to say hello in a variety of ways, one after the other: *Cómo está? Cómo le va? Cómo se acabó de ir? Cómo le fué? Qué tal? Qué mas?* (How are you? How are things going? How did things go? What's going on? What else?)

I tried to get other things accomplished while in El Valle. I traveled to Bucaramanga several times to meet with officials of the Department of

Health to make the case for assigning a public health nurse to work in El Valle. I had no success at this effort. I met several times with officials of the Department of Education to make the case for the construction of three additional schools in the farmlands outside of El Valle, but I had no success at this effort either. I helped the head teacher in El Valle's school to organize a 4-H Club, securing vegetable and flower seeds from a Rotary Club member back home in Mineola. With the seeds, the boys and girls planted a wide variety of vegetables which the children brought home with them and sold the balance in the market.

Women and having sex were constantly on my mind during my Peace Corps experience in Colombia. My first attempt at a relationship was with a former San Gil beauty queen. Salomón and I would typically spend our days driving his jeep or riding horseback into the isolated sections of the countryside and then go into San Gil late in the afternoon. Salomón typically had office work to do at the Coffee Federation office. I would be left to my own devices.

On one day I went into San Gil, to send a telegram to the Peace Corps office in Bogotá, something I needed to do from time to time. I went to the telegraph office on the main square. I found a beautiful woman with a big friendly smile, sparkling brown eyes, and long brown hair sitting behind the reception desk. They belonged to Janeth Navarro Sanchez. I knew as soon as I saw her I'd be continuing my afternoon visits to San Gil and sending lots of telegrams for the next two years. Seeing her became a daily requirement. We talked for hours on end while making eyes at one another. We began to go to the Ritz Café together for *tinto* (coffee). Over the course of weeks and months, Janeth and I became an item in San Gil society. *Pablo tiene gancho* (Paul has a rubber band attached to him) was the expression often used by the townspeople. We'd meet at dances at the country club and private parties. I continued to be a lousy dancer so I simply moved my feet to the rhythmic Colombian music.

Colombians enjoyed hearing gringos speak Spanish. The fact that I was from a working class American family was of no significance. I was the local Peace Corps volunteer, a representative of the US where the streets were paved with gold, and thus I achieved social status. That I was courting one of San Gil's beauty queens presented the romantic idea to people that I would take Janeth away with me to the US and the glamorous life that all Americans were presumed to live.

One Sunday afternoon, Janeth and I went to a matinee movie together. I walked to her house, knocked on the wooden door and was greeted by her 12-year-old brother, who would be joining us to the movies. I waited for Janeth in a parlor and saw her father sitting in an inner room watching television. I imagined him to be a very unhappy camper, what with his daughter dating an American who could only be up to no good. Knowing that I'd love to fool around with Janeth, given the opportunity, I felt guilty just being near him. I'm sure he knew it, too. The theater was crowded because there was a big American feature, *Esplendora en la Hierva* (Splendor in the Grass) starring Warren Beatty and a young, nubile Natalie Wood. I felt very awkward sitting next to Janeth, as if everyone in the theater was watching us. I kept my eyes on the screen to avoid eye contact with her when Natalie was lying on the back seat of a roadster groping with her boyfriend. We had never kissed, or even touched one another except for dancing. I was glad when the afternoon was over. I walked Janeth and her brother home. I knew that Janeth would never be an outlet for my horniness. Somehow, I also knew that the relationship wouldn't last very long, that it was an infatuation for both of us. When I moved to Bucaramanga, the relationship ended.

I also became infatuated with Caroleah Kotch, one of the volunteers living in San Gil. She and her partner Barbara Siani were trained by Peace Corps in health education and nutrition.

They organized women's and girls' classes in various communities. Caroleah and Barbara were very dedicated volunteers and also very attractive. Caroleah was especially attractive to me but despite my many efforts to gain her affections, she didn't want to date me. Other volunteers had their eyes on Caroleah, too. The best we could do was attend parties and dances with one another. My experience with women was common among the other volunteers in the region. The men wanted to date and, of course, have sex, but the women appeared not to be interested. As far as sex was concerned, the men relied on periodic visits to *las casas de putas* (whore houses) in Bucaramanga where we would dance, drink a lot, and have sex.

On November 22, 1963, I went to San Gil to visit Caroleah and Barbara. Afterwards, I drove to Dick Miller's apartment where I found him sitting at his kitchen table listening to his Zenith transoceanic radio. As I entered his apartment, Dick looked at me in a way that indicated something terrible had happened. I was stunned when he told me that President Kennedy had been shot and might die. I sat down to listen to the radio. I listened to the announcer repeat the news over and over again, unwilling to believe what I was hearing.

Time passed. We learned that the President had died. I felt sad and confused. We cried and hugged one another. Soon, Colombian friends came to Dick's house. Colombians were shocked and saddened by the news. They expressed their sympathies to us as if we had lost a parent and, indeed, it felt like we had. That evening, San Gil's principal church held a special mass that I attended. People wanted to know if we would remain in Colombia now that President Kennedy had been assassinated. The Peace Corps was viewed as his program. He was revered in Colombia and respected not only for launching the Peace Corps but for establishing the larger Alliance for Progress program of economic aid. The Colombian President set three days of national mourning in which businesses and schools closed. People flocked to churches throughout the country. It was no surprise when, over the upcoming weeks and months, many schools and neighborhoods throughout Colombia were renamed in the memory of John F. Kennedy.

During training, we had been alerted that many Colombians had intestinal worms (amoebas) of various kinds. We were cautioned not to drink the water nor eat fresh vegetables or fruit unless they had been soaked in iodinized water. Diarrhea was also a common complaint among villagers and Peace Corps volunteers who used an over-the-counter medication called Polymagma to deal with the unpleasant symptoms. While living in El Valle, I developed what I thought was an intestinal illness. I went to Bucaramanga to get help from Dr. Mogollón, the local Peace Corps physician. He recommended that I limit my eating for awhile to tea and saltine crackers and to take medication to settle my stomach. I did so, but the discomfort of not being able to empty my bowels was uncomfortable and sometimes painful. The result was that I had to stoop over, my rear end protruding, when I walked in the village. When Antonio Corso saw my awkward appearance, he cried, *Pablo tiene un chichagui en el culo!* which means that I had a "bug up my ass!" I was very embarrassed and later found out that my suffering had to do with the fact that I had an enormous boil growing on my rear end that had to be lanced and drained. Ouch!

My mother wrote to me often. In the first few months, it was almost every day. Years later, she told me that sometimes she would stop what she was doing—cooking, ironing, or cleaning around the house—and sit down at the dining room table and write me a letter. She remembers that when I was coming home, my father asked what she would do if I got off the plane with a "Spanish" girl. My mother told my father that she didn't care who I got off the plane with, "As long as it's my Paul who gets off the plane, that's all that matters."

My father said that this was proof to him that I was my mother's favorite. She asked him what he would do if I got off the plane with a girl. He said he would do nothing because he would be "dead on the ground."

Isbelia understood from the start how difficult it would be to effect dramatic changes in the community and how people and systems resist change. She accepted my idealism and purposefulness as genuine reflections of my youthful human and charitable spirit. Therein lay the truth about what I and the majority of my colleagues accomplished. We contributed our emotional and physical energy directly to the people of Colombia. The broader social and political changes that have taken place over the past forty years would have taken place with or without the Peace Corps. Unfortunately, the worldwide production and distribution of cocaine and marijuana has bound the words "drugs" and "Colombia" together in the view of the world. However, when I lived in Colombia, drugs hadn't yet become the country's biggest export. I never heard of drug production or use.

My situation was similar to that of many other Peace Corps volunteers during the 1960s. Our group replaced the original Peace Corps group that was sent to Colombia in 1961 when the Peace Corps was established by President Kennedy. In some cases, we were the first volunteers to be assigned to the area. In other cases, our assignments were to continue the work started over the previous two years.

In small, limited ways, they did. Peace Corps contributions can be seen today in the form of countless construction projects such as roads, schools, water systems, and housing for the poor as well as people who learned to speak English, organized cooperatives, and learned marketable skills. Certainly, these efforts contributed towards the improvement of economic and social conditions in some parts of the country. These contributions were also subtle in nature, fostering a climate of hope, expectations, and opportunity as well as creating the potential for understanding and friendship among the Colombian people and American people.

Within a short period of time in Colombia, however, I became a lot more jaundiced about whether my expectations for the redistribution of wealth were realistic. I increasingly identified with those who saw the Peace Corps as a neutralizer of true social change not as a social reform organization. I began to question whether government could be a true agent of change. Instead, I adopted the perspective that the best the Peace Corps Volunteers could do was to do no harm—by not imposing their values and culture on others while doing what they could to make life better in their villages. Adopting this perspective gave greater purpose and perspective to my work. Always looking at my work in the context of social change was just too frustrating.

It was difficult for most Colombians to truly understand the role of a young American Peace Corps volunteer in an agrarian society where economic growth moved at a snail's pace and where 10% of the nation's population had more than 50% of its income; where only one exportable product (coffee) was produced; and where uneducated *campesinos* flocked to urban centers in pursuit of a better life. I often felt useless. I had no skills and was not particularly handy with tools or equipment. According to the Peace Corps promotional material, most volunteers were teaching English or helping to build schools, roads, and bridges, but I knew nothing about these things. I felt guilty about this lack of knowledge and somewhat a fraud for believing that I had something to offer.

During my first few months overseas, Paul Mundschenk and I exchanged many letters. We both expressed our doubts and uncertainties about our work. It was comforting to know that I wasn't alone in my doubts and worries. Actually, these feelings were very common among volunteers when we met. We wanted to believe that we were part of a larger national movement towards positive social and economic change.

It was important to us to believe that the Peace Corps' motivations were noble and genuine; that we weren't, as some pundits and authors believed, simply youthful pawns of US foreign policy, a goodwill gesture to quell the spread of communism.

With my logical mind, compliant nature, and lack of political understanding, I accepted Peace Corps orientation at face value. Here we were, hundreds of energetic Americans with the will and time to make a difference, living in hundreds of Colombian villages and urban neighborhoods. It seemed reasonable to believe that our collective efforts would contribute to the improvement of conditions for the ill-fed, ill-housed, uneducated masses.

Auto accidents were very much part of my Peace Corps experience. The first one occurred only four months into my time in Colombia. Several volunteers, including Dick Miller, Sharon Lake, Dee Neb, and others were thrown from Fred Detjen's jeep in a turn on a rainy road. Fortunately, no one was permanently injured although Dee required a neck brace for a period of time. The jeep was not supposed to be used again until its canvas top and side bar structure were replaced.

However, a month later Peace Corps Volunteer Leader Fred Detjen of Illinois needed to use the jeep to transport newly-arrived volunteers to their work sites. So, despite Peace Corps instructions not to use the jeep, Fred did what he felt he had to do as part of his job responsibilities for the new volunteers. On the way back to Bucaramanga, Fred became very tired and turned the driving over to John Meier, a dear friend of mine from Washington State. John drove the jeep for several miles before entering one of the many sharp turns on the dangerous road between San Gil and Bucaramanga. He didn't know that Fred had fallen asleep in the passenger seat, which had no seat belt.

As the jeep rounded a sharp curve, Fred fell from the jeep. His head struck the pavement hard. John stopped the jeep and ran to Fred who lay unconscious on the road. He lifted him into the vehicle, tied their belts together to strap Fred onto the passenger seat, and raced to the San Gil hospital with Fred beside him, apparently in a coma. When he got to the hospital emergency room, John immediately called me to ask for my help. Before driving to San Gil, I called the Peace Corps office in Bogotá to let them know what had happened. I urged them to send Dr. King, the Peace Corps physician, to see if Fred could be helped. Peace Corps decided to send the physician by plane that evening to land at the small, abandoned San Gil airport located in the hills above the village. The airport had no runway lighting and, therefore, we had to figure out a way to provide sufficient lighting for the plane to land. When I got to the hospital, I comforted John, who was understandably distraught. I got on the telephone and spoke to the manager of the local radio station asking for the opportunity to speak to the public to appeal for help. He agreed. I also called some of our other friends in San Gil and asked them to ask friends to join us at the airport. Dozens of residents responded and arrived in their cars and trucks.

The airport hadn't been used in several years and was basically a grassy field. I directed everyone to place their cars and trucks along the runway every ten yards for about one hundred and fifty yards. There were probably thirty or forty vehicles all together. I arranged for someone to drive down to the city and bring back cold drinks. I asked some of the volunteers to build fires in two oil drums we found at the airport and to place the drums at the two extremes of the field. From time to time, I drove Fred's jeep along the bumpy landing strip to chat with everyone, urging their patience and alerting them to any plane sightings.

Hours went by. One of the drivers indicated that he was a ham radio operator and offered to contact the Bogotá airport manager. When the plane hadn't arrived at the estimated time of arrival, I made arrangements for the ham radio operator to call the Bogotá airport from the San

Gil airport. We learned that the plane had tried to land but couldn't find the airport due to low cloud cover. I was able, after much pleading, to convince the authorities to instruct the pilot to return to San Gil to try to land again. With this information, I was able to encourage the vehicle owners to stay another hour. Finally, after six hours of waiting, the plane located the small airport through the clouds and landed. As the plane bumped along the field, there were shouts and cheers and blinking lights. I immediately drove the doctor down the mountain overlooking San Gil to the hospital.

It was no use. The physician concluded that Fred had suffered multiple concussions and was expected to die soon. John and I slept on couches in the hospital that night. Early in the morning, Fred died. Fred's parents flew from Illinois to Colombia to accompany Fred's body back home. I was very upset and wanted to go to Bogotá to express my condolences to them, but the Peace Corps director denied my request. This was the first time in my life that someone I knew as a friend had died. I was very upset, felt terrible, and cried. It was a powerful reminder about the fragility of life.

My effort to assure beyond a shadow of a doubt that nothing could be done to save Fred's life drew the attention of several Peace Corps officials. I received two letters of recognition, one from the Peace Corps director and one from the regional director. The director wrote, "I have heard nothing but praise from both Dr. King and Matt DeForest for the way you helped out in Fred Detjen's unfortunate accident. One could say that you did what any volunteer would do to help out another in serious trouble, yet I feel that you showed far above average initiative and determination to see that everything conceivably possible was done to help Fred. You obviously did a very fine job of contacting and handling the Colombians in San Gil, enlisting their cooperation for the landing of the plane at night, and in numerous other ways. Your help was invaluable in this time of crisis."

I didn't feel like I had done anything special. Like countless soldiers at war and witnesses to accidents, I did what I felt I had to do. It seemed only the right thing to do to assure that everything possible was done to save Fred's life. A life seemed too valuable to go ignored.

Sometimes one person's tragedy is another's moment in the sun, and so it was to be with me. Two weeks after Fred's death, the Peace Corps director, Chris Sheldon, asked me to replace Fred as Volunteer Leader for the State of Santander del Sur. Filled with doubt and anxiety, I reluctantly left El Valle, Salomón, Isbelia, Antonio, and my other friends. I had never been in a leadership role and questioned my abilities. I knew that Fred was greatly admired by all of the volunteers in Santander del Sur so I questioned how I would be able to fill his boots and handle the inevitable comparisons. He was a natural leader who, I would learn, had attended West Point and received an engineering degree. As a former classmate of his told me years later, Fred's "strong independence and ruggedness were uniquely combined with a desire to be kind and help other people." I didn't feel anyone would have such words to say about me, but I decided to take the job and do the best I could.

My title as Peace Corps Volunteer Leader was *Coördinador* (Coordinator). It was my first serious responsibility and I was determined to do a good job. I remembered how I looked forward to Fred's visits to El Valle. It wasn't an easy role for me to play, with my lack of self-confidence and worldly experience. I was called upon to represent my fellow volunteers to our Colombian counterparts and to give moral support to the volunteers. The tougher stuff had to do with giving advice when volunteers were unsure as to how they could be most helpful in their work. Some volunteers struggled for two years to find what they could contribute. Some volunteers spent their time reading the two hundred books in their book locker, drinking beer or rum with the local villagers, marking dates on their calendars until the next regional meeting, their vacations, and the days left until their termination dates. As was typical of my role as volunteer leader/coordinator, I visited the eleven rural sites in Santander del Sur on a monthly basis to serve as a friend and social worker, and to bring supplies, information, and equipment to the often lonely volunteers. I saw my El Valle friends from time to time. I visited the three volunteer sites in Bucaramanga's poor neighborhoods. Half of my time was spent traveling, and the arrival of my new Willys Jeep was a major event for the children of the villages and the barrios.

Me and my Willys jeep in the mountains

The villages and cities in Santander del Sur were located everywhere from jungles along the steamy, muddy Río Magdelena in oil country to the edges of the snow-capped peaks of the Cordillera Central where wool *ruanas* (capes) were worn twelve months a year. I enjoyed driving, even on the narrow, unpaved roads. Of course, I had some near-death experiences when I was in the process of passing a vehicle, often a big truck or bus that approached from the opposite direction. One of us either had to put on the brakes or speed up. I found Colombian drivers extremely cautious and accommodating in these instances. Of course, there were drunk drivers like anywhere else. Foolishly, I did take my chances from time to time. Driving at night in mountainous areas with switchback roads, I looked ahead to see if approaching headlights were to be seen. If I didn't see any, I cut the switchback corners to save time. Since the jeep had a standard shift transmission, I often drove in second gear. Over the two years, I developed small muscles in my wrists from the frequent tension that I felt from making lots of turns to my left and right driving on bumpy roads.

On one trip, I traveled to the isolated villages of Málaga and Concepción to visit Mike Davis, the volunteer in the village. Concepción is located high in the *altiplano*, an area above the tree line, not too far from one of Colombia's five snow-capped peaks, the Sierra Nevada de Cocúy. It wasn't one of my favorite places to visit due to its isolation. It took about five hours to get there by jeep on narrow dirt roads containing many sharp switchback turns. It took twenty minutes in a small plane. I made the trip on a fairly regular monthly basis only once by plane.

I frequently travelled from Bucaramanga to San Gil where I usually had lunch at the Pozo Azúl, a wonderful riverside restaurant with red and white table cloths below straw roofed kiosks. Before meals were served, the waitress placed a bread basket on the table with a small bowl of *ahí* (a mixture of chopped onion, garlic, green pepper, and oil and vinegar). I would dunk the sliced bread in the *ahí*. It was delicious. The menu featured fried yucca, white rice, seasoned roast chicken, *lengua sudada* (marinated tongue), and, my favorite, *sobre barriga*. *Sobre barriga* is what we commonly call skirt steak but looks like corned beef. The Colombian version is seasoned with crushed garlic, salt and pepper, onion, dark beer, oregano, cilantro, and marjoram. Its seasoning was very different from the Jewish corned beef I ate in New York City. After lunch, I visited volunteers Bob Perkins and Eliot Levine in Mogotes and John Meier and Larry Leckenby in San Joaquín. I stayed in each village at least one night, spending time with the volunteers chewing the fat, drinking beer, and learning what the volunteers were up to and whether they needed my help in some way in Bucaramanga. I shared information with them about what was going on in other Peace Corps sites and gave them advice where I could.

I then proceeded higher into the mountains above *el páramo* (the tree line) to Onzaga. On one site visit to Onzaga, I found Jim Morris and Dave Lightwine, the volunteers assigned to the village, drinking beers in a local cantina and chatting with some village residents. In the course of conversation, someone asked me what I did as a Peace Corps Volunteer Leader. I was taken aback by the question. It wasn't easy to explain my job in English, much less Spanish. With the aid of several beers, I offered the following explanation:

"I live in Bucaramanga and, every month, I travel to the villages where Peace Corps volunteers live and work. I help them plan and implement projects," I said. "I also serve as their representative in Bucaramanga to Colombian officials, and organize meetings and conferences for educational purposes." Feeling that explanation was too long and vague, I tried to summarize my work with a simple sentence that, in English, meant that I had at least one project in every village. In Spanish, I said, *Pues, tengo por lo menos un hecho en cada pueblo.*

This remark was immediately met with uproarious laughter and loud comments from the villagers. One fellow made the sign of the cross on his chest in disbelief at what I had just said. There were pats on my back. The guy sitting next to me sharply snapped his wrist up and down as if to say "Wow!" It was obvious that they were laughing at my expense. I was confused and Jim and Dave were no help. How was I to know that I had just told everyone that I had fathered at least one child in every village that I visited? They hadn't taught me that idiomatic expression in Peace Corps language classes!

On a visit to the village of Mogotes, I had a life-threatening experience. Bob and Eliot had helped to construct a one-room school building about an hour by horseback from Mogotes. We mounted our horses and rode to the school where we were greeted by members of a local *junta* (council) who had built the school building. We drank some beers, ate some food, and attended a short ceremony commemorating the school's official opening. We mounted our horses to return to Mogotes and the trip back to Bucaramanga. On the way, the three of us approached a curved and very narrow 100' gorge where there was no room even for horses to pass one another. As we entered the gorge, we noticed three horsemen ahead of us coming from the opposite direction. What should we do? The gorge was too narrow for us to turn around, so we kept moving towards the horsemen. When we were face-to-face with them, we could see that they carried machetes and that one of them was drunk. They made it clear that they weren't going to turn around. We asked them nicely to turn around because they had just entered the gorge and had a shorter distance to negotiate. They refused. They could tell that we weren't Colombians since Bob had a light complexion with blond hair. The drunk one asked where we were coming from. We told them about the inauguration of the new school. He reported angrily that he lived nearby in another vereda where they also wanted to build a school, but they hadn't been chosen for the assistance. We assured him that we would do whatever we could to help build a school in his *vereda*, but he wouldn't buy it. We sat there at an impasse for what felt like an eternity. Fortunately, one of the other riders convinced the inebriated one to back off. Things could have been ugly but fortunately, they weren't.

Carcasí was the most remote Peace Corps site. Kent Kedl of Wyoming and Ron Auglur of Alabama were partners in Carcasí. I visited there a number of times. On one of these visits, we had another adventure. Kent ignited the Coleman lantern that gave light to the house. The lantern sat on a wooden table in the middle of the room.

As Kent pumped the manual pressure stick to get the lantern ready for a match ignition, the lantern burst into flames searing Kent's arm and burning everything on the table. Ron and I rushed to get blankets to contain the fire and smother Kent's arm. The fire destroyed the card table and some *ruanas*, sleeping bags, a duffle bag, camping gear, and blankets on it. We removed the charred materials to the ground outside the house and then helped Kent bandage his arm. Fortunately, no other injuries or damage occurred.

Volunteers in Latin America were entitled to one month vacation time in the Western Hemisphere, for which the Peace Corps gave us an allowance. We weren't permitted to return to the US. My primary trip was to Ecuador and Peru. Paul Mundschenk, Bob Salafia, and John Meier joined me. We met at Paul and Bob's site in Silvia, Cauca and took a bus to the border, crossing from Ipiales, Colombia to Tulcán, Ecuador. We traveled on the Trans American Highway which, in truth, was a two lane paved, but bumpy, road, over scenic mountain passes on very precarious switchback mountain roads. On a number of occasions, while high in the Andes, the bus stopped. The driver came through the bus, silently appealing for donations to be placed in his hat. The donations were left in a wooden box that was part of a makeshift shrine in memory of the victims of the auto or bus accident at that spot. Superstition had it that if you didn't donate to the shrine you might suffer the same plight as the deceased.

We went to Quito, Ecuador's capital, commonly known as the "city of churches." It seemed as though there was a church on every corner. Quito, at an altitude of 11,000 feet, has a chilly climate in which people normally wear dark wool *ruanas*. I bought a beautiful two-sided *ruana* in the public market. In walking the streets, you could see changes in the facial features of the people from those that were more common in Colombia. Ecuadorians had classical Andean features with prominent noses and reddish brown complexions. Women from rural areas wore black, round dress hats.

From Quito, we flew to Guayaquil, the country's port city and a humid, busy commercial center surrounded by slum neighborhoods consisting of dwellings built on stilts above muddy water. We had dinner in Guayaquil and booked passage for that night to travel by ferry south on the Guayas River to the Bay of Guayaquil and across to the Ecuadorian-Peruvian border and the town of Túmbes. We tried, with little success, to sleep in hammocks located on the ferry's deck. We arrived near a small town close to the Peruvian border. We made a deal with a truck driver to let us travel on the rear of his cargo truck to the Peruvian border. After traveling over muddy jungle roads, we got to the border. We walked over the border and rented a taxi to Aguadillas and then to Túmbes, where we got on a Greyhound bus that took us to Lima, Peru, about a 24-hour ride. The trip was uneventful other than the fact that we passed through a desert that was spotted with lush vegetation which reminded me of areas of Israel that had been converted from desert to productive farm land. We spent two days in Lima. It had the appearance of a European city except for the enormous *favella* (slum area) surrounding the city. We stayed in a downtown hotel and were struck by the many 1940s and 1950s automobiles that were held together with rope and tape. We took a short trip to a nearby beach to spend a nice afternoon.

The next morning we boarded a DC-3 to fly to Cusco, the ancient and beautiful capital city of the Incan civilization. From the airplane, we could see snow capped peaks between the clouds. During the descent to the Cusco airport, the plane flew between mountain peaks onto a small runway. Cusco was founded in the eleventh century and is said to have been plundered by Pizarro in 1535. There are still remains, however, of the palace of the Incas, the Temple of the Sun and the Temple of the Virgins of the Sun. Inca building remains and foundations can still be seen.

We were warned by everyone that we would tire quickly due to the thin air of Cuzco's 11,000 foot altitude. We soon understood why. We took a taxi to our hotel, beginning to adjust to the thin air. After resting, we visited the colorful public market and the many outdoor stalls manned by men and women with classic Andean features. We walked through Cusco's streets that are bordered by polished dry stone walls consisting of 4' x 2' rectangular stones precisely fitted side by side without mortar. The next morning we boarded the train to Machu Picchu, the lost city of the Incas. It is located about fifty miles from Cusco at 8,000 feet above sea level over the Riobamba River in the Urubamba Valley. The train slowly crept between the rapidly ascending mountains. It made two stops to give local women and children the opportunity to offer the train passengers native drinks and food. On one of these stops, I noticed a vendor near the train crouching. When she walked away, she left a small yellow puddle. It served as a reminder of how far away we were from modern sanitation standards.

The train tracks end at Machu Picchu. From there, we took a small tourist bus up a switch-back road to the tourist hotel managed by the Peruvian government. Llamas and alpacas forage in the rich green grass surrounding the hotel and the ruins. Machu Picchu is a remarkable site, standing prominently between two rivers probably two thousand feet directly below. The buildings, like those in Cusco, are made of large stone blocks placed next to one another using no mortar. It was hard to imagine how this community was assembled and constructed. It was an unforgettable experience to be there.

I went on one other trip while in South America. Peace Corps Colombia needed some jeeps that Peace Corps Venezuela didn't need. Five Volunteer Leaders, including me, were assigned to fly to Caracas and then drive the jeeps in a caravan to Bogotá, Colombia. We had a great time wining and dining on Iberia Airlines' cuisine and then in Caracas with our generous meal allowance. We looked up Peace Corps volunteers in Caracas, who held a party to welcome us. We noticed the extreme poverty surrounding the city, featuring 15-story apartment buildings that were recently constructed by the government to house people from the country's interior who had fled rural poverty. They lived in squalor in the apartment buildings, often with goats, chickens, and pigs, and found no decent employment within the city.

Following Peace Corps instructions, we left Caracas after two days. Within two hours of our departure, one of the five vehicles broke down on the highway, requiring a new engine block. We stayed together and made arrangements for the downed vehicle to be towed for repair in the nearby city of Valencia. We rented hotel rooms and wired Peace Corps Colombia to notify them of the situation and to ask them to wire more money. We ended up staying in Valencia for a week, living high on the hog. A week later, the vehicle was repaired and we got back on the road. We brought the vehicles to Bogotá and then returned to our sites.

While living in Bucaramanga, I often hung out with the volunteers living in the city. Some Peace Corps volunteers in Bucaramanga taught English and physical education at one of the city's two universities. Sometimes, rural volunteers stayed in their apartment when in the city. One of them, Tom Tolman, married a Colombian woman. There were also volunteers doing urban community development work in several of the city's low income and squatter neighborhoods.

In the Barrio Santander, volunteers Linda Pierce and Nan Kretchkoff asked for my help to organize a cooperative among a group of women who, individually, were making and selling attractive purses made of *fique*, a hemp used to make a variety of items. With the advice of Dick Miller, one of the volunteers in the cooperative organizing group, I helped the women by finding markets for their products. I traveled to other cities around the country and made arrangements with retailers to accept the purses on consignment. Other volunteers made contact with department stores in the United States and the United Nations Gift Shop in New York City to sell the purses internationally. The cooperative functioned for many years and provided much needed income to the women and their families. The women also learned business skills and built their self-confidence. In 1972, when Karen and I visited Bucaramanga, we visited one of the women who presented Karen with a coop purse. Inez described how the purse income enabled her son to go to the university.

There were two female volunteers in Santander del Sur who lived in Barrancabermeja, who were trained in health education and nutrition. Barrancabermeja, the department's second largest city, was hazy, hot, and humid virtually all the time. I didn't enjoy driving to this city. It was Colombia's oil capital. To get there, you needed to drive four hours on dusty and narrow two-lane roads, always alert for speeding oil trucks. If you were unlucky enough to approach one from behind, you were left in a cloud of brown dust. Then you had to decide whether to stop for a breather or to pass the long truck on the curvy roads, praying that no vehicles were coming from the opposite direction. Poverty in Barrancabermeja was severe, perhaps accentuated by the oppressive heat. Children were usually barefoot and dressed in raggedy clothing. It appeared that most people lived in shacks. Americans, working for the oil companies, lived in country club-like compounds, having little to do with Colombians other than their hired help.

I was fortunate that Bucaramanga had some great restaurants so I had wonderful choices where to eat. By far, my favorite was DiMarcos, a restaurant owned by an Argentine. It was in an upscale neighborhood and had attractive indoor and outdoor dining areas. My most enjoyable meal was a dish called *parrillada*. It featured a *churrasco* (steak) served on a wooden board along with intestinos, kidneys, heart, brain, and salivary glands all broiled on a charcoal fire. For one dollar and fifty cents, I could have this meal along with a bottle of beer and a cucumber salad. My breakfasts were usually at La Berna, a bakery owned and operated by a Swiss family. Whenever I was in town, I was sure to go to La Berna by seven thirty in the morning to get croissants and buns hot out of the oven and a great cup of coffee.

About six months before my Peace Corps term was over, I learned, along with other Peace Corps Volunteer Leaders, that Peace Corps Washington was changing the organizational structure of Peace Corps in Colombia. They were about to assign foreign service staff to be regional directors and eliminate the volunteer leader system. I had felt that this was wrong and had come to believe that leaders played a valuable role that was irreplaceable by paid career staff from Washington. I talked with other volunteer leaders who shared my beliefs.

When Lloyd Gaspar arrived in Bucaramanga to become Regional Director in Santander del Sur, I immediately disliked him. He lived in an expensive, swanky house in an exclusive neighborhood, wore flashy clothing, and didn't show an understanding of Colombia or Peace Corps volunteers and their needs, nor did he fit the image of Peace Corps.

On two occasions, I organized conferences for volunteers in Bucaramanga. They featured meetings with our Colombian counterparts to discuss current and potential future projects. I also arranged for various types of workshop presentations as well as social events that were held at the end of each day. On the second day of one of the events, we had a party at Las Paraguitas, a beautiful retreat in nearby Floridablanca owned by the Tobacco Institute. It had manicured Japanese Gardens, streams with goldfish in them, and a swimming pool. I arranged for the party to be catered and, of course, to include plenty of aguardiente, rum, and beer. I also hired a Colombian music group to provide dance music.

Everyone was having a nice time when conflict arose. My dear friend John Meier got into an argument with Lloyd Gaspar. There had been a history of tension and conflict between John and Lloyd probably having to do with Lloyd's apparent pretentiousness and what we felt to be a take-over style. In any case, the argument led to loud curses, pushing and shoving, punches, and a wild fight in and out of the swimming pool. Eventually we broke up the fight, only to be faced with another problem. Bob Perkins, one of the volunteers from Mogotes, had been drinking heavily and was missing. We later found out that he had wandered off the grounds of the Tobacco Institute and threatened a local homeowner, and nearly got attacked with a machete. He was being detained by the police. Lloyd held me responsible for allowing the party to get out of hand.

Things would only get worse with me and Lloyd Gaspar. Along with many other leaders in other parts of the country, we made it known to the Peace Corps director that we felt that the new system was ill-conceived. We felt that the volunteer leader system worked and shouldn't be replaced by assigning Washington-appointed, State Department-trained staff persons. We felt that volunteer leaders had established positive relationships with their volunteers and that paid people would have great difficulty establishing the kind of trust that volunteer leaders could.

This experience turned out to be the first of a number of career-altering situations where I challenged the status quo and authority figures and acted against my best interests regardless of the consequences. As I've thought back about my attitudes towards Peace Corps policies, I see a terribly idealistic, naïve young man. Conditions weren't so terrible under the regional director system. I was more concerned with being a part of a movement to right what I saw as a wrong. I felt comfort knowing that other Peace Corps leaders shared my attitudes. I wanted to show them and everyone that I stood up for what I believed in.

New Years Eve 1965 was spent partying with other volunteers and Colombian friends. We attended three parties in different neighborhoods of Bucaramanga. At 5AM, I gathered the dozen volunteers to drive them home after a night of dancing and drinking beer, rum, and aguardiente. I had consumed a good deal of alcohol over the course of the evening. Whether it was from too much drinking I'll never know, but I missed seeing a hard-to-see one-way traffic sign and caused an accident in which a woman was injured in the other vehicle. Eventually, the police arrived and instructed me to follow them to the police station. Once there, I was given a sobriety test which I narrowly passed.

Lloyd Gaspar made arrangements to pay the woman's hospital bills and castigated me for my behavior. He immediately relieved me of my duties as volunteer leader and instructed me to pack up my belongings and fly to Bogotá on the first flight. I obeyed and so I was denied the good-byes from the many friends and associates of the past two years in Santander del Sur. Over the years, I have been struck about how compliant I was in this situation. In a month of "house detention" in Bogotá, I never boarded a bus or plane to visit El Valle or Bucaramanga to make my goodbyes. I had been told not to do so and feared reprisals if I was caught. I felt abandoned by the Peace Corps. I had served well for two years but I felt as if I was being given a dishonorable discharge.

When I returned to the US, I lived at my parents' home for a while, but I was very unhappy. I had been on my own for two years. I was critical of my relatives and parents' friends and the superficialities of their lives. My mother once asked me why I couldn't be nicer to them. I told her that I wasn't interested in talking about cars, sports, clothing, who had married whom, and how successful so-and-so was. I also didn't appreciate their chiding me about my liberal views.

My Peace Corps experience gave me direction and purpose. It was a defining experience of my life. For the first time, I had been given leadership responsibilities. When I returned to the US, I could see myself entering a career in public service, perhaps overseas. I came to identify with the Colombian people and have followed the country's ups and downs over the years. I made lifelong friendships and enjoyed the diversity of Colombia's people and its geography.

Forty-six years later, Colombia still holds onto me. Its people were kind to me. They accepted me and made me feel welcome. They opened their hearts and homes to me. I still listen to Colombian music from the 1960s, especially the folk songs of the country's distinct regions. I support small development projects sponsored by Friends of Colombia, a group of former Colombian volunteers who served in Colombia between 1961 and 1982 when the Peace Corps discontinued the program due to rising violence and kidnappings.

CHAPTER THREE
Karen, Sari, Jeremy, Liza, Davi, and Mira

In 1967, two years after the end of my Peace Corps service, I married Karen Wildman. Karen was 22 and I was 27. She lived in Huntington, New York with her parents and siblings and had just graduated the State University of New York at Oneonta, headed for graduate school at SUNY Albany with designs on becoming a school psychologist.

She applied for a summer job at the youth center in Huntington where I was the director. I needed someone to help reach out to at-risk teenage girls in the community and those who already attended the youth center. I interviewed her and found her enthusiastic, intelligent, and sensitive to issues facing teenagers, and someone I could work with.

I called her and asked if she could attend a dance at the center, as a way for me to observe how she got along with young people. At the dance, she easily conversed with the teenagers and was well accepted so I was convinced she would do well in the summer job. After the dance ended, I asked her out for a drink. We went to Finnegan's, a Huntington bar. We made eyes at one another and knew there was strong chemistry going on. Not wanting the evening to end I invited her to the youth center where we played a game that the kids enjoyed called "Kreskin's ESP," which, basically, was a Ouiji board, predicting how a person feels about a given subject. by responding to questions while holding a string with a round metal ball at the end. A player would hold the string, and the ball would lean towards the "yes" or the "no." We asked one another whether we wanted to date again. All our responses indicated that we wanted to get to know one another better.

We enjoyed many of the same things. Neither of us was interested in material wealth. We laughed at the same jokes and couldn't get enough of one another. We dated every day after work and on the weekends. We went to a Mets game, drove in my dilapidated 1958 black Peugeot to a beach in the Hamptons, and spent a lot of time in my $110 a month, one-room Huntington apartment. Karen arrived every morning with coffee and bagels. It was a wonderful way to start each day. We talked and listened to folk music while sitting on the "mattress-couch" in my living room/kitchenette.

I proposed to Karen two weeks after we met. We were kindred spirits. I was very confident that, even though we'd known one another for a very short time, the basic qualities for a good marriage were present. I was also tired of dating and wanted someone to share my life with. I knew that I needed a supportive person who shared my passion for social justice. My parents, who had begun to feel that I'd never marry, were shocked. After all, I was 27 years old, consumed with my work, with no marriage prospects on the horizon. My mother told Karen that she felt I'd never marry.

Karen and me at our wedding, Levittown, New York, 1967

Karen's parents were progressives in the 1930s. Karen describes herself as a "red diaper baby," recalling her parents' admonition not to open their New York City apartment door if she could see men dressed in suits through the peephole, because they might be FBI agents. They felt this way because they were politically active at the time. Both of Karen's parents worked all of their lives. Her father, David, had total recall of everything he read. He was an expert on the Civil War. He sometimes made me feel foolish with his tremendous wealth of knowledge. Karen's mother, Rose, is a nurturing person who passed on her warmth and sensitivity to Karen. She worked for many years as a teacher's aide at the Nassau Center for Emotionally Disturbed Children in Woodbury. Karen worked at the Center during summers while in school. Karen's childhood was highlighted by the role that she played as a "mothering" child.

My love of Karen was based on an intuitive feeling that she would balance my shortcomings. I believed that we had the raw ingredients for a good marriage, and this has certainly been true. Karen surely didn't know, after knowing me for two weeks, what she was getting into when she married me. She had a sense of my mother's powerful role in the family and my father's passivity, but she couldn't have imagined how I would struggle for years to free myself from the often dysfunctional emotional climate in my family of origin. It turned out that our basic instincts were right. We've been married for 42 years and I love Karen more today than I did during those hot summer days in Huntington when we first met.

Karen is Jewish, but from a kind of Judaism that I never knew existed until I met her. She had been raised as a humanist secular Jew. This form of Judaism is home to people that recognize and celebrate Jewish history, values, and cultural heritage but don't practice the religious traditions. When we married, we discussed how we would educate our children about Judaism. My attitude was different than Karen's. I wouldn't have sent the girls to any form of religious or cultural studies and left it to the children to develop their own attitudes towards spirituality and religion. Over the years, Jewish holidays were treated as times for dinners with my brothers and my parents. At Passover, sometimes in our house, we read an English, secular Haggadah that described the struggle of the Jews through history and their liberation. We did not join a temple nor live in communities with higher Jewish populations. My goal was to live as a person of the world.

The summer of 1967 was filled with wedding planning, working together at the youth center, and passion. We married on September 3, a sunny afternoon, in the back yard of friends of Karen's parents in Levittown, New York. Karen looked radiantly beautiful as she approached me under the *chupa*. As Karen came through the back door of the house with her father David, a folk singer and a guitarist played "Black is the Color of my True Love's Hair" and later "Try to Remember" from the Broadway play, "The Fantasticks," a song that we both loved then, as we do now.

The wedding ceremony was led by Rabbi Irving Rockoff who, coincidentally, was rabbi at the synagogue where I was bar mitzvah as well as on the board of the Nassau Center, where Karen's mother, Rose, had worked for many years. Karen, believing in destiny, has always felt that this connection was further proof that we were meant for one another.

After the wedding, my brother Rob and his future wife Liz drove us to LaGuardia Airport for a flight to Denver, Colorado. We counted the gift money in the back of their car to see how much we had to spend on our honeymoon. It was about $700.

When we arrived in Denver, we spent a couple of days with Bob Koehler, a Peace Corps friend who had replaced me as a volunteer in El Valle de San José. We rented a while Ford Thunderbird convertible and took off for New Mexico and Texas. We camped and toured Mesa Verde National Park. We trekked the pueblo ruins at Bandelier National Monument before visiting Taos and Santa Fe. In Santa Fe, we bought four stools with colorful woven seats that we envisioned in our living room around a low, round coffee table that an aunt had given us. We had the stools, our first furniture purchase, shipped home.

On the way to Gallup, New Mexico, I noticed a state campground outside of town. We stopped and bought take-out Kentucky Fried Chicken and drove to the campsite as the sun began to set. Off Route 66 stood a trading post next to a one-story building with a large painting of a big brown bear with "Home of the Bears" on the wall. Karen and I both saw the picture but said nothing, not wanting to scare the other one. We each privately recalled a major news story that summer in which campers were attacked by bears in Yellowstone National Park. Our parents and friends had warned us to be careful, but we were tired and hungry and anxious to set up camp before dark.

We drove a couple of miles to the campground and quickly set up our two-person pup tent. We sat down at the picnic table to eat our fried chicken as it was getting dark, and realized that it was a weekday evening after Labor Day, so we were totally alone in the park. We placed our garbage in the trunk of the car so it wouldn't attract animals and then crawled into the narrow tent. By that time, it was nearly dark.

We listened to the sounds of the forest and began to feel very isolated and at-risk. The sounds of animals disturbed us. Were they skunks, squirrels, raccoons, or bears? We thought of the "Home of the Bears" sign we had seen. With light from our flashlight, we looked at one another and knew that we couldn't sleep there. We quickly took the tent apart and threw it into the car trunk, drove to a nearby motel, and rented a room for the night. In the morning, we decided to visit the trading post near the campsite to buy a Navajo rug. As we approached the store, we saw what was meant by "Home of the Bears." It was the local high school and the picture was of the school's mascot! We felt foolish.

We spent the rest of the day in Gallup and the Navajo Tribal Headquarters in Window Rock, Arizona before traveling to El Paso, Texas, where I had spent my sixteenth summer. There, we lazed in the hot sun and visited Júarez, Mexico a couple of times to tour a museum and visit a cultural center before we headed back east.

By the time Karen and I got married, a couple couldn't afford to live on one income unless the breadwinner earned a lot of money. For the first four years of marriage, we rented apartments in Huntington Village. Both Karen and I worked and, in the early days, were able to save a little. In 1970, we got a mortgage loan to buy a house in Sound Beach for $19,000. We thought of asking my parents for a loan for the down payment but discarded the idea because we knew that there would be emotional conditions attached to a gift or loan. However, they bought us a bedroom set. We were frugal in our spending but we both felt that annual vacations were essential to our lifestyle. So, even if we had to use our credit cards, we went on annual camping vacations, first by ourselves and later with our daughters. The costs of home ownership added to our monthly obligations causing us to get a home equity line of credit to make ends meet. The line of credit was also our ticket to be able to send the girls to college along with student loans and the girls working part-time and during summers.

Karen and me in the late '60s

In the late 1960s and early 1970s, smoking pot was very common. Often on Saturday nights, we got high with friends and ate lots of munchies. We listened to the music of the day including the Beatles, the Band, Richie Havens, Grand Funk Railroad, Jimmy Hendrix, Janis Joplin, Simon and Garfunkel, and folk singers Peter Seeger, Joni Collins, Joan Baez, Arlo Guthrie, Peter, Paul, and Mary, Patrick Sky, and Donovan. Some of our friends smoked pot daily, others smoked on the weekends. It was normal to pass around joints at parties. On a number of occasions, we attended parties where high-level employees working in the district attorney's office and police department were smoking pot with everyone else. We never had an interest in using stronger drugs.

Our friend Karl Grossman had started a small home-based business, the "Aquarius Candle Commune," selling black light-responsive candles to stores on the South Shore. I liked the idea and decided to establish "Pablo's Candle Commune" in the basement of our Sound Beach house. I bought 55-pound slabs of wax, candle molds, wicks, a variety of scents, and a variety of color dyes as well as several black lights. I also had labels printed to be placed on the candles displaying the name of the enterprise. I set up tables in our basement where I made round, square, tall, short, and star-shaped candles. I visited "head shops" in Nassau and Suffolk Counties and made arrangements to sell the candles on consignment. I did this for about a year, almost deciding to buy a ton of wax in order to dramatically reduce the per-candle cost. Fortunately, we decided against this investment. The wax was highly flammable so we could have had a terrible fire and burned our house down.

After three years of marriage, we decided to begin a family. On May 24, 1971, Sari was born in Huntington Hospital. I shared the wonderful experience of a Lamaze birth with Karen. We attended weekly Lamaze classes at a church in Deer Park. Dressed in a green hospital gown and cap, I was thrilled and crying to see our daughter physically come into the world. I took pictures of the delivery and later made a slide show depicting Karen's pregnancy and Sari's birth, which we showed to our friends and relatives. Participating in Sari's birth was the most moving experience of my life. Karen and I were so happy. We cried together at the wonder of new life. We were worried when we had to bring Sari back to the hospital for several days because she had jaundice. Later, when Sari was about two years old, we were upset when Sari developed "lazy eye" and needed an operation.

I loved to spend time with Sari and witness her curiosity and growth. Sari was a happy child who adjusted well and got along nicely with children and adults. We took her camping every summer. Sari particularly bonded with Karen's father, Dave. He had a wonderful way with her, spending many hours telling her stories with his rich imagination. He even wrote an illustrated book for Sari.

In the spring of 1974, we moved to another house in Sound Beach, blocks from our first home. The house was a little bigger and the property larger and flatter. We lived in this house for 25 years. We installed an above-ground swimming pool that we enjoyed for many summers. We added a fireplace and built wood fires on many weekends. I converted an all-purpose room in the basement to the children's playroom and, later, a TV-room and small office. Not liking to care for a lawn, I planted dozens of trees on the property that grew significantly over the years into a forest. The property was part of what once was a tree and shrubbery nursery. The builder let us relocate as many trees as we wanted. I transplanted yews, dogwood and wild cherry trees, and a large mimosa tree. I enjoyed watching their growth over the years knowing that I had successfully transplanted the trees. We enjoyed the company of Ed and Ronnie Kasten, who lived directly across the street. They were wonderful neighbors who especially loved Sari and Liza.

Sari attended school in the Millor Place School District. She enjoyed school and did well in her courses and she was often recognized for academic success. We were very proud of her. She had lots of interests and friends. She played on the school's soccer team and ran the high hurdles on the track team. She took ballet, clarinet and piano lessons, and participated in all of the school's theater productions, where she had important acting roles. She also performed in the school band and rose to become first clarinetist. Later, she served as director of summer youth theater productions in the Shoreham Wading River School District.

Sari was self-directed and knew from an early age that she wanted to be an English teacher.

As a young child, Sari would put on a dress and play the role of teacher with her imaginary friends and stuffed animals in our basement playroom, working at her play blackboard and directing her "students" in their lessons.

As Sari approached 12 years of age, we decided that it would be a good idea to provide her with a foundation in Judaism. Karen learned that there was a Jewish secular school in the area. We registered the girls at the Jewish Secular School of Suffolk where they both completed their studies. We attended all of the school's functions and enjoyed the participatory activities; the singing, the plays, the dancing, and, of course, the Jewish food. Sari loved shul; Liza hated it. Both girls made us very proud when they graduated. We celebrated by having big parties with our family and friends. I was especially touched when Liza participated in her group's play in remembrance of the Holocaust. I was overwhelmed with joy and wept during the ceremony.

The day that we drove Sari to college was a rough one, especially for me. We knew that she was ready for college and would do well. But no sooner did we leave campus and get on the interstate, Karen and I began to cry. We listened to a CD of "Phantom of the Opera," Sari's favorite show, and reminisced. I wrote a short poem about my thoughts. When we returned home, there were days of spending time in Sari's room thinking about how much we missed her.

While in college, Sari joined the Hillel Club at SUNY Geneseo and furthered her interest in Judaism. Later, at Boston University, where she attended graduate school, Sari studied Hebrew and became bat mitzvah. Karen and I were very proud of her as she read her *haftorah* (a portion of the Torah), which she had learned in just three months. Karen and I attended the ceremony and glowed with pride. Our dear friends, Jeff and Joan, were kind enough to join us for this special occasion. I had virtually abandoned religious traditions, but it was somehow comforting to know that our daughter would follow them.

Sari met Jeremy, her husband-to-be, at a friend's engagement party in New York City. It was apparent from the start that this was going to be a very important relationship. Sari and Jeremy got engaged after one year and married a year later at a Great Neck synagogue. Jeremy comes from a wonderful Rockland County family who is very active in their temple and follows Jewish traditions. Through the wedding planning period, Karen and I were introduced to traditional Jewish wedding customs. Sari and Jeremy didn't see one another for a week before the wedding. There was a *tisch* where the men prayed together, followed by a ceremony where Jeremy saw Sari for the first time. Then, Sari circled Jeremy seven times as part of the wedding ceremony under a *chupa* (canopy). After the reception, there was "benching"

for people to say prayers together. It was a
wonderful experience and especially moving
to me when Sari and I waltzed together to the
song "Sunrise, Sunset," from "Fiddler on the Roof."
It was very special to me that Caroleah Kotch,
a Peace Corps buddy from San Gil, and Paul
Mundschenk, my dear Peace Corps roommate
and friend, attended the wedding.

Sari and Jeremy have a kosher home and
practice Judaism in a way that would make
my father and his parents very proud. I am glad
that Sari has found a religious expression that
gives meaning and comfort to her life. Liza, on
the other hand, demonstrates little interest in
Judaism, following in my path. Sari is an English
teacher at Paul D. Schreiber High School in Port
Washington. Jeremy has a Masters degree in
tourism management from New York University
and is Director of Economic Development for the
City of New Rochelle. They live in New Rochelle.
Sari got involved in Barack Obama's presidential
campaign and followed the campaign daily.
She reads voraciously and is well-versed in
minority women's literature. Several years ago,
she was awarded a National Endowment for
the Humanities stipend to attend a Summer
Institute at Yale University on the subject of *The
Canterbury Tales*. Most recently, she was invited
to present a workshop on Chaucer at the annual
convention of the National Council of Teachers

of English. Sari is a wonderful mother. It gives me joy to see how she teaches her children not only information, but more importantly, to be emotionally intelligent individuals who are socially responsible. It is one of the gifts in my life to live to see our grandchildren grow and develop.

Three years after Sari was born, on May 4, 1974, Liza was born. Her Lamaze birth was also very special. I brought my 35mm camera into the delivery room at Huntington Hospital and took photos of Liza coming into the world. I converted these photos into slides, added taped folk music from the 1960s, and showed them to everyone who agreed to see them including my father, grandmother, and great aunt Shirley who were shocked at the shots of Liza's head popping into the world.

Liza was curious, feisty, and sensitive, with definite ideas about things. She loved to draw cartoons and build structures with Lego blocks. Our dining room table was often filled with Legos. Liza loved to wear baseball hats and showed a great interest in sports at an early age. I loved to play catch with her in front of our house and in the school yards. We also played basketball together in the driveway. During snowy days, we all enjoyed sledding down the little hill next to our house and making snowmen.

When she was about fourteen, Liza took an interest in tennis. We were happy about this interest and paid for tennis lessons at the Miller Place Tennis Club. Liza had a natural backhand and showed potential of becoming a good high school and college player. She had great hands at the net. She went on to play on the high school team and won several matches. I was very proud of her. For a period of time, Liza followed the career of Gabriella Sabatini, a beautiful Argentine up-and-comer in world tennis, to whom Liza had a strong physical resemblance. Liza lost interest in tennis in high school but became a passionate softball player. She has considerable skills as a softball player and has played regularly on several teams for many years. Two years ago, she was elected to the Advertising Softball Hall of Fame. Softball is an important part of Liza's life. She enjoys the camaraderie with her teammates and socializing with them. Liza is also a lifetime, avid Yankee fan with a wealth of information about every player, trade, and management decision. She has long surpassed me in her of knowledge of baseball. As an adult, I abandoned interest in baseball, the game of my childhood and youth. I'm so glad that Liza loves sports.

Liza and I had a hard time getting along for much of her adolescence and early adulthood. We had long periods of silence where we were at loggerheads in our relationship. This upset me greatly. I brooded and obsessed and looked for reasons why we were having such difficulties.

I came to see why Liza felt that I neglected her, emotionally. While Liza was in high school she wouldn't permit me to watch her play softball, something that I wanted to share with her. She felt that I would embarrass her in front of her teammates. In hindsight, I was too critical, and too consumed with worry about my work to see how I was hurting my relationship with her. My trouble expressing my feelings resulted in me often not saying what needed to be said at the time, choosing silence and withdrawal.

Recently, Liza and I reflected on our relationship. She reminded me of an incident while she was in college that occurred while she worked part-time at the Ronkonkoma child care center that was one of the three that my organization operated. There was a great deal of organizational financial insecurity and unrest among staff at the time. Staff knew Liza was my daughter. According to Liza, the center director said some very negative things about me that Liza told me about. I didn't believe that Liza understood the whole situation and exactly what the director meant by her remarks. This upset Liza. She saw my attitude as a sign of mistrust and lack of respect for her rather than as a sign of her loyalty to me and a way of protecting me. I didn't know what to believe. I had faith in the director and chose to stand behind her. Liza remained hurt and angry at me for many years. I didn't try to speak with her about her feelings, believing that I would make things worse. While she was in college, Liza and I had little communication. I continued to do the dutiful things expected of a father but without a clue as to why she had such negative feelings towards me. I hoped that Liza would grow out of it and things would change. I wanted her to see how much I loved her and wanted to have a good relationship with her.

Over the past few years, both Liza and I have worked separately to look at our relationship. Today, Liza and I have a nice relationship and can talk about our past differences. Karen and I have gone to a couple of her softball games. On one of these occasions, we drove into New York City's Central Park to see a game. We brought her a surprise birthday cake which she appreciated and shared with her teammates. I was thrilled when she asked me if I would like to hit some balls with her friends during batting practice. During recent years, we went to batting ranges where I watched her hit. I took delight in seeing her methodical hitting style and intelligent analysis of her sport and play. We talk with one another regularly by phone. We also enjoy playing Scrabble together and with Karen. Recently, I was touched by her willingness to go with me to visit my mother in the nursing home where she resides. Not long ago, she introduced me to one of her friends, saying that I could have been a professional baseball player. I knew that Liza was exaggerating my athletic abilities but was touched by her kind remark.

Liza has a strong social network and many friends. She has maintained lasting friendships with some of her high school and college friends. She is a very loyal friend and loves children. She goes out of her way to baby sit her friends' children. Liza very much looks forward to marriage and having children of her own. I know that she will be a great mother.

When Sari was three years old and Liza was a baby, we spent some vacation time at a camp site near Lake Winnipesaukee in New Hampshire. One day, we took a day trip north to see Mt. Washington, the tallest mountain in New England. After parking our van, we released both girls from their car seats. Karen placed Liza in a papoose-type sling placed around her neck. I wore our camera on a strap around my neck and held Sari's hand while we proceeded to view the scenery around us. The views of the surrounding countryside were spectacular so I wanted to take some photos.

I began to get the camera ready. A couple approached me. The man said, "Excuse me, would you take our picture?"

Startled, I responded, "Why would I want to do that?"

Karen laughed. Embarrassed by my misunderstanding, I offered to take the couples' picture.

While the girls were young, we vacationed all over the country as well as Mexico and Prince Edward Island and Nova Scotia in Canada. We camped together in the Berkshires, New Hampshire, the Catskills, and Virginia. We had modest incomes but wanted to provide the girls with all the opportunities we could. They took tennis, clarinet, piano, dance, and violin lessons. They played tennis, softball, field hockey, badminton, and soccer.

Emotionally, the girls and I have repeated some of my family's patterns. I believe the girls feel that I wasn't emotionally there for them. I thought that I gave quality time to them, but my professional career consumed me. I brought my passion for social causes and my financial worries at work back home with me. I was always worried and preoccupied by it. It was not enough that I never missed a concert, graduation, or other special event. The girls fortunately had Karen, a nurturing mother, to comfort them unconditionally and provide counsel when they had questions.

It has taken many years for me to begin to see that I paid a price for my commitment to my career. The tradeoff was that I distanced my children from me and also wasn't as available to Karen as I should have been. That has hurt me for many years. I perceived the reason for the girls' frustration with me as adolescent rebellious behavior. But I felt it went a lot deeper than that. I believed that they were treating me as they felt I had treated them during their formative years—at an emotional distance. Their lack of interest in a relationship with me depressed me. I withdrew or got angry, which only exacerbated the problems.

Seated (l-r): Michaelyn, Liz, Mother, Karen.
Standing: Victor, Rob, Dad, Paul, 1981

In his early sixties, my father contracted bladder cancer and went for many chemotherapy treatments over several years. In early 1982, he entered Long Island Jewish

Hospital and never returned home. At one point, the doctors wanted to do a blood transfusion which required the correct match of blood types. When I offered, mother insisted that I not be allowed to donate, because she stated that she didn't want to "risk the loss of both a husband and a son."

Before he died in April, I visited my father in the hospital many times and brought him the pastrami and corned beef sandwiches that he loved. Sometimes, we played cards. I had hoped for more time with him to recall some of the good times we shared in my childhood. I told him I loved him. When he passed, I felt a mixture of sadness and relief, but my father's death was not easy for me, either. He was a person of his time, a poor Jew who came from uneducated parents whom he rebelled against. He seemed to view life as a series of struggles to cope with and saw himself always as an outsider, using the street smarts that he learned on the Lower East Side of New York to get through life.

Our family suffered another loss in August 1982, when Karen's father died of congestive heart failure. Having served in the Pacific and Aleutian Islands during World War II, he was buried at Calverton National Cemetery on eastern Long Island with a military funeral. His death was particularly difficult for both girls, especially Sari, because of the wonderful times they spent together. As a grandfather today to Sari's daughters, I deeply enjoy the time I spend with them just as David must have with Sari and Liza.

In 1999, Karen and I decided to sell our house and downsize to a condo community nearer to New York City. Both girls had completed their schooling and lived independently. Karen was concerned about the future and the time and effort involved with maintaining our home. She wanted to spend our future enjoying activities away from the responsibilities of home ownership. She found a new condo community in Hauppauge that was very attractive. I agreed with Karen that we should move. It would bring us closer to the girls, who then lived in New York City and Westchester County, and to New York City's theaters and restaurants, which we enjoyed a great deal.

However, I was ambivalent with the move, struggling with leaving the home where we had raised our children. It was filled with fond memories. On the day we moved, I sobbed as I realized we were leaving the "ancestral home." Sari and Liza were very upset about our moving, with all the memories of their childhoods there.

We had hoped we might meet some new people and become a part of a close community. We figured that if we could afford the price, there would be other middle-class, educated people with whom to associate.

We have lived in the condo community for almost ten years and enjoy the convenience of its location and the beauty of its setting. We decorated our new home with Colombian paintings and memorabilia. While we have made some friends in the condo community, particularly the Louises, the Felberbaums, and the Pinedas, the move to this community is not what we had hoped for from a social perspective.

Mira and Davi, 2008

What they say about grandparents' relationships with grandchildren being special is all true. From the moments when I saw the girls as newborns to today, spending time with them has been a joy. Since Davi is now six years old, most of this time has been spent with her. She is a ball of non-stop enthusiasm and curiosity. She calls me "Puh." One of her favorite activities is to pretend to go hiking, an activity I initiated with her years ago. We hike up and down the staircase, into the bedrooms, and kitchen. I make tents out of blankets and chairs and bring plastic food into the tent. When we do this at our house, we carry my real canteen and compass, too. If I don't remember to get them, Davi reminds me. We eat in the tent, imagine we hear the sounds of animals, and take naps. We stop to smell imaginary flowers and watch for deer and other animals. She asks me if we can go "real camping" when she gets older. I've assured her that we will. That's something to look forward to.

I also look forward to attending school events in which she participates and dance recitals in which she performs. Davi is a talented child who is destined to be good at whatever she does and self-confident in doing it. I hope she takes an interest in tennis as she gets older so that we can share time playing together. Of special note is that Davi was selected to be in a Columbia Teachers College bilingual program at her school that continues from kindergarten through fifth grade. Each time we see her, her Spanish vocabulary has improved. Her accent is better than mine. It's wonderful to see my granddaughter follow my path with the Spanish language. Also wonderful, is the fact that Sari and Jeremy now have a relationship with our dear Colombian friends, José and Carolina Ávila. Davi and Mira have become friends with their daughters, Maria and Sari, who was named after our daughter.

Davi loves to call us to tell us what's happening in her life—in ballet classes, about the Jefferson School where she attends kindergarten, and about what she did at Hebrew school and at her friend's birthday parties. She remembers every detail and recounts events sequentially with great enthusiasm. Recently, we were playing with blocks, constructing a Lego tower. She looked at me and said that I made her feel comfortable and that I'm her friend. I smiled at her and thanked her for saying such a nice thing. I told her that I feel the same way about her and gave her a hug.

The most recent gift that Davi gave to me occurred during a phone call. Enthusiastically, Davi informed me that she found a compass/whistle. "Puh," she said, "could we take it with us when we go camping together? So, if I get lost, I could blow the whistle and you could come and find me. We can also use the compass to help us get to where we want to go." I told her that I thought it was a great idea but she didn't have to worry because I would make sure that we always stayed together.

Davi often asks me to tell her a story about when Sari was young. Not so easy for me. I don't recall great details about events in the distant past so I improvise. Davi listens intently and asks questions so I have to be careful not to discuss something that I don't want to describe thoroughly. Most recently, after celebrating Martin Luther King's birthday in school, she recounted a brief history of Dr. Martin Luther King that she learned in kindergarten. I was touched by this and saw how much better her education is, even at her age, than mine was. Davi, in her bilingual kindergarten class, is in the minority, racially and ethnically. I never knew an African-American until seventh grade and had no non-white friends until college. We are so pleased that Davi is enjoying the benefits of a racially and ethnically diverse early childhood so that she will grow up without the stereotypes that we grew up with.

When Mira was born we were thrilled at her arrival. This was a very special occasion in the family. Mira is now three years old and is a wonderful child with a warm smile. It has been a delight to spend time with her and watch her grow. Mira is a sunny, happy child. Like her sister, Mira loves imaginary play and enjoys endless creative games and stories with Karen and me. She has a very good attention span and occupies herself with activities well beyond others of her age group. She is a very social child who enjoys playing with other children, including her sister. She adores Davi and is often seen following her around. She loves Karen and me to read to her and to play with her baby dolls. On two recent occasions, I joined Sari and Mira at Saturday morning music classes. It was so nice to see Mira using the varied musical instruments and singing along with the teacher and other children. We also recently visited the preschool that Mira attends and enjoyed meeting her friends and their parents. She was very proud to show us her school. Mira loves playing school with Davi who plays the teacher. However, when Mira plays with Sari, Mira enjoys playing the teacher and being in charge. I look forward to having many more times with Mira.

During summers, Sari has been bringing Davi and Mira to our place once a week to go swimming in the pool. Davi is building up the courage to swim. When she arrives at the pool, she enters the children's pool before moving to the larger pool where she clings to the sides. I've shown her that the water isn't over her head on the side of the pool where she plays so she's begun to feel comfortable walking away from the sides. She also likes to jump off the edge into my arms. Sometimes, she reluctantly allows me to carry her, clinging to my neck, into deeper water.

I assure her that I won't let her go. I don't want to pressure Davi to swim. She'll learn when she's ready.

Mira, Sari, Jeremy, Davi, Liza, Karen, and me in 2009

CHAPTER FOUR
My Public Service Career

In 1965, immediately after my work as a volunteer in Peace Corps had ended, I went to the Peace Corps office in Washington DC to see if they had any employment openings in Latin America. I learned that I had been black-balled as a "troublemaker" by the Peace Corps Director in Colombia. My personnel file had a letter on top of several letters of recommendation that said that "previous recommendations should be disregarded." Postscript: Twenty five years later, at one of the Peace Corps reunions I attended, Chris Sheldon, the director, apologized to me for the way he treated me.

That I couldn't get a job with Peace Corps was a tremendous disappointment to me. Left with no immediate alternatives and needing money to re-establish my independence, I decided to get a job.

Towards the end of my Peace Corps work in Colombia, I had been thinking about what career path I would take when I returned to the United States. My perspective on traditional American values had changed. I now saw America as a deterrent to social and economic change in the developing world, and I wanted to be part of efforts like the Peace Corps to advance economic and social change. I thought that my Peace Corps experience could help me find work in Washington or New York and eventually take me back overseas on assignments. I returned to my parents' home on Long Island eager to find work and move on.

I found that family and friends cared little to know about my Peace Corps experience. Here I had just returned from a life-altering experience and virtually no one asked questions about what I had done in Colombia and how I felt about my work. I wanted to share my thoughts and experiences as well as my views about America's policies in Latin America. Some people had never heard of the Peace Corps and asked if was like the Marine Corps. Knowledge of Colombian history, traditions, and politics was limited, as was interest in learning more about them. It was American ethnocentricity in action, proof of the biased education we had received about the world around us. People said I was very dedicated and that I had done a wonderful, adventurous thing by sacrificing two years of my life.

And, when someone did ask about what I did in the Peace Corps, it was difficult to describe rural community development. "Help the people help themselves" wasn't exactly a clear explanation to most people. When I spoke to other former Peace Corps volunteers about their experiences upon returning to the US, I learned that they shared my experience that people didn't show interest in their work and the feeling that we had received a lot more in the Peace Corps than we had given.

I searched the *New York Times* for international job opportunities, but there were few jobs posted that met my interests. I interviewed with Tools for Freedom, a nonprofit organization based in New York City that collected discarded industrial tools and equipment and sent them to countries that needed them. I was surprised by the one hundred dollars a week salary and turned them down.

So, within weeks of my return, I went down an unlikely path. In reading the Peace Corps magazine, I noticed that Avis Rent-a-Car's President, Robert Townsend, was on the Peace Corps National Advisory Board. Avis had a job opportunity posted in the newsletter that indicated that they saw former volunteers as potential company executives who could help the company to expand overseas. The ad encouraged returned volunteers to join an executive management training program. Avis' corporate headquarters was in nearby Garden City, so I called and scheduled an appointment. The appointment was with the head of international operations and the company's CEO. I was very impressed. They wanted to meet me the next day. The interview went very well. They offered me a position that afternoon. I think that the turning point was when they asked why I thought my Peace Corps experience was relevant to renting cars. I said that I had learned that if you could sell yourself, you could sell anything. Apparently, that was the right answer. Even though I did not believe that I was cut out for a business career, I accepted their offer, feeling that I would never know if a business career was something I wanted, or not, unless I tried it.

In order to work at Avis, I needed to buy some clothing and shoes. The only clothing I owned was chinos and a pair of worn dungarees. My shirts and undershirts were torn and tattered from two years of washings on rocks along river beds in Colombia. I needed a car, so I bought a red MGB sports car and new clothing with the $2,400 stipend that the Peace Corps had given me for my 24 months of service.

I was first assigned to work for Avis in New York City and, later, in Miami and Atlanta. The plan was for me to be trained for one year in the full-range of company activities from behind the counter sales and customer relations to marketing, insurance, purchasing, and accounting. After the training period, I would be sent to open an Avis operation with twenty-five cars in a Latin American city—tentatively, Lima, Peru. Avis was planning a worldwide expansion as part of being bought by International Telephone and Telegraph.

In New York, I rented cars behind the counter in a midtown garage, commuting by subway into the city. I dated some woman. In particular, I dated Diane, a very nice woman from Mineola who I cared for a lot. In fact, we were quite serious and spoke of marriage. After I relocated to Miami, we corresponded regularly for two months and spoke by phone almost daily.

I soon learned that one of my close Peace Corps buddies, Bob Salafia, woke up one day to discover a lump on his chest. He was diagnosed with a serious cancer and was being treated at Memorial Sloan Kettering Hospital in New York. Paul and I visited with him almost weekly for several months during which time Bob's condition deteriorated until he died. I was very upset by this experience.

I also visited Paul at his home in Hopewell, New Jersey. Paul had married Dee, also a former

Peace Corps volunteer in Colombia. They both worked at a research laboratory. Paul and I continued some of our silly games together. One time, we built a snow woman with enormous breasts, adorning them with big nipples. Another time, Paul, Dee, and I went to an ice cream parlor that sponsored daily contests for ice cream consumption. Paul encouraged me to compete, which I did. The objective was to eat a decanter of ice cream, about a quart, in twenty minutes. If you were successful, you won the decanter. Well, I did it! In the process, I was freezing and bloated. The customers rallied me along with applause through the last two minutes. When I had swallowed the last mouthful, I got up, bowed, and rushed to the men's room where I barfed up the quart of ice cream. We had a lot of laughs about this silly experience.

Paul and I also saw a movie in New York City that remains one of my all-time favorites— "A Thousand Clowns" with Jason Robards and Martin Balsam. The movie had a strong impact on me. We sat through the film twice. I identified with the main character, Murray Burns, an unemployed television writer. Murray, an unapologetically romantic nonconformist refused to work in a job that was meaningless to him. He and Nick, his twelve-year-old nephew, lived in a small studio apartment on New York's Lower East Side. Murray's sister had abandoned

Nick on Murray's doorstep years before. Nick was precocious and more responsible than Murray. Under the threat that child welfare would remove Nick from unemployed Murray's care, Murray searched for a job and reluctantly agreed to return to writing the "Chuckles the Chipmunk Show." One of the most powerful dialogues in the movie occurs when both a psychologist and social worker visit Murray and Nick in their apartment. Murray tries to show the officials how intelligent Nick is for his age and that the boy should be left with him. The social worker, frustrated by Murray's ravings, shouts, "Mr. Burns! You must come back to reality!" With that, Murray retorts. "I'll only come as a tourist!" Murray's brother, a successful businessman encourages Murray to grow up and get a job "like everyone else." Murray was an idealist with no clear direction who had to make some life decisions while people around him tried to tell him how to live his life not unlike my experience before the Peace Corps.

In Miami, I was first assigned to work in the downtown office and later in the airport location. This was a time when Avis was, after Hertz, the number two auto rental company. Their advertising promoted the message "We try harder." I was placed in a newly-created position which involved supervising the men washing and cleaning cars. They were all African-Americans.

It was summer and blazing hot and humid but I stuck with it, demonstrating good work habits. I befriended one of the men and met him for drinks on a number of occasions in his neighborhood. Several years later, I became aware that we had been drinking in the section of Miami where there were strong racial tensions and, during the late 1960s, rioting.

I went to the beach a lot and dated a number of women during my three months there. I invited Diane to come to Miami, which she did. By that time, though, I was dating other people, especially a young woman spending the summer with her grandparents. We spent a lot of passionate time together. So, when Diane came to Miami, it was apparent that I no longer felt the same way about her. She could see it right away and returned to New York the next day. I had never dated more than one person at a time and felt disloyal to be having two concurrent relationships. Over the years, I have thought about how I treated Diane, and I regret my behavior. I didn't have the courage to tell her over the phone that I had had a change of heart and wasn't ready to make a commitment. So, she was understandably very angry with me.

My teeth were in bad shape, probably due, in part, to eating so much guava candy in Colombia and drinking so much Pepsi-Cola. I went to a dentist in Coral Gables to evaluate the situation. In order to pay for the $2400 of dental work I needed—ironically the exact amount I had been paid for two years in the Peace Corps—I had to sell the MGB. Fortunately, Avis provided me with the use of a car so I continued to be mobile.

By the fall, I was assigned to be assistant city manager in Atlanta, Georgia. I rented an apartment in downtown Atlanta and reported for work. I quickly discovered that my boss didn't like me and intended to make my life as miserable as he could. When I first met him, he made it clear that he knew I was making $7800 dollars a year. He told me that it took him fifteen years to earn that income. He had me work six days a week mainly doing tedious tasks like driving cars between locations. It became clear that I would not be working for Avis much longer.

I did a crazy thing. Rather than just quitting, I sent a letter to the President of Avis, whom I considered my boss, describing what I believed to be the racial discrimination of the Atlanta city manager towards his black employees. Naturally, I was fired.

I dated two women in Atlanta. One was the daughter of a friend of one of my uncles. She would have loved to make a match with me but I wasn't interested after a few dates. There were no sparks. With the other woman, though, it was a different story. I met her through some men

I bumped into while playing golf. They invited me to dinner, where this woman was present. She was involved in the arts community. Sparks flew immediately, and for three months, we couldn't get enough of one another. She was from a wealthy family, and it became clear to me that she was accustomed to having everything she wanted. The relationship ended when I left Atlanta, but it was great while it lasted.

The Avis experience made it clear that the business world wasn't for me. I had no interest in sales and profits; my identity was still as a Peace Corps volunteer. I was focused on issues of poverty and justice. I couldn't reconcile the wide disparity between the wealthy and the poor.

I returned to my parents home, again, unemployed. I collected unemployment insurance, slept late, and watched television into the night. I had few interviews and little money to spend. It was a tense and miserable period, but I was determined to find work that interested me. During this time, I again dated Caroleah, the woman I had known in Colombia. I hoped that she would come to feel the way I did about her but it never happened, and it took me some time to get over my disappointment. Caroleah eventually married Jairo Ruíz, a Colombian from San Gil. An accomplished flamenco dancer, she became the director of a nonprofit company that promotes flamenco dance and performs throughout the States.

After about six months of collecting unemployment checks, I revisited the Peace Corps office in Washington, DC, where I met a counselor who took an interest in me. Not long after I returned to New York, he called to tell me about a job opportunity. It sounded great. I boarded a train and rode to Washington to be interviewed by David Dichter, the Executive Director of Sports International and Youth for Development, a nonprofit organization. Dave was a former Peace Corps desk officer in Washington who was hiring ex-Peace Corps volunteers to be counselors in a leadership training program funded by the State Department. Dave hired me as the counselor to the nine Latin American participants from Panama, Colombia, Venezuela, the Dominican Republic, Guatemala, El Salvador, and Honduras. The concept was to provide young, emerging leaders in Third World countries with a confidence-building cross-cultural experience that would equip them to return home with the skills, and the confidence, to assist in nation-building activities. Nation-building involved reforestation projects, raising poultry, erosion control, the construction of farm-to-market roads and bridges, sending teachers and medical personnel into rural areas, and organizing local people in other self-help projects. Before leaving for New Mexico, I translated a training manual into Spanish.

The program was based at a US Forest Service Training Center in Continental Divide, New Mexico about a half hour east of Gallup, just off Route 66. It was in a serene and beautiful setting, a pine forest over seven thousand feet above sea level. There were men from more than a dozen African nations, Korea, and Latin America. We ate together, traveled around the Southwest by bus, and flew to visit San Francisco. We camped, built a small storage building and a bridge over an arroyo, did physical exercise at seven o'clock every morning, and heard lectures given by experts in such subjects as erosion control, raising poultry, urban planning, and gardening. After two months in New Mexico, we returned to Washington where the men boarded planes to return to their home countries.

Before I left New Mexico, I had another adventure. It was decided that the men should be given the opportunity to celebrate, so arrangements were made to bus them to Gallup for the evening to dance at a local night club. I remained behind with Bill Soresby, the camp director, who invited me to go to Gallup with him to have dinner. He had a new, blue Mercedes convertible, which he loved to drive at high speeds. Along the route, we were stopped by a local policeman who gave my colleague a speeding ticket. Bill argued with the officer, who told him to take up his complaints with the judge in Gallup. We drove to Gallup to the courthouse, where a judge met us. Bill forcefully argued his case—that he was driving perfectly safely, that the Mercedes had fantastic brakes, and that no one else was on the road. The judge would hear none of it and levied a twenty dollar fine.

We went to a nearby restaurant that happened to be across the street from the nightclub where the men were celebrating. Bill decided to see how things were going. I waited a few minutes, and when he didn't return, I went out to look for him.

At the gas station adjacent to the restaurant, I saw that my colleague, Bill, was loudly arguing with, of all people, the judge who was getting gas. One of the men in the gas station office was on the telephone while the others watched the argument. Moments later, a police van arrived and Bill was ushered into the rear of it. I approached the police, asking if I could have the keys to Bill's car so I could get home. They said that I could have the keys after Bill was booked at the police station, and gave me directions.

I set off on foot but a block from the police station I saw four men ahead of me barring my way. I ran from them as fast as I could through the unfamiliar streets, but they caught up with me. I recognized them as the men from the gas station. They punched and kicked me until I lost consciousness. I awoke in the police station parking lot bloodied and with some of my front dental bridge work broken. Confused and in pain, I limped into the station. My request for help was met with indifference. I explained what had happened and made a written statement, which included the first name of one of the people who had assaulted me, "Charlie." I identified "Charlie" in a book of mug shots and the police said that he was an alcoholic and local troublemaker.

I couldn't pay the $100 bail that was required to release Bill. I asked to see him, but they refused; they also refused to provide first aid for my cuts and bruises. I asked if I could stay in the building overnight, and they let me sleep on the courtroom floor. In the morning, I called the Forest Service Center camp director, who came to Gallup and bailed out Bill from jail. We then met with a lawyer to discuss our options. He discouraged pressing charges because, in effect, my life would be in danger if I remained in Gallup to see justice done. The bus was heading east that day and I decided to board it, with my missing teeth and swollen and bruised body, despite my feelings that I was allowing a criminal to avoid punishment.

When we returned to Washington, the program director asked me if I would go to Panama to represent Sports International and Youth for Development to Panamanian officials in an attempt to garner support to establish the program there as a Latin American training center. I agreed but insisted on a round trip plane ticket and travel expenses. I spent a month in Panama meeting with several high-level government officials only to find that the Panamanian government would not put up any funding to support the program. I also met with Peace Corps and US Embassy officials without success. It seems that Sports International and Youth for Development had not paid some of its bills in New Mexico and had, therefore, a bad reputation with the State Department, which had funded the program. Without the blessing of the US Embassy and Peace Corps, we could get nowhere. In fact, I approached Jack Hood Vaughn, director of the Peace Corps, upon his arrival in Panama on an official visit. As he was getting out of the elevator of his hotel, I identified myself and requested a meeting with him. He refused, making it clear that I "was in the wrong country at the wrong time." I left Panama with pocket change and returned to my parents' house in Mineola where, again, I started looking for a job.

I decided that I needed to do something about my front teeth and that the best thing to do was go to Florida to have the dentist who built the original bridge do the work. Through a New York City agency whose business was to find drivers to transport vehicles to their owners in

Florida, I made arrangements to drive someone else's car. My plan was to get to Florida ahead of schedule and have the use of the car for a day before delivering it to the owner.

Everything was going fine until I got into Georgia. I was going about 70 MPH on a stretch of two-lane highway that ran along the railroad tracks approaching a long trailer truck. I pulled into the opposite lane to check for traffic and saw the road as clear so I put my foot on the pedal to pass the trailer. Then I saw the school bus immediately in front of the trailer, making a left turn onto a dirt road. I hit the brakes but couldn't avoid bumping the rear fender of the bus. I was shocked. I pulled over to the side, but the bus had continued up the road. What should I do? If I left, I was leaving the scene of an accident. No one arrived, but I decided that it was too risky to continue the trip so I drove into the next town and reported to the police station to explain what had happened. The policeman told me to lock my car and go with him to the scene of the accident. We drove up the dirt road where the bus had gone. The policeman spoke to a school official to confirm my story and that no one had been hurt. He then drove me back to my car and told me that I was lucky that "it was just a bunch of n___s."

I got back on the road to Miami and delivered the car to its owner who flipped out when he saw the damage done to his brand new Pontiac Bonneville. A few days later I drove another agency car back to New York without consequences.

In 1966, I returned broke and, yes, to my parents' house. I quickly applied for a position as center director of a new youth center in Huntington Village, Community Development for Youth (CDY). CDY was founded by the Family Service League and its Executive Director Bob Bergstrom who conducted a youth needs study with Columbia School of Social Work. I was interviewed by the executive director, Tony Romeo, and a board committee, and was hired. My Peace Corps credentials were the key to my otherwise unimpressive resumé. I bought a run-down 1958 black Peugeot and rented a studio apartment in Huntington Village despite my parents' protestations that I could live with them and commute to the job, in order to save money.

The organization had a wonderful board of directors. Some of its members went on to become influential in the development of youth services in Suffolk County, particularly Helen McIntyre and Ruth Corcoran. Helen became the chair of the Suffolk County Youth Board and Ruth was instrumental in founding the Huntington Youth Board. Others, like Walter Spilsbury, were active with the Family Service League, the original sponsor of the youth organization. I respected them and learned a lot from them.

In part, my work was to reach out to at-risk young people whose behavior was disrupting business for the village's storeowners. They were drinking, fighting, using foul language, and were an eyesore to the public. I took the work quite seriously and began to get to know these "troublemakers," hoping I could redirect some of their behavior to more socially acceptable activities. What I found was that these young people were doing poorly in school and either had no fathers or had fathers who were alcoholics. I was able to attract many of them to the youth center building which was located in a commercial area several blocks from downtown. The center was equipped with pool tables, ping pong tables, and various games.

Over the next few months, I organized a boxing program by hiring a former professional boxer. I became aware that the local YMCA had a fully-equipped boxing room, so I met with the Y director and scheduled a visit by some of the kids, most of whom were black or Latino, who wanted to join a boxing club. The director and some of the members of the Y board greeted us and showed us around the facility. We indicated that we would love to establish a program at the Y. The Y officials promised that they'd get back to us.

Well, as promised, they did get back to us. They claimed that there were restrictions in their insurance policies prohibiting non-members from using the facilities. It was apparent to me that this was an excuse—the Y just didn't want these kids at their center. If this experience had occurred years later, when I knew more about the Y, I would have confronted the board with the Y's own national policy which states that they don't turn anyone away because they cannot afford to pay dues. I decided to base the boxing program in the youth center. I bought two heavy boxing bags, a speed bag, and several pairs of leather boxing gloves. The boxing professional gave boxing lessons and supervised boxing matches among the students.

We set up a snack bar and organized some clubs and dances. A fifteen-foot rowboat was donated to the center which the young people painted and named "The Yellow Submarine." We held car washes to raise money to go on local field trips to the circus, an auto speedway, and to Greenwich Village in New York City. The clubs were popular for a period of time, redirecting some of the kids from their exploits on the streets. Fights sometimes erupted inside and outside the youth center over girls and petty differences. It was clear that the center was a safe haven for some of the young people. Nevertheless, many of the young people continued to get into trouble with the law. On several occasions, I went to court with some of them to appeal for leniency for their juvenile delinquency.

During this period, I became increasingly concerned about civil rights issues. In the late 1960s, racial tensions in America were mounting. The 1965 powerful civil unrest demonstrated in the Watts district of California, in Detroit, and other parts of the country, the nonviolent movement led by Dr. Martin Luther King, the emergence of the Black Power movement and the Student Nonviolent Coordinating Committee, began to have their impact on Long Island. Many white people felt that African-Americans were being given preferential treatment in the distribution of federal antipoverty funds. They harbored racist attitudes towards people of color and resented their appeals for greater rights and opportunities. It was a time when many African-Americans were protesting institutional racism, discrimination, and police brutality. High schools were the sites of protests against the Vietnam War, the draft, perceived bad treatment by school officials and law enforcement, irrelevant curriculum, and the materialism of their parents. Many students, both black and white, were involved in protests. Groups were divided along racial lines with few exceptions in all segments of society but particularly in schools.

I joined the Civil Rights Coordinating Council and the Huntington Human Rights Committee. I reached out to African-American kids in nearby Huntington Station. Most importantly, I befriended

Reverend Earl Jordon, an African Methodist
Episcopal minister who was the director of the
local Community Action Agency (CAC). Earl
and my boss, Andy Casazza, who had replaced
Tony Romeo as CDY's director, had reached
an agreement with the CAC for CDY to take
over the Freedom Center, the youth center in
Huntington Station, in a heavily African-American
neighborhood.

I was assigned to reach out to the mostly
black and Latino young people to encourage
them to use the center. I thought that my Peace
Corps experience would serve me well in this
regard. After all, I had been accepted by Latinos
of all colors in Latin America. But I was quickly
reminded that things in America were different.
We practice institutional racism either overtly or
covertly ever since slaves were brought to the
country. I was successful in establishing good
relations with local Latino leaders but to most of
the black youth, I was another white authority
figure. This disappointed me since I had always
felt that I could overcome racial barriers through
my personality, sincerity, and enthusiasm. I began
to question my ability to work across racial
lines. I began to believe that I could be most
effective in the role of developing programs for
all community members as well as in supporting
more progressive public policies.

The CAC operated an employment program, a housing program, and a summer youth program. Earl was a natural leader who earned a good deal of respect for his role during the era's racial tensions. Black students organized demonstrations at Huntington High School but the rightful discontent never boiled over in riots as it did in other communities. Earl was one of the key reasons for this.

At the time, there was a popular saying, "If you aren't part of the solution, you're part of the problem." One summer evening when Earl and I were talking in his office, we agreed to print the phrase in big, bold two-foot letters on butcher paper that Earl used for sign-making. We hung the sign in the CAC's window. We wanted the thousands of suburban commuters who passed the CAC offices every day to see the sign and maybe think about its message.

In the spring of 1967, Senator Eugene McCarthy was running for the presidency and capturing the imagination of America's youth. Many local young people were expressing the desire to be involved in improving conditions in their community. As a consequence, Andy Casazza and I organized the Teen Volunteer Corps. I made arrangements for a big article to be published in *The Long Islander*, the local newspaper, that described me as a former Peace Corps Volunteer who was introducing young people to public service.

I personally interviewed two hundred young people in May and June, and contacted a variety of nonprofit organizations to find suitable volunteer experiences for the young people. I established twenty different projects. Some young people helped children with developmental, disabilities; some volunteered in a home for the blind; some were aides in a day care center; some worked in a day camp; and some helped the frail elderly in a nursing home. Others taught English to Latino farm workers living on local sod farms and nurseries. Several published a newspaper while others helped in a voter registration campaign. It was an exciting period with lots of youthful energy, enthusiasm, and idealism.

During this period, young people were unfairly stereotyped as hitters, hippies, and collegiates. Hitters got into fights and drank a lot of alcohol. Hippies smoked pot, dressed in unconventional, often sparse clothing, and challenged authority figures and lifestyles. Collegiates did well in school, were college-bound, and obeyed traditional values and behavior. The youth center tried to have programs and activities that satisfied, at least, the hitters and hippies. The latter group was primarily attracted to the center on Sunday nights to a coffee house atmosphere which we labeled "Chicago Mollies Last Resort and Sitz Bath." We secured wooden spools from the utility company which we used as tables.

Candles were placed on the tables for light in the darkened hall. Hot cider with cinnamon sticks was served along with other non-alcoholic drinks. Folk singers played their guitars and sang songs of protest.

My first supervisor at the youth center, Tony Romeo, had urged me to get a Masters degree in social work. I was ambivalent about going back to school after my experience at Adelphi, where I had poor grades and study habits. I thought, however, that maybe I would be a better student after my Peace Corps experience and my interest in social causes. I enrolled in a part-time course offered by Adelphi at Adelphi Suffolk (now Dowling College). I found the group work course interesting and, at the urging of the instructor, Gary Rosenberg, applied to the Masters in Social Work program at Adelphi. I was accepted and offered a National Institute for Mental Health stipend that permitted me to stop working while enrolled in the two-year program from 1968–1970.

Anyone who lived through the late 60s and early 70s knows that these were turbulent times in the US. The murders by National Guardsmen of student protesters at Kent State University, the assassinations of Martin Luther King and Senator Robert Kennedy, the Vietnam War, and increasing discontent with American politics and corporate power made for conflict and countercultural thinking by many Americans. The women's movement and the environmental movement along with the emergence of the Black Power movement fueled the fires that fractured families and communities. Traditional values and norms were questioned and authority figures were to be mistrusted. Thousands of returned Peace Corps volunteers joined the Committee of Returned Volunteers to protest the war. The group also saw the Peace Corps as part of the United States' "worldwide pacification program."

The position as director of the youth center was my first employment in the US serving an unpopular cause, in this case young people who didn't fit into traditional molds—the ones who did poorly in school, who didn't conform to conventional standards, and who often came from dysfunctional families. I enjoyed this position and began to learn about their lives and the public policies that often ignored them. The policies viewed it as the sole responsibility of the family unit to raise children without assistance from government other than through the educational system. I increasingly dedicated my career to working with such individuals and families. After all, I thought, this is where I came from, the suburbs. If I could make their lives better and influence public policies here, I would find personal and professional satisfaction. I didn't need to travel and live in South America to be a change agent. This was a tremendous shift in my thinking.

It was during this period that I entered the Adelphi School of Social Work. The academic program at Adelphi divided students into three categories either: casework, group work, and community organization. I chose the community organization concentration. Our readings included such contemporary works as *Reveille for Radicals* by Saul Alinsky, *The Autobiography of Malcolm X* by Malcolm X and Alex Haley, *Soul on Ice* by Eldridge Cleaver, *Black Power* by Stokely Carmichael and Charles Hamilton, *The Uncommitted* by Kenneth Keniston, *Crisis in Black and White* by Charles Silberman, *Do It!* By Jerry Rubin, *Asylums* by Erving Goffman, *The Lonely Crowd* by David Reisman, *The Wretched of the Earth* by Franz Fanon, and *Counterculture in the Making* by Theodore Roszack.

I especially enjoyed my community organization classes taught by Jerry Tavel, Harmon Putter, and Myron Blanchard and the group work courses with Gary Rosenberg. The community organizing classes were sometimes very heated and brought out the polarizing racial divide common in 1968 and 1969. In fact, one of our professors had what appeared to be a nervous breakdown in front of the class as a result of arguments between him and some of the black students about racism in America. That was the way things were during the late 1960s, filled with rhetoric and confrontation.

At the time, many people, especially young people, felt that Establishment institutions needed to be challenged and exposed for their hypocrisies and injustices. Their goal was to secure media exposure, not to effect changes. "Just do it" was a common theme. My focus was to organize individuals and organizations, not to protest in the streets or storm the barricades. I did participate in protests of the Vietnam War and against racism in local housing. Karen and I also went to Washington, DC to be part of the Poor People's Campaign, Martin Luther King's efforts to address economic justice and aid to America's poorest communities.

My fieldwork assignments were with Ed King, a school social worker in the William Floyd School District and with Rick Van Dyke with the Long Island Council of Churches. At William Floyd schools, I was assigned to try to help a ten-year-old boy who refused to attend school and a seven-year-old boy who wouldn't speak in school. I helped the mother to be more forceful with the boy who refused to go to school, which was the key to that situation. As for the boy who wouldn't speak in school, I learned that, when they were children, his parents hadn't spoken in school, either. I tried a variety of strategies to ease the boy into school with no effect. I found individual and family work very difficult and unfulfilling. These casework experiences further confirmed my desire to create new programs, improve ineffective public policies, and work to change societal conditions.

The school social work program was threatened with termination because the superintendent and board of education didn't like the idea of having a social work program—it implied that the district had social problems. So, they announced that the program would be terminated at the end of the school year. My supervisor assigned me to organize students and parents to object to the program's imminent demise. On one occasion, I attended a contentious Board of Education meeting to speak about how important the social work program was to many students. At the meeting, the superintendent of schools made his views public against the social work program. I left the meeting and drove home only to be stopped by a policeman who had me get out of my car while he inspected my car and its trunk. It was clear to me that this was the work of the superintendent of schools who was sending me a message to back off. Ultimately, the district terminated the social work program.

My other placement was with the Council of Churches under the supervision of Rick Van

Dyke, a former Peace Corps volunteer in Malawi. Rick was a very good supervisor and guided my professional development. I served as migrant community coordinator, visiting sod farms and tree, shrubbery, and flower nurseries where Latino men were seasonally employed. The deplorable housing conditions that I visited reminded me of the squalor I had seen in Colombia. I met with farm owners trying to convince them to improve living and working conditions. I organized recreational activities for the workers and English classes, involving high school and college students in the work. In some cases, nursery owners refused to permit me on their property suspecting that I was a union organizer. The migrant workers' plight was one small element of Long Island's hidden poor's circumstances amidst suburbia's generally lily-white, suburban, racially-segregated, middle-class communities.

I completed my MSW work in 1970. Upon graduation, I became the director of the Cold Spring Harbor Youth Center, where my work primarily engaged high school students who were searching for something missing in their lives. The Youth Center was, from the start, the target of criticism by a John Birch Society group and conservative elements of the community who viewed the center as a waste of tax dollars that fostered permissiveness and liberal thinking. I was aware of their attitudes and developed a series of educational events, with guest speakers, to examine topical issues, including the military draft, religion, the counterculture movement, higher education, drug abuse, and music. At the end of the series, we sponsored *Come Together*, featuring a music concert and multimedia show in the high school auditorium that depicted the producer's views of America at the time. He used twelve slide projectors each portraying different slides. The show's theme was that there was a lot to question in American foreign and domestic policy. Among other topics, it depicted the treatment of Native Americans, the shootings of students at Kent State University, and the Vietnam War. I had made arrangements for students to convene in the school's cafeteria after the show to discuss the issues raised in the show. A community resident and member of the Cold Spring Harbor Study Group stormed out of the auditorium screaming, "Stop the show! This is communism."

The event made the front page of *The Long Islander* for four weeks and resulted in a plea at a Board of Education meeting to have me fired. At this meeting, Sam Albanese, a prominent local businessman, asked, "Who hired Arfin?" Some members of the youth center's board were very upset with me, questioning the fact that I didn't preview the show for controversial material. They felt pressure from the community and held me responsible. The young people felt that they had the right to sponsor the show and saw the show's messages as expressions of free speech. At a heated meeting of the board, one woman, the publisher of a local newspaper, gave me a check for five hundred dollars and told me to keep up the good work. However, I was slapped on the wrist by the board of directors, who insisted that I broaden the center's programming to include everyone, not just those identified as critics and hippies. I developed additional programs—ski trips, dances at the high school, and Friday night socials—but the die had been cast. The youth center was seen as politically controversial and needing new leadership. My close-cropped photograph in the *New York Times*, with my full beard and tie-dyed shirt, alongside an article about the youth center, exacerbated the situation. There was no pleasing all of those involved: the board of directors, the leadership among the young people, and the community-at-large. I was viewed as politically controversial, sympathizing with countercultural points of view. I eventually resigned under pressure by the board of directors.

There had been another complication, too. One of the projects I undertook was to help young people to get more in touch with their feelings and their relationships, as a way to redirect them from drug use to healthy behavior and socially acceptable activities. At a Saturday morning get-together at the Methodist church, I led a session that included a number of trust exercises commonly used at the time, known as sensitivity training. In one exercise, I instructed students to guide one another around the room while blindfolded. In another, one person, with eyes closed, fell back into the waiting arms of six others ready to catch him. Later, the students went outside and guided one another with eyes shut being aware of the sounds, smells, and sensations around them. The kids enjoyed the exercises and talked with their parents about what a positive experience it was for them. Some parents, however, felt that these trust exercises were psychologically dangerous for impressionable young people.

Joe Vigilante, the dean of Adelphi's School of Social Work, from which I had graduated, was on the youth center's board of directors. I had thought that his professional status would be an asset in my work. The parents asked the dean what he thought of these exercises. He floored me by indicating that the exercises should only be done by a psychiatrist or trained clinical psychologist. This position stood in stark contrast to the teachings of the director of group work at his School of Social Work. My respect for the dean dropped after this experience. He was just one of the upper-middle-class parents who weren't willing to acknowledge the social and cultural changes going on at that time.

After resigning from the Cold Spring Harbor Youth Center, I tried to get a position at the newly-formed Huntington Youth Board, an outgrowth of Community Development for Youth, where I had worked before graduate school. Andy Casazza, the director, wanted to hire me but reported that the chairwoman of his board felt that it would look bad in the community if they hired me after the controversy in Cold Spring Harbor.

This was a time of great opportunity for the creation of a system of youth services in Suffolk County. A key leader in the effort to form the county's first and only youth board was Lou Howard, a Republican Suffolk County Legislator and a former high school coach in Amityville. He recognized that there were at-risk youth in many Long Island communities who could benefit from youth programs. In addition, an Islip Town Councilman, Jack Finnerty, who would become Suffolk County's Sheriff, and Ann Meade, a former Deputy County Executive, played important roles in convincing the County Legislature to establish the youth board. Resistance from conservative elements in the legislature, however, viewed a youth board as a sign of big government interference in family matters and a waste of tax dollars.

Fortunately, Howard, Finnerty, and Meade, along with youth service advocates, were able to convince enough legislators that the youth board made sense and that they should take advantage of available state financial aid. Andy Casazza, a Democrat, who had formed the Huntington Youth Board, applied for the job but was objectionable to the Republican majority. The common practice of both parties enabled the party in power to fill senior county positions with town political leaders. Islip appointed the head of the county recreation department. Smithtown appointed the head of the social services department. Babylon appointed the head of the labor department. And so it went. As one knowing political leader put it at the time, referring to who would get the youth board director job, "They'll probably give it to some political hack from the probation department." That was exactly what happened. Thus began the development of the county youth board. Casazza's plan to hire three community organizers, Tom Williams, Aldustus Jordan, and me, never came to pass. Under the benign leadership of Charlie Merwin, a political appointee, the youth board began its life as a weak county agency.

Unemployed again, and a child on the way, I needed a job. I learned from Sy Symonds, a YMCA executive, that the YMCA of Long

Island was broadening its mission to include programming for at-risk youth and families. They had secured a $15,000 grant from the Suffolk County Youth Board, one of the first two awarded by the agency. I was hired by the YMCA of Long Island as what was termed a high-risk employee, thanks to the notoriety of my Cold Spring Harbor work. I accepted the position because I saw it as an opportunity to work for an organization with a strong, positive reputation that didn't need to establish a credible identity, with the resources to build services. I also accepted because no other jobs were available and Karen and I were parents with responsibilities.

At the YMCA, I developed youth service and drug treatment and prevention programs and established the first neighborhood dispute resolution center on Long Island. This was a period of expanded youth service and drug programs with lots of competition among agencies for grants. After Huntington established its youth board, Babylon and Islip soon followed. Later, Smithtown, Brookhaven, Riverhead, and Southampton did, too. I served on the ad hoc Islip and Brookhaven Youth Board planning committees, providing advice on the formation of policies and programs.

The YMCA was undergoing a long-range strategic-planning process. I was appointed to be a staff representative to the YMCA's long range planning committee, a position I very much enjoyed. Over a two-year period, we held countless early morning meetings, eventually rewriting the YMCA's constitution and bylaws to make them more inclusionary and democratic. There was a great deal of resistance to our efforts but the changes were supported by key YMCA leadership and therefore moved forward to be approved by the Board of Directors. The opposing forces felt that the YMCA should exclusively continue its traditional programming focused on athletic and leisure-time activities for dues-paying members. They viewed the new programs, primarily funded by government, as undesirable additions that diverted corporate attention from the essential YMCA mission.

I always felt that my Peace Corps leadership experience provided me with the self-confidence to work with corporate executives, superintendents of schools, and civic leaders in reforming the YMCA. It was my position that the YMCA's original mission was to assist young people fleeing rural poverty in England by providing them with housing, employment, and other aid. I saw the YMCA playing an important role helping youth and families cope with the changing social conditions of the 1970s. I felt I was contributing to making institutional changes at the YMCA that would be lasting. I hadn't been able to effect systemic changes in the Peace Corps but I could do so at the YMCA.

I was also involved in establishing the Suffolk Youth Services Coordinating Committee, an informal networking and advocacy organization. The Committee's members included a number of individuals who went on to be leaders in Long Island's nonprofit world including Dick Dina, Tom Williams, Carol Tweedy, Barbara Strongin, and Marty Timin. We shared common values and a passion to create a comprehensive system of youth services. In 1975, as Committee Chairman, I led an effort to sponsor a conference at Stony Brook University on juvenile and criminal justice issues. Four hundred people were in attendance to hear keynote speakers Harry O'Brien, the District Attorney and New York City District Court Judge Bruce Wright. Judge Wright was a controversial figure with a reputation for leniency in sentencing so inviting him to the conference was a politically sensitive action. His nickname was "Turn him loose, Bruce." The judge was the subject of a front page *New York Times* article. I was pleased that the YMCA didn't object to his participation at the conference even though one Y official from New York City tried to convince the Long Island Y to cancel Judge Wright's participation.

An important outcome of the conference was the formation of a group to try to implement some of the recommendations generated at the conference. Fortunately, the Veatch Program of the Unitarian Universalist Congregation at Shelter Rock, with deep pockets from a wealthy benefactor and a progressive agenda, provided funding to the group. I worked closely with Ed Lawrence and Dave DiRienzes of the Veatch Program during this period. The major result was the establishment of The Community Mediation Center which was originally formed as a program of the YMCA of Long Island, as part of my responsibilities. With the guidance of Jonathan Gradess and Bob Saperstein, two young Hofstra Law School students, we convinced the District Attorney, the Chief of Police, and the head Administrative Judge, that the Community Mediation Center should be supported as a project funded through a federal Law Enforcement Administration (LEA) grant. We then lobbied all eighteen Suffolk Legislators for their support. This effort took about two years and was fraught with resistance, primarily from the probation department who wanted control of the program and conservative elements who saw the program as another waste of tax dollars. At a meeting with probation department officials who were mostly social workers like me, I was asked if I felt that Probation Officers were part of the criminal justice system. I shocked them by saying that I felt they were and that the mediation center should, therefore, not be part of the probation department but rather be operated by an independent, non-governmental agency. My position on this matter didn't make friends for me with many social work colleagues.

Once funded, the center became very successful. After two years, it was separated from the YMCA, becoming an independent nonprofit community organization. The mediation center served thousands of people involved in civil disputes, enabling them to amicably settle their differences without entering a courtroom.

Another example of the climate of the times and my efforts to create community service projects occurred when we applied for a grant from the Suffolk County Criminal Justice Coordinating Council. The Council reviewed grant requests for federal funding to support projects to reduce juvenile and adult crime. We put together a YMCA-sponsored counseling and support project and were invited to make a presentation to the Council at one of its monthly meetings. The Council was made up of the police commissioner, the district attorney, the sheriff, the youth board, the probation department, and some elected officials. I asked a member of the YMCA Board of Directors to join me to make the presentation. I selected a very Establishment-looking man who worked for Long Island Lighting Company. He probably had the world's shortest crew cut and wore tailored suits. After the presentation, which was at the end of the meeting, he and I walked to my car.

We noticed an official car approaching. It was the county sheriff. He approached us slowly and appeared to be taking down my license plate number. My colleague was noticeably shocked. It was no surprise when he called the next day to let me know that he could have nothing else to do with the project in light of its apparent controversial nature.

While at the YMCA, I also established a strong relationship with Lee Lawrence of the Long Island Community Foundation, which made several grants to my work. Sometimes, Lee called me to invite a grant application saying she had some extra money to spend. Of particular note was the funding of a family advocate position which was ably filled by Richard Sass. The project conducted an ambitious community study of Brookhaven Township that sociologist Marty Timin led. At the time, parts of the township were experiencing home foreclosures amidst a rise in unemployment. The study projected the township's housing and other needs based on demographic projections and a telephone survey of 450 town residents. The study was covered in *Newsday* and became the subject of much public policy discussion.

During this period, I was invited to become a member of the Board of Directors of the Suffolk Community Council. I served on this board for seventeen years including terms as

Secretary and Vice Chairman. Since the 1930s, the Council has served as an umbrella agency advocate for Suffolk County's hidden poor. Ann Meade was Executive Director for many years and was a highly-respected person. When Ann left, the Council hired a number of executive directors including Ed Ross, Helen Gould, and Ruth Kleinfeld. I, along with many others, were disappointed with Kleinfeld's performance. We tried to convince the board's executive committee to dismiss her with no success. I was very frustrated by the situation and decided to put myself on the line by writing a white paper and distributing it to board members and calling for a meeting of the executive committee without the executive director. My actions outraged the majority of the board with the result that I was removed from the board. In addition, a number of colleagues wanted nothing to do with me for many years, feeling that I had acted improperly as a board member. I have never had any regrets about what I did. Sometimes, someone has to take an extreme position to get a group to act.

I was dismayed when one of my peers was accused in a major *Newsday* article of misappropriating funds under contracts with county government. I had noticed his well-decorated offices, with attractive art work displayed on the walls, and expressed concern about the appearance of such largess, but it fell on deaf ears. The YMCA was front page news for several weeks. One legislator called me, asking if he should visit my office to see if I had art work as well. I encouraged him to visit if he wanted to see my children's drawings because that was all the art work on the walls of my office. Ultimately, the accused was fired and relocated from Long Island.

At the same time, the YMCA was in serious financial trouble and conducted a number of ambitious campaigns to raise its charitable contributions through various events and individual appeals. However, in 1978, the YMCA's executive director, Bob Schmidt, was fired. This was a classic example of a board of directors holding an executive director accountable for an agency's financial problems, instead of the board stepping up to the plate to raise the necessary funds itself.

The YMCA directors, including me, met in secrecy to discuss the situation. The majority agreed that Bob was no longer able to command the leadership to lead the organization out of its crisis. I felt bad about this, but hopeful that the organization would hire a highly-qualified YMCA executive to heal the wounds and generate the needed support. The board created a search committee and went through the motions of a national search. They interviewed YMCA directors with proven histories of success in other regions of the country, but these candidates didn't stand a chance against the powers who wanted the YMCA to get back to its business of fitness and leisure programming.

The board hired a Long Island traditionalist, Bill Jenkins, who quickly made it clear that my YMCA days were numbered. Jenkins didn't support the expansion of the outreach services that I had cultivated. He also knew that I had encouraged one of his board members to present a white paper documenting that the YMCA wasn't being truthful to the United Way about how it was spending its allocation (not on its outreach programs). Jenkins blamed the government-supported outreach programs for the YMCA's serious financial problems, despite the balance sheet that showed that many of the traditional YMCA centers were experiencing lower memberships and attendance and large deficits.

On a Friday morning in March 1978, Jenkins came to my office with his executive secretary and fiscal director and told me to immediately vacate the premises. Our four-year-old daughter Liza was in my office playing on the floor when Jenkins came in my office and handed an envelope to me with a termination letter and a three month severance check. Liza was spending the day with me since her preschool was closed.

She watched me take my photos and plaques off the walls and pack my books and other belongings and leave the office. In the car, I explained that I wouldn't be returning to work with the YMCA anymore because the YMCA didn't like the way I was doing my job. Years later, Liza told me that this experience, of seeing her father fired, was upsetting to her. Who wouldn't have been upset at the way the YMCA handled the situation? They could have been sensitive to Liza's presence and asked me to leave with her and return the next day to pick up my things.

Over an eight-year period, I was instrumental in founding YMCA outreach programs, from the original youth center in Bay Shore with a $21,000 budget to a multi-site organization with a $500,000 budget with centers in Bay Shore, Coram, North Bellport, Shirley/Mastic, Shoreham, and East Hampton. These programs exist today under the name YMCA Family Services.

After leaving the YMCA, I collected unemployment insurance. It was strange to be unemployed and spending a lot of time alone in our house. I received calls from supportive colleagues but no job offers. I knew that it would be very difficult to find a comparable position. I decided to join forces with Jill Rooney, an experienced childcare leader, to establish CPC, the Community Programs Center of Long Island. We believed that we had complementary skills and could develop corporate supported childcare centers throughout Long Island.

For a while, things worked out. However, the partnership was fraught with interpersonal conflicts and misunderstandings and did not last long. Jill left the organization and I remained as Executive Director for twenty-three years, building the organization from nothing to a $6 million enterprise employing 160 people at three sites. They were extremely stressful years of funding uncertainties when I worried from payroll-to-payroll if we would survive.

In 1980, when CPC was incorporated, we believed that the timing to establish corporation-supported childcare centers was perfect. Ronald Reagan had become President and was promoting public-private partnerships. We learned of the opportunity to set up a childcare center in a school district-owned community center. When the child care center's enrollment didn't meet expectations, we were forced to stretch out payments to suppliers, sometimes over six months. Eventually, everyone got paid but there were many unhappy suppliers, some who refused to make deliveries anymore. It was difficult and unpleasant all around.

When we were hired to do a needs survey by *Newsday* and LILCO (Long Island Lighting Company), we were confident of success in securing the support of businesses. We developed a business advisory committee consisting of representatives of several businesses including *Newsday*, ADP, Chemical Bank, and Fairchild Republic. Meanwhile, we searched for a suitable site to establish a center in the Melville area. We visited a number of excessed school buildings and churches and decided that the opportunity in the Half Hollow Hills School District was the best. The district had closed down the New Hills Elementary School two years earlier due to declining enrollment and planned to sell the building and property. It was located on busy Deer Park Avenue within view of the Long Island Expressway and just four miles from Melville, home to many corporations. The school district was willing to lease a large portion of the building to us for a very modest amount so that vandalism of the building could be minimized and their insurance rates would be lower. We had virtually no funds but decided that the opportunity was worth the risk.

We hired teaching, kitchen, office, and custodial staff and purchased classroom, office, and kitchen equipment. We spent thousands of dollars on advertising, especially in local editions of the *Pennysaver News*. Our only committed funds were from *Newsday*, which pledged $10,000. Another $5,000 was donated by several other businesses. In addition, I made arrangements for a $30,000 loan from the

Veatch Program of the Unitarian Universalist Congregation in Plandome, which supported the center as an effort to develop childcare for Long Island industry. We continued our appeals to businesses to pay for part of their employees' childcare costs as a way of recruiting and retaining valuable workers but they felt that they didn't need to offer this fringe benefit and chose to see the center as just another charity to which they might associate their names for a modest contribution. Even the Grumman Corporation, for years Long Island's largest employer, refused to support the center. I was told by informed sources that the vice president of human resources didn't believe in childcare, feeling that a woman's place was in the home. The human resources director of another large company told me that "the old man doesn't buy it," referring to the CEO.

So, there I was again, appealing for support for another unpopular cause. It became clear that the center had to survive in the marketplace like any other childcare center. Fortunately, enrollment income grew monthly as workers and area residents learned about the center and visited the facility. We employed an experienced childcare center director as our first director. He gained the trust of the parents and hired some very good childcare workers.

But the center had some very serious financial problems. We lost over $75,000 in the first year and thus had to "borrow from Peter to pay Paul" every month. I was constantly receiving calls from vendors and suppliers who wanted to be paid. If it weren't for Chemical Bank's willingness to give us forbearance when we didn't have enough in the bank to cover our payrolls, we would have filed for bankruptcy protection within the first year. I drew no salary for more than a year. Meanwhile, staff members were paid starting salaries of $3.85 per hour. Until Social Security required us to pay into the program, workers weren't covered by Social Security. We fell behind in lease payments to the school district that, for months, ignored our defaults. Staff grew increasingly unhappy, pointing to the enrollment growth and ignoring the debt that we carried and, at one point, threatened to unionize. Although the parents knew of our precarious financial situation, they did little to help raise funds or make connections with their employers. In addition, the tension between Jill and me grew to a point where the board decided that they needed to eliminate one of us. Jill left and achieved substantial success operating several child care centers in Nassau County.

The organization struggled throughout its life, never recovering from its original indebtedness. I continued to seek financial support from businesses. We raised enrollment fees. We offered discounted fees for advance payments.

We developed a summer camp program that produced positive cash flow, which helped. I hired a local couple with camp administration experience to direct the camp. For two years, at the beginning of interest in computer learning, we created "Compu-Day Camp." The camp was very successful after I secured full page *Newsday* coverage of the program, which offered a teacher for every three campers and four hours of hands-on computer teaching daily. The camp also offered weekly trips to the beach and recreation and sports at the center.

In 1984, I facilitated a board retreat in which one of the organization's founding board members, Mary O'Hagan, suggested that we develop an adult daycare program. Mary was a board member of the Syosset Senior Day Care Center. I visited this center and became intrigued by the potential of operating a center for both children and older adults. I sought startup financial support for the project and found that the timing was right to apply to the Suffolk County Office for the Aging for a grant to develop one of the first two social adult daycare centers in Suffolk County. We received a $15,000 grant and thought the center would immediately be successful. But, of course, it wasn't. We publicized the program wherever we could afford to. I secured a State grant to hire a public relations firm to publicize the center. We were featured on a major television news show as well as on local radio and newspaper feature stories. Nevertheless, enrollment grew slowly, partly because families needed transportation to and from the center for their parents and relatives. After a year, we made arrangements for transportation services to be provided by a van service and later a taxi service. It was essential to engage the children with the older adults on a consistent basis so we developed activities for their daily engagement. Over the years, we expanded the adult day center to our three child care centers, naming the elder care programs Day Haven. The program serves the frail and impaired elderly, including people with Alzheimer's disease. It has earned considerable praise and recognition due to its uniqueness since it features daily interaction between the very young and very old. It is apparent to me that both generations benefit from such interactions. In fact, a good deal of research has documented the case including a study that I secured for CPC in the late 1990s. The federally-funded observational research study presented a series of recommendations to apply in other programs. I presented these findings at several national and regional conferences.

I involved a number of very dedicated people on the board of directors, including Mary O'Hagan, Christopher Burns, Denis Feldman,

Keith Merriwether, Bill Jaeger, Patrick Halpin, Larry Maltin, Richard Turan, Bob Ciovacco, Vince Polimeni, John Westerman, Pat Feder, Warren Wartell, Gil Schwab, Charlie Schneck, Matt Crosson, Marvin Tolkin, Mary Chisholm, Don Hoffman, Cecilia Teng, Ellen Volpe, and Eric Redin. However, we were never successful in establishing a financial commitment to the future of the organization either from government, businesses, or individuals. In those years, public funding for childcare was solely dedicated to the very poor. Childcare centers didn't have the acceptability that they have today. They were seen as programs for the poor, not the middle class. So, the fact that our centers featured children from both low and moderate income families was a deterrent for many middle-class families. Furthermore, our centers were in former public school building that needed repairs, thus not giving the appearance of middle-class institutions, and we were not able to capture the attention and support of wealthy individuals to help us raise funds to offset our operating losses. Raising our fees meant limiting our access to many working families.

We had periods of success and relative stability but, ultimately, the board and staff grew to believe that I would "pull a rabbit out of the hat" and rescue the organization every time we had a crisis. Over twenty-three years, I had done it many times with grants, fund raising events, and loans.

Over the years, my affection for Day Haven grew. I started most of my days greeting elders in the morning and chatting with them. I appreciated their individuality and understood the reasons they came to the center, and how they benefitted from their experiences at Day Haven. These people would otherwise be sitting home alone if it weren't for the program. The research on such programs supports my feelings that there are not only psychological but physical benefits from the routine activities of dressing, getting in and out of vehicles, walking into and out of the center, and from the organized physical and mental activities that we offered.

I also began to see the possibility that, someday, I might need some form of personal care. Of most concern has been the fear of contracting Alzheimer's disease. I have heard so many stories about its suddenness and its consequences that it is easy to project myself into this condition. But I also have real appreciation for people afflicted with the disease and the importance of treating them with respect, patience, and understanding.

Day Haven has taught me to find humor even in the horrors of Alzheimer's. James, a 50-year-old Alzheimer's patient, a former insurance executive, came in the front door every day and went to the office staff to greet them and wish them a good day. As far as he was concerned, he was still in his business office.

Then there was the time when Gus, a World War II veteran, was in the program for several years as his Alzheimer's disease progressed. He was a cheery fellow who greeted all visitors with a friendly smile. We received a representative of the Japanese government on a tour of US senior centers. At the end of his tour, Gus approached the Japanese visitor and reached his hand out in friendship, saying, "I just want you to know that I don't hold the war against you. We are friends." The interpreter explained Gus' statement and the Japanese authority bowed and reached his hand out in friendship. When the visitor left the room, Gus said to me: "Goodbye and good riddance, you Jap bastard!"

One morning, a newly enrolled four-year-old came to the child care center with her grandfather, who was dropping her off for the day. When she saw some of the elderly program participants passing her in the hallway, she said to her grandfather, "Grandpa! Maybe when you get old you can come to my center, too."

Over the years, we became like family, an extended intergenerational family of children, staff, and elders under the same roof, eating the same food, subject to the same weather, celebrating one another's birthdays and national holidays, and grieving life's losses.

The other key organizational decision was to establish a federally-funded Head Start Center. I learned of grant funding being available from the US Department of Health and Human Services. With the help of Glen Winters, a Suffolk resident who was retiring from a career with the Head Start Bureau, we submitted an application. We secured a $96,000 grant to establish a center in Selden to serve 34 children in low income families who were residents of northwest Brookhaven Township. Despite major financial and housing challenges, the program grew over the years to serve over 150 children in two centers with a budget of over a million dollars. The program was housed in seven school buildings and churches and struggled to convince the federal government to expand the program despite the considerable and documented need among the area's low income residents. I always had special feelings towards our Head Start program as I witnessed the positive life-changes among the children and parents involved in the program. Staff reached out to parents who wanted to better their lives and didn't know how. Their patience and skills uplifted thousands of parents. We were able to employ many parents over the years in the Head Start program as teachers, assistant teachers, and family workers. We also subsidized their continued educations. Meanwhile, Head Start's wonderful children's program has provided thousands of children with a solid early childhood education.

A major decision I made was to hire Sara Pokross as our full-charge bookkeeper. Sara proved to be a hard-working, intelligent, and loyal employee who helped me tremendously to manage the budget and the organization. As the organization grew with funding from a wide variety of sources, I needed someone like Sara to trust and rely on. During her interview, I asked Sara if she had experience dealing with angry vendors who wanted to be paid. I made it clear that we were carrying a lot of debt. Sara not only served as bookkeeper, she helped at our fundraising events and even worked in the kitchen when the cook was out sick. She aided me in thinking through many sticky personnel decisions. I don't think the organization would have lasted for twenty-three years without Sara.

Making hiring decisions about program directors at CPC were not easy. With my strong need to be honest and forthright with job candidates, I told them about our financial challenges even though doing so might scare some from pursuing employment with us. Fortunately, some very talented people joined the organization including Paul Chinn, Donna Tudda, Marie Mason, Glenn Winters, Lucy Gluck, Nancy Picart, Lise Eccleston, Margaret Brown,

Toby Wiles, Denice Karotseris, Denise Fereira, and Elizabeth Geary. Many others did not work out and had to be let go. Each of the firing decisions was difficult for me and never got easier as the years passed.

In the mid-1980s, the organization continued to struggle. I saw no light at the end of the tunnel. I consulted with others to see if there was some way out of the abyss. I learned that nonprofit organizations could create separate business ventures to produce profits to benefit the parent company. I took a course at New York University on the subject to help me develop a plan. I decided that there was a growing need for leisure-time services to the growing older-adult population on Long Island. I envisioned a business that provided social, educational, and recreational services to older adults. Our board of directors liked the concept and supported moving forward with it. I learned about a model program operating in Washington, DC, so I traveled to Washington to meet with the director. He had established a membership-based service organization that became the exclusive retirement program for a national retirement group. I returned to Long Island to meet with a potential funder who might help us establish a subsidiary business corporation. I was able to secure the pro bono legal assistance of a former college fraternity brother, Bob Ciovacco.

He helped us to incorporate the Apple Glow Corporation, as a subsidiary business corporation with design on generating profits that would be donated to the charitable organization. I also secured a grant from the Veatch Program of the Unitarian Universalist Congregation as well as a pledge of $75,000 if we secured an additional $150,000. I wrote a business plan with the help of a business advisor, Richard Dundore, and spent a great deal of time seeking investment capital to support the business. I made presentations to the Long Island Venture Group and made contacts with investment banking firms in New York City. With the assistance of Bob MacMillan, a partner in a prominent law firm, I was able to make a presentation to three senior vice presidents of Avon Corporation who showed interest in our business plan. Avon was creating business enterprises geared towards what was called the "maturity market." We thought we had gained their support but were notified a month later that they didn't want to invest in labor-intensive business ventures. With this disappointing news and our lack of success in finding the needed investment capital, we abandoned the business venture project.

In 1987, we were notified that the Half Hollow Hills School District was selling the building in which we had been housed. They gave us a six-month notice to vacate the building. We had occupied the building under the threat of leaving for seven years but the moment of truth was before us. We decided that we had to appeal to a judge to give us time to relocate. The school district was angry and fought our appeal. The judge gave us an additional three months to vacate. I assured the judge that I had made arrangements with the Deer Park School District to relocate to the former Abraham Lincoln School about ten minutes away from the Hills School. I spent the three months garnering support for a $50,000 grant from all eighteen Suffolk County Legislators. I met personally with each Legislator on both sides of the aisle, sometimes passing them notes during the legislative sessions, and urging them to vote in favor of the requested grant. I was also able to secure a $30,000 grant from the Veatch Program of the Unitarian Universalist Congregation. To save money, I also served as general contractor to get the work completed at the new school rather than hiring someone to do this job. This included securing estimates to do major repairs to the heating system and plumbing system, the installation of kitchen equipment and a central alarm system, and numerous repairs to the floors, windows, and doorways. I virtually lived in the Abraham Lincoln School through the winter months of 1987. The furnaces had been shut off five years before and were in disrepair. While electrical, plumbing, maintenance, roofing, carpentry, flooring, and heating contractors did their work, I loaded refuse bins with broken equipment, furniture, and debris, coming home every night exhausted. I lost twenty pounds during the three months of preparing the building for occupancy. When the state day care licensing inspector visited the building before the work started, she asked me when I expected the work to be done. I told her ninety days. She laughed and said that I was a "very enterprising young man." Ultimately, with the help of many staff members who volunteered their time, we met the deadline, vacating the New Hills Schools over a weekend to occupy the Abraham Lincoln School by Monday, when the licensing inspector returned to complete her inspection and give us a temporary license. She was amazed at what we had done since her inspection visit three months before.

Life at the new school was also filled with uncertainties. It took a year to build the enrollment with people living closer to the building. The costs of building renovations exceeded our estimates, as they always do. We fell behind in payments to the school district as we had done in the Half Hollow Hills District, resulting in eviction threats. We knew that our major challenge was to own a building, but we were stymied by how to achieve this objective.

We thought we had a benefactor in Angelo Campanella, an extremely wealthy local real estate developer who pledged to help us buy the school building. Campanella ultimately reneged on this pledge despite the fact that he made the pledge in front of several board members and a development expert we had hired to help us organize a capital campaign.

During this period, my ability to juggle multiple issues and competing forces was tested. One day, I got a phone call from someone who identified himself as a New York State trooper. He reported that a member of my board of directors had been in an auto accident on the New York State Thruway and asked the trooper to call me and ask that I send him $250 by Western Union. The trooper said that the board member gave him the name of a fellow board member as a way of confirming the legitimacy of the request. The trooper gave me instructions on where to send the funds. I wondered whether this was a scam, but the use of the other board member's name convinced me to honor the request. In addition, I knew that the board member seeking my help was having an affair and thus, he couldn't call his wife for money. It struck me that this fact was somehow involved in the bizarre situation. When I called the board member the next day to check on his medical condition, he informed me that he hadn't been upstate and knew nothing of the incident. It turned out that I had been scammed. I contacted the FBI who, after investigating the situation, determined that an interstate group obtained the public records of nonprofit organizations, which included the names of the members of their boards of directors. I felt used. My intentions to help someone in need, despite troubling circumstances, were seen by friends and colleagues as foolish; they thought I trusted people too much.

In another instance, we received a call from our bank indicating that they weren't going to cover our payroll that afternoon because we were short by $30,000. They indicated that we had to deposit $30,000 by 3PM. Normally, the bank assumed that we would make a last-minute deposit so their call was a shock to us. With no other income anticipated that day, the only way to make the deposit was to find individuals to lend the organization the necessary funds. I made a number of calls to board members with the result that Mary O'Hagan and Mary Chisholm made loans of $10,000. With no other alternative, Karen and I decided to take $20,000 from our line of credit and lend it to the organization. It took about two years to pay back the three loans. If we didn't make the loans, staff wouldn't have gotten paid which would have spiraled into a staff and consumer crisis that would have hit the newspapers and TV and caused the demise of the organization. I couldn't let that happen even though I knew that, in theory, it was the board who should address the financial crisis.

Not too long after this crisis occurred, I had to make another critical financial decision about meeting a payroll. The only alternative I could think of was to delay payment of the organization's share of senior employee pension fund contributions. I explained the situation to staff and got their reluctant approval assuring them that the funds would be restored with interest. Eventually, these funds were deposited but not for many months and with a good deal of employee discontent.

In 1990, I read about Computer Associates International's (CA) plans to build an international headquarters building in Suffolk County so I wrote a letter to Charles Wang, the company president, expressing interest in becoming the daycare center operator. I felt that the organization had to diversity its sources of income in order to survive and that, one way of doing this, was to operate other centers, which would share the organization's central administrative costs. I also figured that a contract with a corporation could provide a nice management fee. One day, I received a call from Lisa Mars, CA's Vice President of Human Resources. Wang asked her to check us out. She visited the Deer Park center and later indicated that she would like CPC to serve as center operator. We negotiated a deal that paid us a fee of about $65,000 a year. This fee became the income to help us survive our operating losses at the other centers. I spent a good deal of time at CA while the center was being constructed advising the contractors, selecting and ordering equipment and supplies, and hiring a director. It was strange to be in a position where money was no object. I had always sought the best prices when making purchases. CA instructed us to pay the center's teachers and assistant teachers about $5,000 per year more than we paid our current staff. At first blush, this requirement seemed untenable. How could we pay different salaries at our different centers for the same work? We decided to agree to the terms, seeing the situation as an opportunity for upward mobility of our current staff as well as an opportunity to improve salaries and benefits for all of our employees. We offered our existing staff the chance to apply for the new positions. We made it clear that we couldn't guaranteed how long we would remain CA's childcare provider and that we would leave hiring decisions to the director of the CA center. I hired Lucy Gluck, one of our former Head Start directors, to serve as the center director. Lucy hired staff and did a great job of managing the center.

Within a matter of months, it became obvious that CA was enamored with Montessori philosophy and methodology. We made it clear from the outset that we practiced a balanced approach to childcare and were not a Montessori School program. We integrated Montessori, Piaget, and Dewey's thinking into our programs. CA management began to place demands on us that we did not feel comfortable with. Ultimately, CA decided to run the center themselves. After about one year, CA took over the center. On a Friday afternoon, I was called to the CEO's conference room where I was expected to sign papers permitting CA to take immediate control of the center. Knowing of CA's influence as a major employer on Long Island, I signed the documents and was later physically escorted to my office by an attorney. I boxed my belongings and was escorted by the attorney to my car. It felt like a hostile takeover.

Some colleagues felt that we should have done whatever CA wanted in order to maintain the contract. I felt that our childcare program served children very effectively and that we shouldn't vary from our beliefs and methods regardless of the financial consequences. I left CA with my head held high and offered to assist the company to make the smoothest of transitions. It made no sense to burn bridges. Months later, a senior CA official, Don Hoffmann, expressed interest in joining our board and served as our treasurer for many years. He also personally contributed to the organization and secured financial support from the company.

In 1991, we were invited by Larry Cohen, CEO of LUMEX/CYBEX, to establish an intergenerational center in Ronkonkoma. We thought that by expanding our services we could achieve an economy of scale by spreading our administrative costs among the centers. We were also able to secure bond financing to purchase this center as well as to build a Head Start center in Port Jefferson thus providing long term housing for our Head Start center. Over a seven year period, the Head Start program had relocated from a church basement to the Unity Drive School, the New Lane School, the North Coleman Avenue School, a commercial building, and the Port Jefferson Junior High School. These moves produced tremendous uncertainties for me, staff, and parents through the years.

During the 1990s, I joined the American Business Associates, a networking organization. I attended monthly meetings and met a good number of businesspeople. Ellen Volpe, the Executive Director, joined CPC's Board of Directors as did Denis Feldman, a commercial real estate broker. They helped me to further network with other businesses which resulted in cost savings on some of our purchases and goods and services.

In 1999, we experienced a major challenge at the Ronkonkoma center when a steam exhaust pipe at an adjacent plant exploded causing a very loud burst of air. Our children were playing in the nearby playground. The explosion caused some ceiling tiles to fall. Fortunately, no one was hurt. However, the incident was the subject of considerable media coverage and parent concern. We held many meetings with parents and representatives of other businesses near the plant. Visits were conducted to the plant to educate everyone about the company's operations. We were able to prevent a crisis of confidence with our parents with only three families deciding that they didn't feel comfortable with the safety conditions.

Over the years, I reached out to local elected officials on both sides of the aisle, establishing a solid reputation as a reliable doer and advocate for community services. Of particular note as supporters of our programs were Suffolk County Legislators Jim Morgo, Greg Blass, Bill Richards, Sondra Bachety, John Foley, Vivian Viloria Fischer, and Paul Tonna as well as New York State Senator Owen Johnson; and State Assemblymen Jim Conte and Steve Englebright.

I continued to take steps to build the organization's board of directors. Most significantly, this involved gaining the commitment of the former Suffolk County

Executive, Patrick Halpin. Patrick attracted the participation of others, including Vincent Polimeni, a commercial developer of office buildings and shopping centers. Polimeni loved our intergenerational programs and pledged to help raise funds. He described us as "Long Island's best-kept nonprofit secret." Polimeni's involvement in the organization began an exciting five-year period in which we held gala annual dinners at the Garden City Hotel and the Meadowbrook Club. We honored people in the business community. The first event generated the support of John Westerman, a senior partner in a prominent law firm. In the next four years, we honored Jack Bransfield of Roslyn Savings Bank and John O'Neill of Fleet Bank, Donald Axinn, another major developer, and Matt Crosson, head of the Long Island Association. We also honored Vince Polimeni. This event produced a whopping net profit of $175,000. Polimeni went all-out to support the organization. The income from these events helped the organization to continue to function. It didn't, however, help us to reduce our operating losses, much less build a reserve fund.

The relationship between a nonprofit board of directors and its executive director is often a subject of tension and disagreement. Some see the executive director as the organization's chief operating officer and as solely responsible for the programmatic and fiscal welfare of the organization. According to this view, if the organization has financial problems, it is up to the CEO to correct them. The CEO could seek the help of the board to address the problem but, ultimately, it is his/her responsibility. The other view sees the organization's welfare as a shared responsibility and emphasizes the board's responsibility to raise funds and the other resources needed by the organization. Over the years, I saw many good executive directors fired because the organization didn't have enough revenue to meet its obligations while the board did little to face its fiscal obligations to raise funds or evaluate its executive director. Thus, as I see things, a healthy state of affairs exists when there is a dynamic tension among the board and its executive director. Otherwise, you either have a board or its executive director exercising too much control of the organization. Successful executives involve their boards in an educational process in which they are invested in the organization and, thus, feel ownership and responsibility for the organization.

Another major development was the involvement of other board members and professional associates, particularly David Boone, a retired banker whom I had met years ago. Dave and Denis Feldman showed me how we might be able to secure financing to buy a building.

With their significant help, we secured industrial revenue bond financing, which permitted the organization to leave the Lincoln School and construct a new building in the Heartland Business Center on the other side of Deer Park, as well as a new building in which to house part of our Head Start program. The unavoidable problem was that the newly-raised funds had to be used to cover current operating expenses during extensive construction delays, which were exacerbated by delays in securing county and state permits. Month by month, the deficit increased with no end in sight. The result of this very serious problem was a loss of confidence in my leadership on the part of some members of the board of directors. This was a time of great stress.

A serious threat to the survival of the organization occurred around the turn of the century and placed me in an ethical and political dilemma. At the behest of labor unions, church groups, and the Long Island Progressive Coalition, a number of Suffolk County legislators spearheaded a movement to establish a fair wage bill. The impact would require companies and nonprofit organizations that did business with the county to pay their employees at least $10 per hour plus health benefits. With over one hundred full-time employees and a number of contracts with the county, CPC would be dramatically affected if the bill passed. In fact,

I calculated that we would have to come up with over $200,000 annually to meet this additional cost. We would either need to raise fees substantially and thus reduce affordability of our programs for working families, or, raise more charitable dollars. There was no way to reduce our expenses to cover the increased costs. Our survival as an organization was at risk. I went to several legislative committee meetings and the full legislature to discuss our opposition. I made it clear that we supported the legislative intent but, without legislative financial support, the fair wage bill would put CPC out of business. Before the jeers of bill supporters, I made our case. It was difficult for me to oppose the bill, especially as the son of a life-long member of the Teamsters. I wanted to stand on principle for low-income working people and let the government figure out how to fund the program, but I couldn't. I was too enmeshed in assuring the survival of our services and the employment of our workers.

This was an example of the dilemmas I often faced in my professional career. There were so many levels of accountability to be faced—to the children and elders we served, their caregivers, our employees, our suppliers and vendors who needed to get paid, the public and private funders of our programs, the local communities we served, and the individual donors who supported the organization. There were often conflicts balancing the expectations of these forces and elements. It was, thus, inevitable that one or more parts of the equation would not be satisfied.

The organization continued to accumulate annual deficits. Several members of the board felt I wasn't managing the organization effectively. They were tired of being expected to raise funds to bail out the organization out and started to feel that that their time could be better spent elsewhere. People also don't like to associate with organizations that are constantly in financial trouble. They pointed to for-profit childcare firms who were, by outward signs, making a profit. They weren't satisfied with my explanations regarding what the for-profits were doing to cut corners and compromising the quality of care.

Many businesspeople often believe that nonprofit executives are unwilling to make tough decisions—that they are too idealistic and waste money because they don't manage their organizations as businesses. Many of my professional colleagues did, indeed, see a business approach as anathema to social work practice, sometimes creating programs that were unsustainable. I saw the business model as consistent with social work values. After all, satisfying the needs of the consumers with high-quality, affordable services is good business *and* good social work. I was cautious in our spending and didn't create programs that we couldn't afford, but our services were underfunded by government at a time when society didn't recognize child and elder care as preventive services that reduced the future costs.

Over the years, there were many instances in which conflict arose around the business and nonprofit models. One illustration occurred when we submitted a proposal to operate a new childcare center in a leased building located in a corporate park. I drafted plans for the interior layout of the center's rooms. I placed all of the children's rooms along the building's perimeter, allowing for windows in each room. The representative of the business community, a member of our board, expressed anger when he reviewed the draft plans. He said that I didn't understand how to run a business efficiently. He wanted classrooms in the middle of the building so that the maximum number of rooms could be accommodated. He would have nothing to do with the importance of sunlight, fresh air, and the children's immediate access to the outdoors. He expressed this business point of view when he said: "I don't care what you have to do to make the organization survive, just do it!" It was no surprise when, years later, this board member was found guilty of unethical fiscal practices in the organization he led.

During this period, I worked closely with the board chairman, Charlie Schneck who did a great job to keep the organization together. The only way that we could see to save the organization from bankruptcy was to find another organization to take us over. Fortunately, I learned from Matt Crosson, one of CPC's board members and the head of the Long Island Association, about United Cerebral Palsy of Suffolk's plans to expand its operations. This $35 million multi-purpose agency wanted to expand its child and elder care programs to serve the population at large not just serve those with disabilities. I contacted Kathy Maul, UCP's Executive Director, inviting her to meet to discuss a possible merger. UCP conducted due diligence and decided that they could operate the programs more efficiently than CPC so they offered to take over the organization in 2002.

It was difficult to know that UCP thought I was operating the organization inefficiently and that they knew how to do a better job of it. They were convinced by a team of business consultants that they could operate the organization profitably by eliminating sixteen full-time workers while complying with state regulations. I knew it could be done on paper but not in practice. I was ultimately vindicated, since no positions were eliminated. In fact, they were forced to shut down one of the centers completely. They were able to negotiate a very good real estate deal with the bondholders who had invested in the centers. Based on UCP's credit-worthiness, they were able to extend the debt repayment period from twenty-five to forty years at a lower interest rate. They also purchased the building for $1.5 million less than its appraised value. They centralized some of the work that Sara and I did into existing positions at UCP.

The handwriting on the wall was clear for me over the upcoming months before the legal takeover. I was being relieved of my leadership roles and responsibilities. I could see that there would be no place for me once UCP took the reigns so I began to weigh my options. I knew that I couldn't function as a middle manager in UCP's administration. I had always been an executive director. I was also tired of the pressures and stress of agency leadership.

I didn't want to, or could afford to, retire. I decided to establish a not-for-profit called Intergenerational Strategies as an advocacy and consulting organization to provide assistance to other organizations. I felt I had a lot to offer and wanted to avoid the inevitable uncertainties of funding, staff turnover, and being responsible for facilities. I met with people I respected and trusted, most of whom agreed to join the board of directors of the new organization. They included Al Jordan, Tom Williams, Lucy Gluck,

Nancy Marr, Dick Dina, Marcia Spector, Luis Valenzuela, Deborah Weiner, Bob Mulvey and Pegi Orsino. Later, Warren Wartell, Nick Felix, and Pam Giacoia, all who joined the board and provided valuable insight and support. Nick secured annual support from Capital One Bank where he is a branch manager.

Leaving CPC was, of course, bittersweet. I was its founder. I lived and breathed it every day for twenty-three years. Rationally, I knew that I had enabled the organization to survive and continue to serve the community. Emotionally, it was hard. I felt isolated and alone, not having been recognized for the work I had done to create the organization and get it through difficult times. A retirement party was held where some kind words were said. I was disappointed that my work wasn't recognized by state and public officials who well knew of my contributions to society. It wasn't the way I had hoped to end my full-time work life. Intellectually, I knew that UCP wasn't going to sponsor an event that gave me the recognition I deserved, but it hurt anyway.

The Long Island Community Foundation agreed to provide start-up funding to Intergenerational Strategies. Under the leadership of Lee Lawrence and, later, Suzy Sonenberg, the Foundation's Executive Directors, had supported a good deal of progressive projects, so I met with Suzy and found that she would recommend support for the new project. I believed that my experiences over the years could be helpful to other organizations while providing a source of needed part-time income for Karen and me since I have a tiny pension. Fortunately, Karen has a very good pension as well as a private psychotherapy practice. We met with a financial advisor to determine how much I had to earn in order to maintain our current lifestyle. Until the international financial crisis that hit millions of Americans beginning in September 2008, we could look forward to a stable financial future. But, like millions of people, we lost a great deal of our retirement savings and must reduce our expenses and work longer than we had planned.

Since 2002, the organization has established itself as the Long Island leader in the promotion of intergenerational programs and policies as well as the leader in the civic engagement of older adults. Significantly, several *Newsday* editors and reporters, including Noel Rubinton, Ron Roel, Bob Koehler, and Jim Smith have sought out the organization's views for upcoming articles and editorial issues. In addition, I have written several published op-ed articles and letters to the editor. The organization has sponsored four conferences and more than two dozen workshops and seminars. I've also been able to establish a very positive relationship with John

Kominicki, publisher of the *Long Island Business News* and his editor, David Reich-Hale. I've been a contributor to many other articles on subjects ranging from housing, the perception of aging, the employment of older adults, the need for community programs to enable older adults to age-in-place, intergenerational issues, and the civic engagement of older adults. My work has also featured numerous speaking engagements and presentations at local, regional, and national conferences. Last year, I was retained by the Nassau library system to conduct several workshops and an Aging Summit.

A major undertaking I launched with Steve Levy, Suffolk County's Executive. I proposed that he establish a Commission on Creative Retirement for the purpose of studying the needs of the county's aging population and develop a series of action recommendations. Levy asked me to chair the Commission which I did. I chaired monthly meetings for a year, conducted a great deal of research, and held public hearings. I then wrote a detailed report for the County Executive. Many of the Commission's recommendations have been implemented either by the county, or by various nonprofit organizations. The Commission's report has been downloaded from the internet several thousand times and was widely acclaimed by planners, policy makers, and those in the aging field.

Last year, Donna Butts, Executive Director of Generations United (GU), the country's pre-eminent intergenerational organization, invited me to work as coordinator for Seniors4Kids in New York State. Donna and I had become colleagues over the years as I became increasingly interested in intergenerational policy and practice. Through my GU association, I have also met and benefited from associations with other leaders in the intergenerational field including Matt Kaplan at Penn State, Nancy Henkin, Andrea Taylor, and Bob Teitze of the Center for Intergenerational Learning, as well as Jeanette Bressler and Valerie Kuehne, dynamite researchers in the field. As part of Seniors4Kids, I recruited over 130 adults aged 50+ to serve as advocates for the expansion of pre-kindergarten funding in New York State. I recruited folks in Rochester, New York City, and Long Island into the project including the New York City Grey Panthers Network. These individuals have enabled the project to achieve its measurable objectives and generated a good deal of positive publicity around the importance of pre-kindergarten programs. Most significantly, I was interviewed by former New York City Mayor David Dinkins on his weekly radio show. GU has asked me to continue this work for another year.

I was also invited to join The Long Island Progressive Coalition's Board of Directors. I served

for about two years and was very impressed
with this small organization's effectiveness by
targeting a small number of critical issues and
using community organizing tactics to institute
changes. David Sprintzen, Lisa Tyson, and
Diana Coleman and the other members of the
board are doing important work that no one
else is. I admire their political acumen and their
commitment to a world view and social change.

In 2008, I established a partnership with
Dowling College. In August 2007, Tom Williams,
Nick Felix, and I met with Bob Gaffney, Dowling's
president, to discuss my proposal to join forces.
Gaffney, who was Suffolk County Executive and
a state assemblyman, was enthusiastic about
the idea and commissioned Mike DeLuise, a top
aide, to move forward. We soon met with three
prospective corporate contributors who showed
real interest in supporting what I named the
Center for Intergenerational Policy and Practice.
They donated $55,000 to the college to start the
center.

Over the following months, we decided that
the center should be a new entity, not part
of any existing college institute or center. We
also decided that Intergenerational Strategies
should serve as an independent contractor to
the college rather than me becoming a college
employee. The director of the college's sociology
department, Dr. Susanne Bleiberg Seperson, was

appointed the center director, with me providing her with technical assistance.

With the academic assistance and expertise of Kevin Brabazon, President of the New York State Intergenerational Network, we drafted a syllabus for a three-credit introductory course in intergenerational studies and a non-degree bearing course directed to older adults seeking employment or volunteerism in the nonprofit sector. We made arrangements for a website, three educational seminars, and a conference to be held at the college. We also searched to identify other financial support for the center, which, of course, was essential to its survival and growth. It was envisioned that the academic program would grow to become a degree or certificate-bearing program in intergenerational studies.

Since the center got off the ground, dramatic changes have occurred. The college has decided to operate without Intergenerational Strategies' assistance. I made it clear that I wasn't willing to continue to serve the very active role I played in 2008 without being compensated during 2009. Therefore, I refused to make presentations on behalf of the center at two national conferences nor as coordinator of the Long Island Intergenerational Network in a voluntary capacity. So, when it became abundantly clear that the college wouldn't raise additional funds for the center, I concluded that the original concept, that the partnership would help Intergenerational Strategies, didn't have a future. I also felt that the college had treated me unprofessionally by not being upfront with me about its plans. I, therefore, decided to limit my association with Dowling College and its Intergenerational Center. I did continue to teach a continuing education course for the Dowling Institute. This course, "Nonprofit employment and volunteerism in life's next chapter," began recently with seventeen enthusiastic age 50+ students wishing to switch careers from the for-profit to the nonprofit sector. The unique course, the first of its kind on Long Island, promises to continue and generate new volunteers and job candidates needed in the nonprofit sector. This effort is a gratifying extension of my Peace Corps experience, bringing new people into public service.

I can look back on many professional accomplishments during my post-Peace Corps years. In so doing, I believe that it was the desire for recognition and approval that fueled the constant quest that drove me to achieve what I did. My childhood perception that I was an underdog who had to do more and better than the next guy was deep and powerful. I was successful at taking ideas and organizing them into realities. I was successful in finding people who believed in what I was doing and allowing them the freedom to operate fairly independently. I generated a lot of loyalty among staff and the people who joined the boards of directors that I brought together. I was successful in also forming positive relationships with many elected and appointed officials, foundation leaders who granted funds to the programs I developed, and members of the press.

Not working in a traditional agency setting has been an adjustment, since I function alone most of the time. No water cooler or coffee pot present where I can talk to others. No one right there to bounce ideas off of. No children to play with. No elders to chat with. Most everyone I know is working full-time with considerable demands on their time. Sometimes it feels like I died or moved away. Fortunately, I love the challenges of studying new issues and developing strategies to address these issues without the day-to-day worries of agency management.

Reflecting back, my professional career has been consumed with building community-serving organizations. In the Peace Corps, it was the Communal Theater and a handbag coop. At Community Development for Youth, it was a youth center, as it was at the Cold Spring Harbor Youth Center, followed by a Latino social club in East Northport. After that, I was instrumental in establishing a family service division within the YMCA of Long Island with centers in Bay Shore, Coram, Mastic, Bellport, and East Hampton. Part of this work included the establishment of the first interpersonal dispute resolution center in an American suburb. At the Community Programs Center, I created three intergenerational child and adult day care centers. During the same period, as President of the New York State Adult Day Services Association, I established Advocates for Adult Day Services (AFADS), a lobbying arm of the New York State Adult Day Services Association. AFADS was successful in securing a $1 million New York State grant program from New York State government to fund ten new adult day service programs around the state, which continues to date. Most recently, I brought the concept of home sharing to Long Island and helped Family Service League and Family and Children's Association to launch HomeShare Long Island. It was my advocacy and determination that brought the Center for Intergenerational Policy and Practice at Dowling College to exist as well as Seniors4Kids in New York State.

I recognize the above accomplishments and the dogged determination I had that was the impetus to move them forward. I worked countless hours in these endeavors.

The political resistance to the establishment of these programs, seen by many as frivolous public spending, was often great. This resistance prompted my fundamental urge to challenge the status quo while also satisfying my desire to be of service.

My missionary zeal to build sometimes didn't make friends for me. I believed that I had to decide where my priorities were—in building organizations or building relationships with individuals, not both. This is not to say that it wasn't important to build trust with staff, board members, and colleagues. But I made many choices in how I spent my time and energy between fostering close relationships, building organization capacity and credibility, and enjoying time with my family. I imagine, therefore, that this is why I have not enjoyed close associations with many professional colleagues.

I made these choices based on an assessment of my strengths and weaknesses and my life experiences. I was driven to focus on finding solutions to problems faced by groups of individuals rather than problems faced by individuals, individually. From my training as a Peace Corps volunteer, I developed this thinking about the larger picture—to concentrate on community issues rather than individual issues. My strength, perhaps, has been to understand individual needs enough to develop strategies to address a problem while not being consumed with them. Fortunately, I was able to find and employ people with the compassion and qualifications to work with the individuals that I couldn't help myself.

I recognize this quality as a strength that many people don't possess. To be a person who earns the trust of his coworkers while building for the future is a gift. It has been rewarding in some respects and frustrating and disappointing in others. I would have liked to be appreciated more than I was. I think that people had the impression that, because I was a trailblazer in the work I was doing, I didn't need or want to be closer to the people around me. I very much wanted and needed it.

I received recognition for my work from other sources. I was elected to the Long Island Volunteer Hall of Fame. Karen, Sari, Jeremy, Liza, and both our mothers joined me at a wonderful public recognition ceremony at Bethpage State Park. I was also selected as "Pioneer of the Year" by the New York State Adult Day Services Association for my work in behalf of the expansion of adult day services in the state. I was given a special award by the Intergenerational Caucus of Early Childhood Professionals for my work creating intergenerational daycare programs. Former Governor George Pataki selected me to receive an "Art of Caring" award at a ceremony at the Governor's Mansion in Albany. Most of Long Island's elected officials at the federal, state, and local levels associate my name with intergenerational issues and programs and sometimes call upon me for my thoughts.

Over the years, I have enjoyed relationships with a number of Long Island's nonprofit leaders including Tom Williams, Rick Van Dyke, Al Jordan, Bob Detor, and Dick Dina. Each of these colleagues has been an important part of my professional career.

CHAPTER FIVE
Returning to Colombia: 1996 and 2008

In August 1996, Karen, Sari, and I flew to Colombia to visit my Colombian friends. I felt emotionally obligated to go when I learned that Isbelia Martinez had suffered a serious stroke. Isbelia was a dear friend during my first seven months in the Peace Corps in Colombia in 1963. She had welcomed me to her home and provided friendship and understanding as I adjusted to life in her small, rural village. I couldn't imagine never seeing her again, so we ignored the recommendations of family and friends not to travel to Colombia.

As it was when I left in 1965, Colombia continued to be plagued by economic and political crises. People of the lower economic class are paid very low wages and have few opportunities for upward mobility. The illegal cocaine and marijuana industries had grown tremendously over the past thirty years, and these drugs were, by far, the country's major export products. Powerful drug cartels and extremist military groups had taken over parts of the country. Some believe that the lucrative worldwide cocaine market was the catalyst that brought the country to the verge of financial and social chaos during the past few decades. By 1999, the State Department would rank Colombia as the most dangerous country for Americans to travel in, due to the frequency of kidnapping.

But my experience living in Colombia had been powerful; it had had a dramatic impact on what type of person I became and the career path that I chose, so I discounted everyone's trepidation and assured Karen and Sari that everything would be fine. Sari was especially uneasy about the trip, since she was just engaged to Jeremy and anticipated missing him. She phoned him every evening. As it turned out, Sari returned home early to be with Jeremy.

From the air, it was clear that Colombia's cities had exploded in growth. The population had tripled since the early 1960s. On the ground, I could see how city centers had mushroomed with high-rise apartment housing developments. The cities were surrounded by makeshift squatter dwellings, sometimes called *zonas negras* (slums), occupied by the massive underclass that had fled rural poverty in the country's mountains—only to find worse conditions in the cities. Today, some of these neighborhoods are controlled by the drug cartels that extort poor people, under threat of death, to kill, steal, and kidnap.

During my Peace Corps training, an economist recommended that volunteers think of Colombia's economy as a "pie." He urged us to concentrate our efforts on making the pie larger, rather than trying to divide the pie more equally among social classes. The Colombian economic pie had grown. And more people had a piece of it. At the same time, the contrast between the very rich and upper-middle class and the poor remained striking.

While the cocaine and marijuana trade proliferated, the economy produced other exportable products, especially cacao, bananas, sugar cane, palm oil, cotton, tobacco, potatoes, beans, grains, fruit, flowers, petroleum, coal, natural gas, iron ore, copper, gold, nickel, platinum, and emeralds. Coffee was no longer king, Colombia's only export, as it was when I was in the Peace Corps. Multinational companies could be seen all over the country. Modern equipment, such as the weed whacker, had simplified the work of rural farmers. Transportation around the country was easier due to better commercial vehicles, and more and wider paved roads with safety barriers.

Driving into the cities of Bucaramanga, San Gil, Popayán, Bogotá, and Cali, we could see a plethora of television antennas. Mazda was said to be the most popular car in the country. Choices available to people—from air travel to packaged food—had grown substantially. As the population has aged, so has the number of nursing homes and retirement communities. Modern shopping centers abounded. You could have your photos developed in an hour in small cities like San Gil and Silvia. I was informed that the Church unofficially encouraged families to have only enough children as could be educated. Most school children we saw in the cities and small villages were better dressed and often wore wristwatches.

I was especially excited to take Karen and Sari to Bucaramanga, San Gil, and El Valle so they could become familiar with the places and people that meant so much to me. When we arrived at the airport in Bucaramanga we were greeted by ten people on a workday night who had come out of their way, including Isbelia's son Tomás, who drove five hours to be there. There were warm hugs and kisses along with tears of happiness. For ten days, we were treated like visiting dignitaries.

While Isbelia's stroke had fueled my desire to spend money we didn't have to visit her, I had wanted to return to Colombia for many years.

We never could afford the airfare and it wasn't exactly the type of vacation the family preferred. Visions of Dad speaking Spanish with old friends in remote villages didn't get high marks when compared to camping in the Berkshires or spending time in the sun at the beach. We lived a typical middle class lifestyle with a mortgage, cars, and educational loan payments. Life was good but international trips were out of the question, no matter the purpose.

Our friends had made arrangements for us to stay at the Bucaramanga Country Club, a world-class hotel with a golf course, Olympic swimming pool, restaurant, and tennis courts. They were eager to know what we wanted to see and do as well as our food preferences. We drove to nearby Girón and Floridablanca to show Karen and Sari what typical villages were like. Girón is unique, because town officials over the decades have maintained the village's architecture just as it was centuries ago, with gas lighted street lamps, cobblestone streets, and wooden balconies. In Floridablanca, we enjoyed a wonderful, typical Santanderean meal of broiled meat, chicken, *yucca frita* (fried yucca), and *plátanos* (plantains).

It's no surprise that an important element of our trip was to visit Salomón's gravesite. The cemetery was on the outskirts of Bucaramanga, in a tropical garden of flowers, palm trees and mowed grass. Salomón and his family had left

El Valle years ago to settle in Bucaramanga, where Salomón continued to work for the *Cafeteros*.

Karen, Sari, Tomás, and Vicki, Salomón's daughter-in-law, accompanied me. As I approached the gravesite, I began to shake. I stood there and looked down silently. I began to weep and then sob. The last time I felt this way was when I visited my father's grave many years ago. Without thinking, I began to talk in Spanish while staring down at the gravestone. Words and phrases came to me. I thanked Salomón for being my friend, for his wisdom and support during my youth. I expressed regret that we had not kept in touch. I spoke of the wonderful legacy he has left in his children and educated and concerned people.

After our stay in Bucaramanga, we traveled with Tomás and his driver to San Gil through the Chicamocha Canyon. Tomás, Sari, and I sat in the rear while Karen sat up front. It was a hot, humid day and the jeep had no air conditioning. As we ascended the canyon on the switchback roads, Sari began to feel faint so she transferred to the passenger seat next to the driver. Naturally, she and Karen were unaccustomed to the bumpy jeep ride and the heat, not to mention the switchback roads. At the top of the canyon, we stopped for soft drinks at a small restaurant and continued uneventfully to San Gil where we had lunch in the Pozo Azul, my favorite restaurant for Colombian food. The *sobre barriga* and *yucca frita* were just as I remembered them from over thirty years ago.

After lunch we traveled the short ride to El Valle de San José. During the visit, I walked Karen and Sari around the main square and to the mayor's office, where I introduced myself. I was struck by the presence of a roof top satellite dish, a new computer, and a secretary reading a Microsoft Excel manual. El Valle's streets had been paved since I was last there. The central plaza, which had consisted of a water spigot on a concrete platform and scrubby grass and dirt paths, had been rebuilt with red brick walkways that crisscrossed in the middle where attractive wooden benches were placed. The village now had a small hotel, a vocational school, and a modest agricultural center where farmers brought their produce for sale and distribution. I was especially touched to see that a bronze plaque with Salomon's picture had been placed in the tourist hotel, which also served as a cultural center. The inscription spoke of Salomon's contribution to the community.

Me and Isbelia at El Mesón, 1996

The short trip to El Mesón, Isbelia's farm, was on an unpaved, rocky road, typical of rural roads. It had apparently rained recently so we had to creep through some muddy spots. Karen and Sari were feeling uneasy with the trip and the fact that we would be spending two nights in this isolated rural location. When we arrived at El Mesón, I could see Isbelia on the second floor patio. I rushed up the stairs to greet her. The results of her stroke were apparent. She was seated in a wheelchair, and an aide stood near her. Her left side was paralyzed and her speech was impaired, but it was clear by the smile on her face that she recognized me. We kissed and hugged. I had tears in my eyes.

After settling in, we left our bedrooms and went to the dining room at the end of the long patio. It had already begun to get dark, so the one light bulb was turned on. Isbelia was wheeled by her aide to the head of the table. I could see that Karen and Sari weren't happy or comfortable when they saw moths and flies hovering on the hanging dim light bulb and some of them lying dead on the table below. Things got even more uncomfortable when the main course, some form of ground chicken loaf, was brought to the table by the cook who placed the main course in the middle of the table below the light bulb. In that location, dead moths began to fall on the food. The chicken loaf tasted awful. We cautiously picked at the food but mainly ate the potatoes and carrots that accompanied the chicken loaf.

Spending time with Isbelia and her family was also time in which to recall the Colombia music that I learned forty years ago. This music has been enjoyable to me throughout my life. While in Colombia, I bought a number of 33 rpm record albums featuring Mariachi singers. One of my favorite Mexican songs was *Llegó Borracho el Borracho Piendo Cinco Tequilas*

(The Drunk Arrived Drunk Ordering Five Tequilas).
On vacations to Latin American countries,
I often pay mariachi bands a few pesos to
sing these laments while I accompany them.
Colombian folk songs that I continue to sing are
Campesina Santandereana (Santander Farmer),
La Tabaquera (The Tobacco Woman), *Pacito*
(Slowly), and *Mi Pueblito* (My Little Town), as well
as *Cuatro Caminos Hay en la Vida* (Life Has Four
Roads) and *Tu y las Nubes Me Tienen Muy Locos*
(You and the Clouds Make Me Crazy). I also
love the ballads of Mexican folk singer Chavela
Vargas, my favorites being *No Volveré* (I Won't
Return) and *La Llorona* (The Weeping Woman),
songs I know by heart forty-five years later.

The next day was spent relaxing at El Mesón
and touring the farm. Tomás showed Karen and
Sari how sugar cane is cultivated and processed
in a *trapiche* (sugar mill). The following morning,
as we loaded our bags into the jeep for the ride
back to Bucaramanga and our flight to Cali,
Tomás approached us with a rifle in his hands.
A wild boar, he said, had escaped from his pen.
Tomás was looking for him so we waited. About a
half hour later, we heard the crack of a rifle shot
in the nearby woods, and Tomás came out of the
woods with the dead boar. He offered to cook
the delicacy for lunch, but we thanked him and
reminded him of our travel plans. This experience
was disturbing for Karen and Sari and culminated

their experience with rural life. Tomás' driver then drove us to Bucaramanga.

In Bucaramanga, we stayed with Salomón's son Alberto and his family. He had arranged for a dinner that night at one of my favorite restaurants, Di Marcos. I had eaten there dozens of times feasting on their Argentinian steaks. They surprised me by finding Antonio Corso, the fellow who had helped establish *El Teatro Comunal* in El Valle, to dine with us. It was so nice to reminisce and share our common bond. They got a kick at how much I remembered about them and the times we had shared.

The next morning, after many tears shed with Tomás, Alberto and their families, we boarded a plane for Cali to visit with Isbelia's daughter Nohora, her husband Manuel Camacho, and their children Nora Patricia, Juan Carlos, and Carlos Manuel. Manuel is an Engineer with a degree from the University of Houston and owner of a successful international business producing veterinary medicines for farm animals. Nora is a dentist and owner of a dental clinic. They have a beautiful home in the Cali outskirts. They were thrilled to see us. In the car heading to the city, they gave us a briefing about Cali. They explained that it was advisable to avoid many sections of Cali, which were considered too dangerous for strangers even to drive through. The poor people who lived there had been bought off by drug cartels. Under threat of severe reprisals, either they did what the cartel bosses ordered or suffer potentially deadly consequences.

Cali is one of the two major cartel centers, Medellín being the other. Manuel and Nohora told us about what life had been like when the cartels were in power. There were guerrilla actions in the nearby Cauca Valley, including the kidnapping of Americans. They had to drive a circuitous route from the airport to their home to avoid travel in a section of the city controlled by the cartel. They pointed out buildings, shopping centers, office buildings, and factories owned by the drug lords. Our friends, in fact, lived in the neighborhood where many of the bosses also owned houses. Their homes are heavily guarded and surrounded by ten foot high walls. Some homes, or better-said, fortresses, have never been occupied. The cartel families aren't welcomed by Cali's upper class society. One of the cartel families tried to gain membership in the very-exclusive *Club Campestre de Cali* (the Cali Country Club) but was denied membership by an anonymous committee that votes in secrecy. He responded to this rejection by spending millions of dollars to construct an exact replica of the elegant *Club Campestre* but never used its pools, golf course, tennis courts, restaurants, or polo field. He just wanted to send the message that he didn't need them.

The cartel families often sent their children to the best American and European colleges. They returned to operate legitimate businesses owned by the families. Colombia's President at the time, Ernesto Samper, remained shrouded in controversy over his alleged connections to cartel money during his election campaign two years earlier. The United States had cancelled Samper's visa to visit the US. Major business groups urged Samper to resign due to the rampant corruption and Colombia's loss of foreign investments. Meanwhile, peasant farmers, dependent on the cultivation of coca (cocaine) and the safety that the cartels offered them, were angry at the nation's military that burned and fumigated their coca fields. They staged uprisings and ambushed civilian cars, trucks, and buses.

Meanwhile, Colombian life continued. There was great public concern about environmental issues such as air, water, and noise pollution as well as the preservation of the country's bountiful antiquities. Unfortunately, the country's instability prevented public expenditures for little more than military personnel to combat the drug trade. At the same time, I was struck by the proliferation of private social and economic associations dedicated to improving the quality of life. The Colombians I knew were enterprising, industrious, and friendly people who were committed to educating their children and to fostering a better distribution of the nation's considerable natural and human resources. They were embarrassed by Samper's presidency and felt that he didn't represent the views of most Colombians nor did they feel that he could lead the country out of its political and economic crisis.

On the personal side, my trip reawakened deep feelings of love and respect towards the Colombian people, who had dramatically influenced the direction and quality of my life. My friends reflected with me on those years as a time of hope where we worked together to improve life in Colombia. We spoke of the difficulties we encountered and how determined we were. After thirty years, we still continued to be filled with fond reminiscences of that time, and with a sense of progress, friendship, and shared purpose.

My reunion with Isbelia and Isbelia's children, Nohora and Tomás, helped me to see and appreciate how they felt about me, the Peace Corps, and the US as a whole. During my ten day visit with them, I learned that they maintained strong, happy memories of the 1960s. Her children were teenagers then and weren't personally involved with Peace Corps volunteer projects. As middle-aged Colombians today, they consider that decade as I do, a period of energy, hopes, high expectations, and national purpose. I don't believe that those feelings have been witnessed during another decade of this century. They were open and forthcoming with me, as if we were family with few pretenses. They could not do enough for us to make us feel comfortable and welcome. They had asked me in letters to let them know what I wanted to eat, where I wanted to visit, and who I wanted to see. I was touched that the bonds with Salomon's and Isbelia's children and grandchildren were so strong after over thirty years of time. They were part of a very special period in my life. I was glad to find out that this is the way they felt, too. I was especially grateful that our daughter Sari had come with Karen and me. Sari easily connected with everyone and had the chance to briefly experience the feelings of which I had often spoken as she was growing up. It was as if Salomón, Isbelia, and I had begun a series of relationships that were destined to continue for generations to come.

These thoughts brought me to the conclusion that my primary Peace Corps legacy was that I had emotionally touched a number of people in one remote Colombian village. This relationship had significance in their development, as it did in mine. It was so gratifying to have this validated.

It was a gift. My spirit of cooperation and dedication to my work was remembered and appreciated. It's not easy to find unconditional love and respect in life, and I was so grateful to learn that it was reciprocal. Perhaps this is the true legacy of the Peace Corps for me. They hadn't forgotten me and I hadn't forgotten them.

Nohora and Manuel Camacho at PANACA, 2008

During the summer of 2008, Karen and I again traveled to Colombia to spend a week with Nohora and Manuel Camacho at their home in Cali. We learned that some of the top drug cartel leaders had been killed or incarcerated. Most significantly, the Colombian President Álvaro Uribe Vélez had been able to generate public support for his policies towards the cartels and the military groups that maintain control of remote sections of the country. In addition, the mayors of Colombia's largest cities had taken control of their cities, enabling the public to live with less threat of violence and kidnappings. In fact, the number of kidnappings had dropped eight-fold. While drug production and distribution had infiltrated all levels of society, both rich and poor learned to endure the dangers of kidnappings and the murders of politicians and journalists who challenged the power of the drug cartels.

On our trip to the recreational areas north of Cali, we observed a good deal of commercial traffic on the expanded highway system. We also learned that Colombia was becoming a tourist destination, taking advantage of its abundant beauty and natural resources. Mountain climbers, white water rapids aficionados, fishermen, history buffs, and others are finding Colombia a wonderful education and recreational tourist destination. It has world class beaches on its Caribbean side with numerous choices for accommodations and eateries. We traveled with Nohora, Manuel, and their driver on paved highways into coffee country, passing through Cartago and Pereira, visiting El Parque del Café, a spacious, well-designed, and well-organized tourist attraction that depicts the history of coffee through music, dance, and other cultural exhibitions. We also visited *the Parque National de la Cultura Agropecuaria (PANACA)*, a spacious, educational, and recreational complex filled with displays and demonstrations featuring farm animals, wildlife, and plants indigenous to Colombia.

Lastly, we spent a day relaxing at beautiful mineral baths at the *Hotel Termales del Ruiz* not far from one of Colombia's five snowcapped mountains, the 17,000 foot high *Navado del Ruiz*. We arrived in the evening, got into bathing suits and put on our overcoats for the walk to the mineral baths. The air was a chilly 50°. The water was over 90°. The sulfur stung our skin but made the bathing quite relaxing. We took cold showers next to the pool to wash the sulfur off our bodies and rushed back to our rooms.

We had a wonderful time with Nohora and Manuel, talking about life in El Valle, Peace Corps memories, current Colombian politics, and our families. We also visited the parents of our dear Colombian friends José and Carolina Ávila, a very special occasion filled with happy tears.

A highlight of our trip was when Ingrid Betancourt was liberated by the Revolutionary Armed Forces of Colombia (FARC) who had kidnapped her six years ago. Betancourt was a senator, an anti-corruption activist, and a Nobel Prize nominee. It was thrilling for Karen and me to experience the excitement and joy as the Colombian people celebrated this event. We watched the interviews of Ms. Betancourt on televisions wherever we were. Nohora and Manuel called their children to share in the celebration.

When President Kennedy and Sargent Shriver designed the Peace Corps in 1961, they envisioned the possibility that Peace Corps service might have significant, far-reaching benefits beyond whatever the volunteers, individually, may have accomplished overseas. They believed that the impact of the volunteers on the US might be in itself highly significant. I am not aware of any scientific way of measuring the accuracy of their vision and it's unlikely that an objective study will ever be conducted, so what we have is anecdotal, unquantifiable data. Certainly, we can point to public figures like presidential candidates and US Senators Christopher Dodd and Paul Tsongas, six US Congressmen, eighteen US Ambassadors, *Vanity Fair* Special Correspondent Maureen Orth, and American news anchor and political commentator Chris Matthews, all of whom served in the Peace Corps.

This list just scratches the surface of the body of volunteers who returned to careers in public service. At Peace Corps reunions, I heard about volunteers working for the World Bank and other international agencies serving the Third World.

But, unfortunately, we will never know how much further the Peace Corps has influenced life in the US. Can we measure the degree to which those public personalities influence national public policy and alleviate some of our economic and social ills? Can we measure the impact of returned volunteers who are public officials at state and local levels and who brought their worldview and understanding of the needs of other nations to other Americans? Can we measure the impact made by almost 200,000 returned volunteers who are teachers, nurses, nonprofit executives, and government officials who are sharing their worldview with those whom they work for and with? Do the Americans who married, worked with, or were born to these former Peace Corps Volunteers act in the voting booth and in their personal and professional lives with a greater understanding of the needs of other nations? I really don't know the answer to these questions but I strongly believe that their influence has been substantial..

I am hopeful that our new President, Barack Obama, will expand the Peace Corps at this point in world history when so many nations are at odds with one another and where America's reputation has been scarred, especially in the past eight years. President Obama appears to have a Peace Corps worldview and may be able to transcend some of the divisions that separate people, just as Peace Corps Volunteers sometimes did during their public service. We need the Peace Corps to become a more important part of our economic and social policy towards other nations along the terms envisioned by Sargent Shriver and President Kennedy. If this were the case, we would be better able to challenge some of the stereotypical assumptions that many of the world's citizens have of the US. If this were the case, we would be targeting significant resources down to village levels in the form of community development workers, along with micro-lending, small business development loans and technical assistance, the construction of educational facilities, health centers, and scholarships for educational advancement. These investments are humanitarian efforts, but also in our own interest.

CHAPTER SIX
My Life Today

In July 2009, I will be 69 years old. Unlike many others, I make no secret of my age. I do this because I feel healthy and alive and want to do my part to demonstrate that getting older can mean feeling good about yourself. I perceive myself as having the appearance of a younger person even though my beard is almost completely white and I only have a crown of hair on my head. I walk erectly with determination and can still move well on the tennis court compared to most people my age. It makes me feel good when people are surprised when they learn how old I am. I still perceive myself as a youthful Peace Corps volunteer.

My father died at age 67. Recently, I had some fleeting worries about whether I would live to be older than him. Reaching 67 was a small milestone for me although I'm often concerned about my health, more specifically about my heart disease. I also have some concerns about memory loss and recently visited a neurologist. I discussed this with the doctor. I described the loss of keys, eye glasses, and other items; the difficulty remembering dates and names as well as movies and Broadway and off-Broadway shows we had seen. He asked me a series of questions to test my memory. Afterwards, he assured me that the brief test results were signs of normal aging, not early-stage dementia. I'm not confident of his diagnosis and worry anyway. It may be that the memory loss, as Karen feels, is symptomatic of the medications I take, and what I believe to be a learning disability. I have chosen not to want to know whether I should be more concerned about memory loss. I just hope that remaining both physically and mentally active will delay the onset of further deterioration.

On January 1, 1993, I got a call from Paul Mundschenk, my closest friend in the Peace Corps. We had lost contact with one another. I looked him up and found that he lived in Illinois and was a professor of religious studies at the University of Illinois. We talked for an hour as if it hadn't been 28 years since our last connection. We decided to meet at the Grand Canyon that June.

Me and Paul Mundschenk about to hike the Grand Canyon, 1993

The following is an essay I wrote on the return flight home:

Hiking the Grand Canyon at age 53 is not something I figured on ever doing. But when my best friend from Peace Corps service got in touch several months ago, a trip through the Canyon seemed a nice way of reuniting, reflecting, and taking stock and being with nature and self.

Paul and I were roommates in the Peace Corps training at the University of New Mexico in the early 1960s, full of idealism and hope for the future, for the possibilities of contributing to social change. We were free spirits who, like most Peace Corps people of the time, got a lot more out of their overseas' experiences than they gave. We soon learned that the Peace Corps was an extremely modest and limited humanistic endeavor, not an agency of social change. Paul always knew he was headed for an academic career as a thinker and teacher. I didn't have a career in sight. I became a social worker and nonprofit organization director. During the Peace Corps, we had fun together. Our reunion revealed that we were both relatively successful in our professional fields. We loved Woody Allen films, Dustin Hoffman, the film "A Thousand Clowns," eating spicy foods, making puns, and talking about our wives and children. We share non-materialistic values. We agree that there are no right and wrong answers but right questions. We agreed that if we won a big lottery prize, we would use the money to expand and enrich the work we do, give a lot to those who need it, and travel more often. We agreed that the world is more messed up today than twenty-eight years ago. Greed prevails with only glimmers of generosity and rational planning in the best interests of the world community. The Grand

Canyon was more of a spiritual journey than a physical one to my friend Pablo Primero. (I'm Pablo Segundo because I'm shorter). For me, the journey was more of a test of stamina and will. My brother told me I was stupid to endanger myself by going down the Canyon. I did no special physical training but I did heed Paul's good advice by packing the right foods, clothing, supplies, and plenty of water.

The trip down from Hermit's Rest in the mid-day sun was the most arduous part of the four-day trip. Paul had been to the Canyon eight times earlier and knew the trails well. For our first two days, he chose The Boucher Trail, a non-maintained trek featuring narrow switchback stairways of boulders, rocks, stones, and pebbles that crisscrossed down the Canyon walls to Columbia Point, our first-night's destination. We noted the irony of going to Columbian Point after our experiences in Colombia. The uncertainties, doubts, and fears began for me quickly on the steep descent. What had I gotten myself into? The trail was dangerous, non-existent in some places. How could I minimize my losses without ruining Pablo's annual journey? Where could an emergency helicopter land to return me to the rim?

The forty-pound knapsack on my back weighed heavily on my back. I slipped several times in precarious situations. I called to Pablo for help when blood oozed out of my hand from catching myself in a fall. I had two muscle cramps, one in a calf and the other in my right thigh. My tennis ankle injury of three weeks earlier was acting up. Wobbling, step-by-step, we made it to our first night's destination by early evening.

Eating dehydrated turkey tetrazzini, chocolate pudding and coffee, I began to see the possibility that I could make it back and enjoy myself on the way. Pablo made it clear to me that no one carries anyone out of the Grand Canyon. During our first night in the Canyon, I sat at a cliff edge and witnessed the physical terrain we had covered on the first day. I woke up five minutes before sunrise to photograph the beginning of a new day. What grandeur and beauty in one place! How unfathomable to try to understand how this all came to be over billions of years! At Hermit's Creek camp on the second night, we waded au buffo, four thousand feet below the rim. Two middle-aged men having fun together on a thirty-three mile hike over four days. Playing trivia games about music and TV shows from our childhood. Catching up about marriage, children, family, and careers. About our mothers and fathers and selves. About some of our private thoughts. Conversation flowed like it used to.

The next three days of hiking were a transition from feeling insecure about my abilities to feeling relatively secure. "I can and will do this," I said to myself as we trekked through rain and desert heat down the Tonto Trail to Indian Gardens and the five mile, totally uphill test of the cardiovascular system called the Bright Angel Trail. While I enjoyed the companionship, I came to solitude, too. I went ahead of Pablo by half an hour. I felt the periodic wind gusts, the chill of the morning air, and the intense heat of the sun. I saw lizards, deer, ants, and birds going about their lives as I went about mine. I listened to the sounds of the rushing Colorado River. I stopped to observe the variety of flowers and plants that make this natural treasure we call the Grand Canyon.

The journey was testimony to the friendship that Pablo and I continued despite the twenty-eight year hiatus. How fortunate I am to be able to have a friend like him to meet again and have fun with; to verbally and non-verbally go through time and space together; to symbolically take steps together across the canyon, across the years, across the ages, to share moments of joy and wonderment; the ease of renewed comradeship.

My brother was very wrong. For me, the hike through the Grand Canyon was more a test of the human spirit than of the human body.

Eleven years later, in 2004, while playing tennis, I had a heart attack. I didn't experience the typical symptoms. I felt pressure in my abdomen and later in my chest, pressure that I had never experienced before. So, I stopped the tennis match, packed my bag, went to the tennis center office, and asked that an ambulance be called. An ambulance promptly arrived with emergency medical technicians who quickly diagnosed the situation and gave me a nitroglycerine pill and placed me on a gurney which was pushed into a waiting ambulance. Within an hour, a cardiologist at Stony Brook University Hospital administered a balloon angioplasty. I was rushed to an operating room where two stents were placed in my left anterior artery. I was told that the artery was completely blocked and that I was fortunate to have rushed to the hospital for treatment. I spent three days in the hospital with Karen at my bedside every hour she could. During this time, I wrote the following essay:

> As I sit here in my hospital bed three days after my heart attack, I continue to disbelieve that THIS has happened to me. So far, my life has consisted of a limited amount of illnesses and injuries but nothing like a Heart Attack. The big one required angioplasty, or the clearing of the plaque that had closed off my left descending artery, and the placement of two "medicated stents" to keep the artery clear. I now must look forward to medical appointments, cardiac rehabilitation, and a life as a patient of one of life's scariest events: the sudden stopping of your heart. My vocabulary has been expanded to include such phrases as "drug-eluding stents;" aggressive cholesterol reduction; and "ejection fraction." I will now take Plavix, one of the drugs promoted on TV to improve the functioning of the stents, as well as several other medications to keep my heart healthy.
>
> How do we lose our identity when we enter and get processed by an institution? From everything from the bare-back

hospital gown (somehow gown isn't descriptive of this item) to the multitude of attending staff attending, each with her specific task to accomplish on a highly-regimented basis. Everyone is in a rush to be somewhere else. Don't misunderstand me. This is all important stuff but it has consequences that discourage wellness.

As one way of coping with this process, I asked Liza to bring me the hat that she recently earned as Most Valuable Player in the Sports Illustrated World Series of Softball in Orlando, Florida. She also was elected to their Hall of Fame. I asked Liza to bring the framed color photo of Davi that I had taken so I could keep it at my bedside. I also wanted my date book within reach so I could call the people I worked with so that I could remain in touch with what's going on. I took the color photocopies of myself atop Mt. Wheeler and Mt. Humphrey and clipped them onto the curtain next to my bed.

The men of medicine who are now in my life say that I could have died last Sunday morning. But the fact is that I didn't and I have a strong will to live. I am exuberant about life despite its crises, setbacks, and disappointments. I think about the bright side of events, looking for something positive to hang my hat on. On the surface it may be rationalizing and denial but I think it is fundamentally a healthy way of facing life. At times like these, I heavily rely on a wonderful support system of Karen, Sari, Liza, Jeremy, two-year old Davi. I have already had moments where something triggered weeping. One of them was when Sari brought a video of Davi, Jeremy, and Sari lighting the first Chanukah candles Tuesday night. The sight of my wonderful grand daughter attentively and curiously sitting in Jeremy's arms while he and Sari sang a prayer, brought happy tears to my eyes. What joy they bring to my life! What satisfaction to see them on their own dealing with the complexities of life! I am so happy for them. I can't imagine a greater feeling than to know that your children can take care of themselves and are loving people. Flowers. Visits from relatives and friends. Phone calls. Signs of concern and love. The daily calls from my brother have been important to me and the renewal of our relationship. They are reminders of how fortunate I have been to have a series of relationships that have lasted the test of time most especially my friendship with Jeff Bloomberg who drove down from Albany in terrible weather to see me. And to hear people talk about my stamina, energy, and the purposefulness that I bring to my work. They remind me that I make a difference. They inspire me to be a better person. They especially encourage me to be a nicer person to people I have a hard time with and to better control being judgmental of others. The experience makes me think of some of the prominent public figures of our time who have faced physical and emotional challenges. President Kennedy's perseverance with his chronic back problems, Lance Armstrong and his battles with cancer while bicycling on a world-class level, the will-power of Mickey Mantle to play baseball despite the pain in his knees, the strength of Jackie Robinson who withstood cancerous racism, and Monica Seles and her ability to come back to the tennis courts after being assaulted with a knife in a public arena. I remember 80-year-old U.S. Senator Jacob Javits in a wheel chair and an oxygen tube in his nose and how he demonstrated exuberance continuing his life of public service despite a debilitating illness that lasted for many years.

I don't excel in anything like these people but I do have the drive to compete; a strong will; the desire to do good deeds; and to set an example of caring and citizenship for those that will follow. These public figures are inspirational to me in their determination to overcome physical and emotional setbacks.

I think of how vulnerable we are to illness. That I could have had a one hundred percent blockage of one of my arteries is hard to fathom. I have always prided myself on being healthy. I thought that I took care of myself reasonably well. Except for being twenty pounds overweight, I am fine. I lift weights and can do seventy-five pushups in five minutes. I play competitive tennis three times a week. I talk about my feelings. I have planned for our future and don't feel stress about our economic security. I remain deeply in love with Karen, the love of my life, and am profoundly grateful for her sensitivity to my needs and her unconditional love in the form of countless acts of compassion. She has passed on these qualities to both of our daughters who are wonderful people. I am part of a community of concerned people who try to make a difference in the world; to reduce the impacts of injustice, poverty, and racism. So, despite the fact that I know that bad things happen to good people, I am now an example of such a fate. I will do my best to move forward with exuberance to fill the next half of my life with love and good deeds and to be grateful for every moment I have in this pursuit.

Since the heart attack, I have been more responsible with my food intake by eating less red meat and more fruits and vegetables as well as regular exercise, although I continue to weigh more than I should. I take daily medication religiously. My cholesterol levels are within the limits for someone with heart disease. I follow the cardiologist's advice and have annual stress tests. In fact, I am doing better on the stress tests after the heart attack that I did before it occurred. Attention to my health status has really been led by Karen who makes sure I take my meds and watch my diet. I have discontinued my mountain hiking out of respect for Karen's feelings. She is anxious that something will happen to me on a mountain, miles from medical care. I understand her concern and am honoring her feelings, but part of me feels that I should go on with my life as I wish.

The last few years have been filled with wonderful vacations with Karen. Karen retired from her social work position at Eastern Suffolk BOCES in June 2005, giving us more flexibility in when we can travel and for how long. Karen's friends organized a wonderful retirement party for her at the Three Village Inn in Stony Brook. I surprised Karen by arranging for two folk singers to entertain us with folk music from the 1960s. I also shocked her with a gift of dancing lessons for the two of us at Arthur Murray. She got a big kick out of the gift, since I have avoided taking dance lessons. I knew it would be a special treat for Karen if we danced together as we age. The lessons turned out to be fun. I wish I hadn't been so reluctant years ago.

Together, Karen and I developed a list of places we'd like to visit before we get too old to travel. We have taken two- and three-week summer vacations to Costa Rica, Mexico, England, Scotland, Ireland, France, Spain, Hawaii, Italy, Switzerland, Austria, and Greece; several of our National Parks in the West and Southwest; and a wonderful trip in the summer 2008 to Colombia. In winters, we have been going to Puerto Vallarta, Mexico where we bought a time share property. We love the reliability of Puerto Vallarta's weather, its friendly people, its laid-back atmosphere, its great restaurants, and the opportunity to speak Spanish and enjoy Mexican culture.

On our most recent trip to Puerto Vallarta, we drove to a beautiful surf beach. The sun shone. The white sands and a beachside restaurant with *pallapas* (straw umbrellas) were inviting. After a nice lunch of *quesadillas,* beef *tacos,* and a beer, I decided to ride some waves. Over the years, I surfed waves without a body board. I noticed that there were body boards for rent at the restaurant. I made an inquiry and found out that the cost was only $1.50 for half an hour. I had some hesitancy about being thrown for a loop but decided to take a chance. The waves appeared to be no more than six feet in height. I was thrilled to be able to ride several of them into the beach. The waves had punch, some of them propelling me about fifty yards. I figured that eight rides were enough and I was going to call it a day after one more ride. I patiently waited for a nice wave. As it approached, I mounted the board and held on. It was the most powerful wave yet, taking me towards the beach at a much faster pace than I expected. The wave overtook me. I was hurled over the board, soundly hitting my mouth and nose on the sand below. The first thought that came to me was that I had broken a tooth. I struggled in the white surf to get to my feet at which time I became aware that my lip was swollen and it and my nose were bleeding badly. I held my nostrils closed to stop the bleeding and quickly walked to Karen who was sitting on a white, plastic armchair under the straw *pallapa* where we had enjoyed lunch. She got some ice and tissues from the waiter to hold on my nose. We packed our things in the rented car and drove back to Puerto Vallarta while my lip continued to swell. Over the next two days, my physical body healed from the powerful blow it had experienced. At the same time, I fretted about what could have happened, namely a concussion, a broken jaw, or worse. So, I now added body surfing to my growing list of forbidden physical activities, along with mountain climbing.

Me atop Mt. Wheeler, Taos, New Mexico, 2004

Two adventurous vacations before my heart attack were spent out West. We first traveled to

Glacier National Park where I trekked to 9,500 feet. Inspired by this accomplishment and the beauty of the experience, I hiked Mt. Humphrey, the highest mountain in Arizona, at 12,636 feet. It was a wonderful day and took me through pine forest, plains above the tree level, onto rocky terrain for the last 500 feet. The view from the summit was thrilling. I felt so healthy and alive. The following year we traveled to Taos, New Mexico where we spent time with Bob Bodenhamer, a former Peace Corps volunteer. Several years prior, Bob retired from his career as a newspaper editor and bought a funky little hotel in Taos. Bob showed us around this scenic town including its restaurants and art galleries. We bought two paintings and a poster from Ed Sandoval, a native artist whose paintings feature Southwestern scenery and people. I also was challenged to trek up Wheeler Peak, New Mexico's highest mountain at 13,101 feet. This hike turned out to be very challenging. I wrote the following essay about my adventure:

Karen woke me up at five fifteen in the morning in our room at the Kachina Lodge in Taos, New Mexico to begin my long-awaited hike of New Mexico's highest mountain peak. Ever since last year's ascent of Mt. Humphrey, Arizona's tallest mountain and hiking the tallest trail in Glacier National Park in Montana, I set my mind to hike Mt. Wheeler. I surfed the internet to learn about Wheeler Mountain visiting several public and private sites. It is located in the Sangre de Cristo Mountains just east of Taos. It is situated in Carson National Forest an area consisting of one and a half million acres. According to the National Park Service, big game animals roam the Forest including mule deer, elk, antelope, black bear, mountain lions, and bighorn sheep. My research indicated that the hike involved a more gradual ascent than the ascent to Mt. Humphrey. The rise, that is, the elevation to be climbed from the starting point was similar, over three thousand feet, with Wheeler's rise was over 3900 feet.

The day before the hike I purchased climbing poles to ease the pressure on my knees and generally make it easier going up and down mountains. I brought with me a first aid kit, my cell phone, a towel, Advil, zinc oxide for rashes, toilet paper, my Swiss army knife with all of it many features, and baby powder. I also bought Gatorade, several bottles of water, nuts, high-protein bars, and string cheese. I wore one of my brimmed caps and a beige hiker's jacket and pants both which could be disassembled with zippers at the knees and shoulders for various climate conditions. My sturdy ankle-high hiking boots gave me comfort that they would reduce the likelihood of spraining an ankle. I brought my 35 mm camera with loads of film because I love to document for myself and the people I care about the wonders of nature and how I achieved my goal despite being 35 pounds overweight and at age 64 when most people want to relax and not face challenges and uncertainties.

Emotionally, I was anxious especially about the fact that didn't know if I would find someone to hike with. I had never hiked alone. I didn't want to hike alone but I very much wanted to hike Wheeler, a 13,000 foot mountain. One simple slip of the ankle or knee or one ill-advised step on rocks and pebbles could find me falling and catching myself on my hand and twisting a wrist. Or worse. Being in such a situation was a concern but not one that I was going to permit me to cancel my plans.

Weather conditions in August in the Taos area added another uncertainty. Afternoon storm clouds with rain and lightening are common realities. Everyone advised to begin the hike at day break and get down into the tree line by no later than two o'clock in the afternoon. Lightning strikes the tallest objects so if you're below the tree line, the trees will be struck. Of course, that is unless you're unlucky enough to get hit by a falling tree.

Based on the time that it took me to hike Mt. Humphrey, I estimated that it would take about five hours to hike Wheeler. Thus, I planned to begin the hike at six o'clock in the morning, leaving enough time to get down to the trail head well before dark. I was also advised that the Wheeler hike is a popular one so I could expect to meet plenty of other hikers. This eased my worry a bit.

Karen and I hugged and kissed in the dark hotel room and I was off for my adventure. She was very supportive and understanding of my need to move forward with my hike but I knew she also was very worried that something bad might happen. I assured her that I would be careful and would call when I reached the peak. I carried my loaded knap sack to the car where I had left the hiking poles the night before. I got on the road and drove the half hour in the dark to the Taos Ski Valley where the hike was to begin. The printed instructions seemed clear but they weren't and delayed the hike by about forty-five minutes so what was to be a six o'clock start turned out to be six forty-five.

My morning routine usually involves "bathroom time." So, I figured, this was one issue that I wouldn't have to deal with on the trail where no toilet facilities are available. But sometimes our greatest plans fail. This was the case two hours later when I had a "bathroom emergency" where I suddenly had to relieve myself at an altitude of 11,000 feet on a narrow path with my butt in full view of any onlookers on the trails above and below.

My anticipation grew as I drove the winding roads and entered the parking lot adjacent to the trail head. The spot was located in the Taos Ski Valley which is surrounded by a pine forest. I got out of the car and put my knapsack on my back and adjusted the straps for comfort. I placed the camera straps around my neck so that the camera would be easily accessible. I locked the car. I approached the nearby trailhead sign and took a photo to record the first steps of my adventure. I walked no less than thirty yards and stopped due to a serious shortness of breath. I felt like I was having an anxiety attack. How could I continue to have shortness of breath for several hours? What was I doing here alone at six forty five in the morning in an isolated and unfamiliar place? Could I do this? What was I trying to prove? Most of the people I associated with would never embark on such a journey. Was I letting my desire to feel and be athletic take charge of my reason? Was I being insensitive to my wife and children? My other hiking experiences were with other people: with Paul Mundschenk at the Grand Canyon, with two people at Glacier National Park, and the experience at Mt. Humphrey where I joined up with someone with whom I matched well, a surgeon from Winslow, Arizona. His medical experience added a sense of security for me. The camaraderie was a nice addition to the experience.

So I worried about what would happen at Wheeler. I looked at the mountains that surrounded the valley and felt small and alone. Do the right and sensible thing and return to the safety and security of the familiar. I then recalled having the same feelings at the beginning of my other hikes and decided to proceed. I moved forward until the shortness of breath became too much for me and then rested for 1–2 minutes. As I moved forward, I decided to count the number of strides that I took before I ran out of breath. Fifty seemed right so I stopped every fifty paces. I did this even though I knew that this wasn't going to be easy and would add a lot of time to the hike. But I had no choice other than turn around—an idea that, in the first hour, came to mind frequently. I decided to set a goal of getting to a place where going back no longer made any sense. My map gave me short-term goals, to get to Bull of the Woods Pasture and then to Bull of the Woods Mountain, a distance of about two and a half miles. My downloaded information said that once you passed Bull of the Woods Mountain you were "ready for the final ascent to Wheeler Peak." Common sense said that this wasn't going to be as easy as it sounded. Common sense proved to be right. At Bull of the Woods Pasture, I drank some water from my canteen and rested for ten minutes, sitting on a fallen tree in the shade next to a small pond. A mountain jay joined me, perched on a branch no farther than five feet away. He seemed to pose as I took his picture. The trail from the Pasture to the Mountain was surrounded by Douglas Fir, Ponderosa Pine, and Blue Spruce trees. I often used my many rest periods to witness the surrounding panoramic beauty. I listened to the silence of the forest sometimes interrupted by the sound of a brook's rushing water or that of a passing breeze. These moments of solitude in the forest and being "on top of the world" were special. I often looked behind me to draw satisfaction from the distances I had already hiked. This was a way of offsetting the temptation to look forward too often and become overwhelmed by how far I still needed to go.

I also looked for and found a four foot length of wood to be used to ward off threatening animals and help me ascend steep and rocky passes. It really didn't help very much in these ways and served as more of a companion during the hike than something of practical value. I saw no threatening animals.

The 'final ascent' took about four hours involving numerous switchbacks in the above-the-tree line trail that rose from Bull of the Woods Mountain at 11,300 feet to 12,300 feet. I continued to stop to rest whenever the oxygen deprivation was too much for me even if it was after taking only ten paces. I remarked to myself that my legs felt fine, that I hadn't experienced shin splints as I had in the past, and that the trail was clearly marked and not too rocky. I needed some assurances.

Some experiences worked against any feelings of assurance and confidence. One was a forty-something fellow, without a water bottle, in shorts and a tee shirt, jogging past me. The others were thirty-something men and women passing me on the trail. At the same time, I was glad to see other human beings from time to time. I hiked with a pleasant couple from Albuquerque for two hours but their pace was too much for me. It became clear that I was the last hiker of the day on this trail. In the final ascent, I could see the others that had passed me as they approached the rocky summit at Mt. Wheeler and then as they descended to Williams Lake over a very rocky, severe forty-five degree decline. This was to be my way down, too, because the thought of returning over the same trail for eight miles seemed too much to endure. The trail, however uncertain, to Williams Lake, was only three miles in length.

As I approached Wheeler Peak, I was visually tricked by three 'false peaks' ahead of Wheeler that were close in height to Wheeler and hid the ultimate

ascent from view until the last half hour.
The view from Walker Peak, the last
mountain before Wheeler, reminded me
of the view of Macchu Picchu in Peru as
I recalled seeing it forty years ago when I
visited there on a Peace Corps vacation
trip with Paul Mundschenk, Bob Salafia,
and John Meier. The scenery around me
was dramatic and filled with contrasts;
distant green pine forests; barren red rock
formations; and rolling hills. Above the
tree line, the changing sky was always
in sight usually composed of blue sky
with rolling cumulous cloud formations, a
constant reminder of the unpredictable
climatic conditions that I had no control
over. I kept telling myself to keep plugging
away one step at a time. I felt grateful
that my weight-lifting had paid off. My
body was sound. However, nothing
could have prepared me for the oxygen
deprivation other than spending more
time in similar conditions. Living a life at
sea level was the issue at hand. What I
was experiencing was to be expected.

Upon arriving at Wheeler Peak, I
was filled with joy and a deep sense of
accomplishment. I had a wide grin on my
face. I decided to take two pictures of the
small metal plaque indicating that I was

on Wheeler Peak. However, the camera's battery indicator showed that the camera was dead so I couldn't have one of the other hikers use my camera to take my picture at the peak. Fortunately, a young man from Virginia offered to take two photos and forward them to me. I called Karen on my cell phone and told her I was okay. The signal was poor so we didn't speak much. I also called and spoke briefly to Jeremy, my son-in-law.

I proceeded to eat half a ham and cheese sandwich and drink some water and Gatorade before beginning the descent by way of the William's Lake Trail. I was surprised that I wasn't hungrier than I felt. I was also excited to start the decline.

This portion of my adventure turned out to be the most challenging and dangerous. The trail is ill-defined and filled with scree (slate particles), boulders, rocks, and stones. Thus, I had to constantly negotiate numerous slippery areas. I fell on my backside a number of times after losing my footing on the scree, sliding several feet before stopping my falls with my hands, feet, and body weight. One time, I sprained my wrist, as I caught myself falling backwards as my legs slipped forward under me. This fall caused a black and blue spot where my spine meets my rear end. Throughout the forty-five degree decline to Williams Lake, I noticed that dark clouds were moving in replacing the puffy, cotton-like cumulus clouds that passed through the deep blue sky so far. So I began to worry about how fast I could get down to the tree line and the shelter it provided from lightening. On the way down, I joined a number of statuesque mountain goats who were silhouetted against the mountain slope and sky above as well as furry black and brown marmots who bobbed their heads from their burrows over the wide expanse around me. As I descended, I could see Williams Lake below, a bluish green body of water that is more like a big pond. During this two-hour period, I saw only two people racing along with the assistance of hiking poles. As I approached Williams Lake, I passed an emergency medical team attending to a woman who sprained her ankle and needed to be carried down the mountain. Apparently, her mates had gone down to the trailhead earlier to seek emergency aid. As I passed them on the trail, I was comforted to know that, if something happened to me, they would be following me. From this point, the hike was uneventful, on fairly smooth, gradually declining trails, all down hill. I picked up the pace and breezed to the end of the trail. My hiking poles were waiting for me on the car's trunk where I had left them.

Was it worth it? Would I do it again? Logical questions. Yes, it was worth it. The feeling of personal accomplishment was extremely gratifying. I set a goal for myself, did my homework, and focused on my past successes overcoming adversities. If I had given into the fears I was feeling, I would have felt unfulfilled. I proved to myself that, despite being overweight, I am in very good physical condition and my spirit is strong.

Would I do it again? Certainly not alone. The risks that I took were very dangerous and insensitive to Karen and her feelings and concerns.

But the moments of joy are tempting to me. As I think about these moments, I think of other very special moments in my life, like the births of our two daughters and physically being witness to the wonder of childbirth. I think of Karen and the courtship we shared thirty-seven years ago and the continued bond we share. I think of the courage it took for me to leave my family and join the Peace Corps as a

naïve, idealist twenty-three year old and
how this two-year experience affected
my worldview and goals for life. I think
of the pleasure I experienced when our
daughters performed in sports and in the
theater and completed their educations,
and when Sari and Jeremy married. I also
think of the joy that entered my life with
the birth of our granddaughter Daviel.
Moments with her are precious. I then think
of moments of accomplishments in sports
that were important to me like hitting home
runs with the bases loaded or executing
a suicide squeeze play to win a game or
throwing out a runner with a precise throw
from the outfield. Tennis has had wonderful
moments when I hit decisive shots that
determined the outcome of matches.

So my hike of Wheeler Peak is another
milestone in my plan for the rest of my life,
to not slow down but to speed things up.
It is my personal expression of the notion
that we only live once so we better get
the most out of it while being a good
member of society in the meantime. I
recognize that, while I might live another
twenty or thirty years, the odds are pretty
good that I won't be hiking Mt. Wheeler or
Mt. Humphrey in my eighties and nineties.
So if not now, when?

During the summer of 2007, we took a trip to Italy to celebrate our fortieth wedding anniversary. It was the trip of a lifetime. We flew to Venice where we immediately got our rented car and drove to Lake Cuomo, in northern Italy. The lake is long from north to south with small villages next to the lake. The city of Lake Cuomo is set at the southern end of the lake. The villages, built on the sides of the surrounding mountains and hills, are connected by narrow, two-lane roads and a very efficient ferry service. The setting is simply beautiful. We stayed in a lakeside hotel for a week, consuming more gelato and pasta than we should. We took ferry rides to some of the towns, bought baguettes, salami, and cheese that we ate on the ferry. On another day, we took a road trip to Salzburg, Austria on the autobahn through Switzerland, Lichtenstein, and Austria to hear an evening Mozart concert. The concert was held in the Stiftskellar in the church of St. Peter's monastery in Salzburg's old city. The Stiftskellar is the oldest restaurant in Central Europe. We dined on traditional foods of the seventeenth and eighteenth century at candelabra-adorned tables. The musicians were accompanied by a tenor and soprano dressed in period costumes singing Mozart arias. In the morning, we took a bus tour of Salzburg and then headed back to Lake Cuomo.

The trip back to Lake Cuomo resulted in a unique vacation experience. We drove back using a different route, through the Italian Dolomites, past snow-capped peaks, switching back and forth on hairpin turns, and going through long tunnels. As we approached Lake Cuomo, traffic crawled to a stop. I questioned a policeman about what was going on and found out that the city's streets were closed to auto traffic for the night because the city was celebrating their annual festival, a common event in Italian cities. The streets were filled with loud music, people dancing, drinking, and frolicking. So the question was how do we get to our hotel, which was in the center of the city along the lake. We were routed to the other side of the lake, surrounded by people walking into the city. Getting hungry and tired, we stopped at a small lakeside hotel to eat, rest, and consider our options. We were greeted by the receptionist and explained our circumstances. She called the hotel owner who then greeted us and encouraged us to sit down and have dinner while he figured something out. He asked us where we were staying and assured us that he would be helpful. After dinner, he reported to us that he had contacted our hotel who had faxed a letter to him on their letterhead indicating that we were foreign guests staying at the hotel and asking that the police provide every courtesy to help us to get back to the hotel. It sounded like a good plan. But the more I thought about it the more I questioned if it would be successful in convincing police at five barricade points to let us through. So I came up with another idea. I asked the hotel owner: "How do you say in Italian: 'I'm a cardiac patient and I need to take my heart medication?' He told me how to say this phrase. We thanked him for his generous help and went on our way. Well, the plan worked. At each barricade, I handed the letter from the hotel to the police officer and said (more or less in Spanish/Italian), *Perdone, sono Americano qui es paciente cardiatico. Necesito mi medicina* (I'm a US citizen who is a heart patient. I need my medicine.). The police instructed us to follow them into the city. As we entered the city, the crowds got bigger. The police turned on their sirens and revolving red and blue lights. We entered some back alley ways and ended up behind our hotel. We profusely thanked the police for their kindness and generosity.

After our stay at Lake Cuomo, we returned to Venice where we boarded a Costa cruise ship for an eight-day cruise of the Greek Islands of Santorini, Mykonos, and Rhodes, and Dubrovnik, Croatia. The cruise was compromised by the very hot and humid conditions we found during the land tours we booked. In both Rhodes and Dubrovnik, we left the tours due to the unbearable heat. On Rhodes, however, we thoroughly enjoyed the jeep ride around the island and the snacks at a small taverna in a little town. The ship had few American passengers so we met many European vacationers with whom we had dinners and pleasant conversation.

I'm not in love with cruise vacations but Karen adores them so we compromised on having a half-vacation by land and a half-vacation by sea. I was eager for the cruise to end because I had planned a big surprise for Karen upon our return to Venice. I had arranged for Sari, Liza, and Jeremy to meet us when our ship returned to Venice. Six months before the trip, I decided that the best way to celebrate our anniversary was for the family to be together in a very special place. Karen and I had booked our trip to Italy and Greece but I decided to arrange for the kids to join us for four days. I didn't tell Karen about the kids joining us so, for six months, I kept the secret. I told everyone else about the surprise, though—my friends where I played tennis, our hairdresser, Jennifer, Karen's mother and sister, my mother, and various friends.

After docking in Venice, we got our luggage, and boarded a water taxi for a brief ride to our hotel near the Grand Canal. We got off the water taxi, unloaded our luggage, and ascended to the dock and sidewalk along the Grand Canal. As Karen turned around, she saw the kids approaching her with glowing smiles on their faces. It was wonderful. We all had tears in our eyes. I had kept this secret from Karen successfully for six months.

We spent three days together in Venice. We visited the former Jewish ghetto from the Nazi regime. It was chilling to be in the footsteps of Jews who were victims of such horrors. We also visited the island of Murano, internationally famous for its exquisite glass productions, where we bought a beautiful vase that sits on our dining room table. We also splurged and took a half-hour gondola ride to get to a splendid outdoor restaurant. The trip was a statement on how I wanted to spend the rest of our lives—living the life we wanted while spending down what we had saved. We had decided that we weren't going to be one of those couples who regretted not doing the things they'd always wanted to do, always putting things off. Time is too precious. Fortunately, our children are able to take care of themselves and don't expect or require an inheritance. They will get the condo property that we will leave behind.

I hate to think of life without Karen. It is also painful to me to think of Karen living alone without me. It's hard to fathom. We've spent over forty-two years together and I want them to continue for many years to come. "It's not that I'm afraid of dying, it's just that I don't want to be there when it happens" is a Woody Allen quote that I identify with. Woody's films, with themes of self-effacement and feelings of being the outsider, have always been among my favorites.

Not believing in an afterlife, I figure that we die and that's the end of it. I feel no compelling need to become religious at this stage of my life. I sometimes wonder how I'd feel if I were diagnosed with a terminal illness and suffering in pain. Will I regret my skepticism then? I think not.

I also think about becoming dependent due to a physical disability. This troubles me. My career emphasizes the importance of positive thinking, healthy living, remaining active, and pointing to illustrations of people who are busy and contributing citizens well into their seventies, eighties, and even their nineties.

My mother and me, 2002

I find it difficult when I visit my mother in the nursing home to see her physical and mental condition deteriorating. I see the institutionalizing policies and procedures that nursing homes impose on their patients. Everything around her care depersonalizes life—the white plastic bib that's placed around her neck when she eats, the restriction that prevents her from sitting outside viewing the comings and goings of visitors and staff, the weekly bathing she receives from a nurse's aide in an over-sized bathtub, the limited menu choices of bland food, and the loss of privacy where people don't knock before entering her room. As I walk down the hallway, I'm sensitive to the sounds of moaning and the all-too-often emaciated patients rigid in fetal positions. It's disturbing to know that half the residents in nursing homes have Alzheimer's disease or other forms of dementia. The thought of losing the memory of your past and your very identity reminds me of the many people I knew at the Community Programs Center as participants in our adult day care program. They were people who were going about their lives when they began to experience memory loss and gradually, or suddenly, became dependent on others for their most basic needs. These thoughts, and the feelings associated with them, raise questions about whether I want to live a long life facing the possibility of spending my last years in such a state.

Frequently, my mother is sad and withdrawn. At these times, she says, "Take me Lord. This is no good." I know that she may be trying to make me feel guilty for allowing her to live in a nursing home, but I can understand her sentiments. While she visits her children and grandchildren from time-to-time, she mainly spends her time sitting in a recliner next to her bed. Fortunately, she continues to be an avid book reader, reading for hours at a time. But her life, and that of the other nursing home residents, is dull, boring, and impersonal and a life I don't want to live.

But, of course, the rub is that we don't have a choice about how long we live and what illnesses or disabilities we will experience. I know that if you exercise regularly, watch your calorie intake and cholesterol counts, your odds for healthy living may be better. But we all know lots of folks who follow all the best medical advice and have heart attacks, get Alzheimer's disease, or contract cancer well before older age. Now, whenever I visit a doctor, whether it's the urologist, the cardiologist, the orthopedist, the internist, or the podiatrist, I wonder if my life will change dramatically if very negative test results come back.

So, we're left with basic choices about how we spend our lives with these choices heavily dependent on things we can't control. In my case, this primarily means coping with heart disease and mild depression. I continue to work on finding balance between my desire for fulfilling relationships and my desire for solitude.

I struggle with the experience of solitude associating it with loneliness and personal failure, confusing aloneness for loneliness which is really a sense of loss, not simply being apart from others.

I don't have a strong religious foundation. I seek no comfort in a belief in a higher being and never have. My life will end when my heart stops beating. I developed this view at an early age. I never learned to love a god or to be comforted by one. I never absorbed a deep Jewish identity. I clearly am Jewish and identify myself as such to others but feel no urge to practice the religion. While there are many aspects of life I cannot explain that others see as acts of a god, I look for rational explanations to life's exigencies. When I can't find them, I conclude that I don't have the answers to many questions and believe that things have evolved over the millennia by random selection. Therefore, organized religion isn't part of my life. I respect the many good and decent people with strong religious beliefs whom I've known, who act charitably out of compassion and concern for others. To me, the soul is a concept created by people to give them comfort about dying, a concept that I don't relate to.

My ethical foundation is based on social work principles that promote the general welfare of society from local to global levels, the meeting of basic human needs like health, housing, and a decent income, and the development of individuals and their communities while respecting and celebrating racial, ethnic, and cultural differences. This foundation promotes informed citizen participation in the public arena and the self-determination of people over their communities in their pursuit of social justice.

What my life is about now is enjoying times with Karen, the children, grandchildren and close friends, along with continuing my community work while playing tennis and traveling and trekking to beautiful places. Knowing that my life will end and that nothing follows gives me a framework in which to live life on earth to the best of my ability.

Karen is the emotional glue that keeps me and our family together. With her natural motherly abilities and her trained therapist's skills, she is a source of unconditional love and comfort to each of us. She visits with her mother in the nursing home twice a week and assists her in countless ways. Due to the job insecurities that I experienced in my work life, Karen has been our family's more stable breadwinner. If it weren't for her pension and psychotherapy practice, we couldn't afford to live the way we have and provide for our children's education. For eighteen years, she lovingly cared for Ifka, a neighborhood calico cat that happened on our doorstep around the time that Sari left for college. Sari named Ifka after one of her many imaginary childhood friends. Karen adopted and loved Ifka and provided her with everything she needed. Ifka required twice-daily insulin injections that Karen administered religiously for many years. I liked having Ifka around the house but never experienced the type of warm relationship that Karen had with her. Two years ago, at 18, Ifka's condition seriously deteriorated. It was very difficult for Karen but, ultimately she did what had to be done to ease Ifka's pain. We both witnessed and wept while the veterinarian injected Ifka to put her to sleep. The veterinarian commented that Ifka enjoyed such a long and happy life because of the loving care she received, especially from Karen. It is no surprise that Karen's psychotherapy practice has grown over the years and that she has many close friends. She is such an empathetic and skilled therapist. She had many good friends at Eastern Suffolk Board of Cooperative Educational Services where she counseled children with special needs.

We have had the gift of special friendships during our marriage. For forty years, we have enjoyed a friendship with Karl and Janet Grossman. In the early nineteen seventies, we became friends with the Grossmans. More recently, Karen and I have enjoyed annual trips to the Grossman home on the South Fork and sailing with them on the Peconic Bay of Eastern Long Island. These have been peaceful, relaxing times shared with friends. Karl has been a significant advocate for protecting Long Island's environment and an international authority on nuclear power. I have always admired his ability to investigate issues, write about them, and get political support for his causes. I sometimes feel like my causes pale in comparison. He has dealt with environmental pollution, nuclear power, and world peace. I admire Janet's commitment to her work and her positive attitude towards life. I am very grateful for the perceptive poem she wrote about me in the front of the book.

Special friendships include José and Carolina Ávila and their beautiful children Maria and Sari. The Ávila family arrived in the United States about ten years ago from Colombia fleeing unsafe conditions caused by the violent drug trade. They came to CPC seeking affordable childcare so that they both could seek employment. Fortunately, I was in the center when José visited. With my cherished feelings towards Colombia, I made José an offer he couldn't refuse, to provide childcare for Maria. José and Carolina had good professional positions in Colombia. They left the country to escape the dangerous conditions caused by the international narcotic trade. We have very much enjoyed time with the Avila family. José is involved in numerous community activities and is my computer consultant. We often talk about their struggles as undocumented individuals and how much they want to become US citizens. We attend Maria and Sari's annual birthday parties and celebrate holidays and other special occasions together. I am so happy to know that Sari and Jeremy have become friends with José and Carolina and have begun to cultivate friendships among Davi and Mira and Maria and Sari. It represents a continuation of my ties to Colombia.

Over the years, I was always looking for father figures and big brothers. In the Peace Corps, it was John Maier and Paul Mundschenk. Later, it was Andy Casazza, Marty Timin, Dick Dina, and Tom Williams. Never feeling completely satisfied with my work nor the recognition I received, I often felt lonely and isolated. My quest for acceptance caused some to distance themselves from me and others to ignore me with the end result that I became a loner who, even though I accomplished a good deal in creating community services and employment for many people, never felt good about myself, continuing to seek validation from others and often feeling like I was in an emotional turnstile. My anchor was always Karen, a source of unconditional love.

Someone with whom I became close and to whom I sought much counsel and support for many years was Dan Panessa, a quiet, humble man of simple tastes. Dan served as CPC's chairman for many years. Dan contributed thousands of dollars to CPC when it desperately needed funds to survive. Tragically, he contracted cancer and died suddenly fifteen years ago. I was very upset by his untimely death and tried to comfort his family in their grief by writing a lengthy obituary published in Newsday, letting them know how important Dan was to me and our organization. I wanted the family to know how much he would be missed.

I also established close relationships with two social work colleagues, Mary O'Hagan and Rosemarie Fischer. They were members of the board of directors of Community Programs Center, the organization I led for twenty-three years. Through thick and thin, they were sympathetic, understanding, compassionate, people who supported my work for many years. They were the heart and soul of the organization diplomatically challenging those who only saw the organization as a business enterprise.

Another friendship that I have cherished is with Paul Mundschenk, my Peace Corps roommate during training in New Mexico. Paul lives in Carbondale, Illinois and flew here to celebrate Sari and Jeremy's wedding with us. A few years ago, he sent me a notice that he had been selected as Distinguished Lecturer at Western Illinois University in Carbondale. As a surprise, I flew to Illinois to celebrate Paul's accomplishment with him. While we haven't seen one another much over the years, we keep in touch by phone and email. Our common bond in the Peace Corps together remains strong.

Another part of my life for the past twenty years that has been special to me is playing tennis. As a child, tennis was viewed as a "sissy" sport unlike baseball, basketball, and football. In my late forties, I decided that I would enjoy a competitive sport. I had played golf on and off over the years and found it very frustrating, time consuming, and expensive. I chose to learn tennis and play regularly. I took lessons from the pros at the Miller Place Tennis Center and later joined the Port Jefferson Country Club where I've met a lot of really nice people. In addition, at a surprise fiftieth birthday party planned by Karen, Sari, and Liza, Jeff and Joan Bloomberg gifted me four days of tennis instruction at the Dennis Vandemeer Tennis Academy in Hilton Head, South Carolina. There was one condition to the gift: that Jeff accompany me to the academy. Jeff and I had played recreational tennis over the years when we visited their upstate home. He always beat me which was frustrating. At the academy, I actually won a match against him for the first time. We went out to dinner that night with other players. I bought a bottle of champagne and asked to be toasted for my victory over Jeff. I got a lot of laughs from this silliness. Over the years, I became more competitive and, on rare occasions, actually beat Jeff again. Our friendship was always more important than the competition.

Tennis is like life. You work hard, practice, and struggle. You use your mind and body. You assess the abilities of your partners and your opponents. You do your best and sometimes win and sometimes lose although I like it a lot better when I win. But in tennis, unlike life, after the match is over and you leave the court, there are clear winners; the work I did in my career was filled with vagueness and incomplete fulfillment. I have been a member of local tennis clubs, usually playing doubles. I'm a pretty intense and competitive player and have struggled when playing with people whom I don't get along with off the court or have on-court habits that annoy me. This impatient behavior has caused a number of players to stop playing with me. My tennis time is special, so I don't want to spend it with people I don't enjoy being with. From time to time, I also play with Bill Baffa, a high school buddy with whom we've enjoyed a warm relationship ever since we reunited at our twenty-fifth high school reunion. Bill is a stronger tennis player than I am, having played since high school. We've become dear friends with Bill and his wife, Arlene, sharing many trips to Broadway shows, dinners out, and a wonderful Mediterranean cruise.

In October 2008, Karen and I attended my fiftieth high school reunion with Bill and Arlene and Jeff and Joan Bloomberg at the Knights of Columbus Hall in Mineola. I very much enjoyed talking with some of the "kids" I knew in high school and finding out what ever happened to them. I especially enjoyed reconnecting with Paul Mariani and his wife, Eileen. Paul is an English professor at the University of Massachusetts and an accomplished poet. Our relationship is such that we simply pick up where we left off since the last time we saw one another as if there hadn't been years in between.

Friends of Colombia members parading to JFK gravesite at Arlington National Cemetery to commemorate the 40th anniversary of the Peace Corps, Washington, DC, 2001

I have also attended every Peace Corps reunion, which has been held every five years since the twenty-fifth anniversary celebration of the Peace Corps in 1986. I dropped whatever I was doing to attend these three day events in Washington, DC. Each one was special with its reflections, catching up, and searching for my dear Peace Corps buddy, John Meier, whom I've lost contact with. At each reunion, the Colombian Ambassador in Washington hosted a gala celebration at the Colombian Embassy in honor of the Peace Corps with Colombian food, music, and dance.

Sargent Shriver, first Peace Corps Director, and me at the 30th anniversary of the Peace Corps, Washington, DC, 1991

At one of these reunions, I had a conversation with Sargent Shriver, the original Peace Corps Director and brother-in-law of President John F. Kennedy. He was very engaging and in good health. It's sad to know that, years later, he contracted Alzheimer's disease. One tradition at the Peace Corps reunions is a walk from the Lincoln Memorial to Arlington National Cemetery. We walk behind country-of-service banners. We pay respect at President Kennedy's gravesite and then attend a touching ceremony in the outdoor rotunda. I always tear up at these events. I return home with wonderful memories.

Karen and I have traveled around the country to spend time with several of my Peace Corps friends. We've spent time in Seattle with Larry Leckenby, Dick Miller in San Francisco, Caroleah Kotch and Dee Gamble in North Carolina, Bob Koehler in Denver, and Bob Bodenhamer in Santa Rosa and later in Taos, New Mexico. On each of these occasions, I am reminded of the special bond that we shared as former Peace Corps volunteers.

Despite, and because of, my psychological makeup and interpersonal shortcomings, I did accomplish a great deal during my post-Peace Corps years. I continued to identify with values and strategies I learned in the Peace Corps. I was successful at taking ideas and organizing them into practical realities. I was successful in finding people who believed in me and what I was trying to accomplish. I generated a lot of loyalty among staff and people who joined the boards of directors that I brought together. I was also successful in forming positive relationships with many elected and appointed officials and foundation leaders who granted funds to the programs I developed. I recognized that getting anything worthwhile done takes hard work, doing your homework, and patience. I was willing to put in the time and effort to make things happen even though I often felt unappreciated by society for the roles that I, and others like me, play in society.

Social workers are often treated like barnacles feeding off the problems of others rather than people who contribute to a stable society. We are often dismissed as do-gooders who have no understanding of the "real world" of business and competition. A common attitude is that since nonprofits are charities, anyone can do the work; some donors believe that they know better than nonprofit executives since they're giving of their time and money. It has been somewhat insulting to witness the respect that a successful corporate executive receives when he enters a room as compared to a social entrepreneur. The inequality in compensation afforded social work is an issue that has troubled me for years. Social workers who improve conditions for the poor and disenfranchised should be rewarded at least as well as individuals who achieve economic success. It is a sad statement on our priorities.

Looking back almost fifty years, I see the significant changes that have taken place in the world—some good and some bad. The gap between the rich and the poor has grown wider. I see how much more dangerous the world has become in no small part due to American policies towards other nations. We must take dramatic steps to counteract the perception that we believe that might makes right. I have witnessed enough of life's cruelties and injustices to have a sense of the evils that may lie ahead. In the 1960s, Peace Corps volunteers were assigned to countries like Colombia, Iran, Pakistan, and Afghanistan. But, due to political turmoil and violence and our economic exploitations and military actions in these nations, Peace Corps assignments in these countries have been discontinued. I also understand that Peace Corps volunteers no longer are trained as community development workers like they were in the 1960s. Countries arrange for Peace Corps volunteers according to their technical and professional expertise. The Peace Corps should be dramatically expanding its community development work along with its technical assistance aid.

So life goes on. The world is a wonderful place that is primarily filled with caring, hardworking people who want to be self-sufficient and provide for their children. But the world also includes very serious dangers that threaten our survival. I am hopeful that the world's economic and political leaders will, sooner rather than later, see that there is something larger than nationalism and religious fervor.

We are all speeding through space together, collectively vulnerable to threats, many of which are beyond our control. I trust that future generations will understand the importance of looking beyond artificial boundaries to find common ground and the strategies to work successfully in common cause. Then, perhaps, my grandchildren will enjoy the benefits of racial and ethnic diversity in their schooling, their employment, and in their friendships.

In my younger and middle years, I regarded life as consisting of limitless time in which to accomplish things, have new adventures, heal poor relationships, and deal with unresolved issues. Life seemed to stretch before me without end. I lived in the future, not the present. But as Gloria Steinem, in her essay *Doing Sixty and Seventy,* so eloquently puts it, "Without an everpresent sense of death, life is insipid."

As I look back at my two years in the Peace Corps, I see them as filled with exciting times when everything was fresh, new, and possible. I represented my country and tried to make America seem less foreign to people who had no knowledge of Americans or had mere impressions, both good and bad. Today, I consider myself extremely fortunate to possess many sweet memories of my life in Colombia in the 1960s. My Peace Corps experience launched my career in public service, forged lasting friendships, and created a powerful bond between me and the Colombian people. For this, I will always be extremely grateful.